Feminist Dilemmas
in Qualitative Research

Feminist Dilemmas in Qualitative Research

Public Knowledge and Private Lives

edited by

Jane Ribbens and Rosalind Edwards

SAGE Publications
London • Thousand Oaks • New Delhi

First published 1998

 SAGE Publications Ltd
6 Bonhill Street
London EC2A 4PU

SAGE Publications Inc.
2455 Teller Road
Thousand Oaks, California 91320

SAGE Publications India Pvt Ltd
32, M-Block Market
Greater Kailash – I
New Delhi 110 048

British Library Cataloguing in Publication data

A catalogue record for this book is
available from the British Library

ISBN 0 7619 5664 6
ISBN 0 7619 5665 4 (pbk)

Library of Congress catalog card number 97-069262

Typeset by M Rules
Printed in Great Britain by Redwood Books, Trowbridge,
Wiltshire

Contents

Contributors' Notes

Pam Alldred is a Lecturer in Psychosocial Studies at the University of East London, UK, and in Women's Studies at the University of North London, UK. Her PhD is about contemporary politics and policy surrounding parenting, the production of knowledge about, and the circulation in popular debates of, psychological ideas about gender, sexuality, development and 'fitness to parent'. She is a co-author of two multi-authored books which challenge the idea of individual authorship (and publishers to accept them!) and allow her to acknowledge the support and influence of her co-authors and her PhD supervisor: *Challenging Women: Psychology's Exclusions, Feminist Possibilities* by E. Burman, P. Alldred, C. Bewley, B. Goldberg, C. Heenan, D. Marks, J. Marshall, K. Taylor, R. Ullah and S. Warner (1996); and *Psychology, Discourse, Practice: From Regulation to Resistance* by E. Burman, G. Aitken, P. Alldred, R. Allwood, T. Billington, B. Goldberg, A. Gordo-Lopez, C. Heenan, D. Marks and S. Warner (1996).

Linda Bell is a Senior Lecturer and Researcher in the School of Social Science, Middlesex University, UK. She currently teaches research methods to undergraduates and postgraduates taking professional programmes in social work, mental health, nursing and herbal medicine. Her research interests include community care; multi-agency and inter-professional training and practice (health and social care); gender, time and work; parenting; male violence; research methodologies and methods applicable to professional practice. Her PhD was an anthropological study of mothers' support networks. She has a son and a daughter.

Maxine Birch is a Lecturer at University College, Suffolk, working in the sociology of childhood. Her research interests centre on the exploration of life stories and self-identity. Her PhD looked at the reconstruction of self-identity stories in alternative therapy groups that promised self-discovery. Maxine lives with her two children and partner on a shared organic farm.

Andrea Doucet is Assistant Professor in Sociology and International Development Studies at St Mary's University in Halifax, Canada. She has a BA in Political Science, an MA in Development Studies and she received her PhD from Cambridge University in Social and Political Sciences. Her current research is centred around the methodological, epistemological and theoretical aspects of research on gender divisions and relationships within households while her own household life is centred around parenting three daughters.

Rosalind Edwards is a Reader in Social Policy at the Social Sciences Research Centre, South Bank University. She has particular interests in motherhood and families, as well as feminist methodologies, on which she has published widely. She is currently researching lone mothers' uptake of paid work; parenting and step-parenting after divorce/separation; and children's understandings of parental involvement in their education. Her major publications include *Mature Women Students: Separating or Connecting Family and Education* (1993); *Mothers and Education: Inside Out?* (with M. David, M. Hughes and J. Ribbens, 1993); *Single Mothers in an International Context: Mothers or Workers?* (co-edited with S. Duncan, 1997). She is co-editor (with J. Brannen) of the *International Journal of Social Research Methodology: Theory and Practice*, to be launched in early 1998. Her personal interest in balancing motherhood and education (as paid work) has recently been extended to incorporate grandmothering.

Melanie Mauthner works as a Research Officer at the Social Science Research Unit, Institute of Education, London University, UK. She has carried out a number of empirical research projects with children and adults in schools and households on family life, parenting and health. Her current research in sexual health involves reviewing the methodology of evaluations of process and outcome interventions. She also teaches Feminist Methodology on the MA in Women's Studies and Education and the Doctoral Studies Programme at the Institute, and is about to complete her PhD in Sociology, 'Kindred Spirits: Stories of Sister Relationships'.

Natasha Mauthner is a Research Fellow in the Research Unit in Health and Behavioural Change, University of Edinburgh, UK, where she is responsible for a programme of work on mental health. Her doctoral (Cambridge University) and postdoctoral (Harvard University) research explored women's experiences of motherhood and postnatal depression. Her current research interests focus on children's experiences of changing parental employment patterns and labour market conditions; employment patterns, family life and mental health; mental health promotion and methodological and epistemological issues in qualitative research. She lives outside Aberdeen and enjoys hill-walking.

Tina Miller is a Senior Lecturer in sociology at Oxford Brookes University, UK. She has a BA in Social Theory and an MSc in Research Methods. She is currently working on her doctoral thesis which is a longitudinal study of women's transition to motherhood. Her interest in the sociology of health and illness and the increasing medicalization of aspects of everyday life – the area in which she teaches – arose from living and working in the Solomon Islands and Bangladesh. Tina has three delightful daughters – Hannah, Freya and Lydia – and now lives in rural Oxfordshire.

Janet Parr is Lecturer in Education, Training and Development at the University of Sheffield. This is a distance-learning Master's degree, which is offered in the United Kingdom, Eire and Singapore. Embarking on her degree in sociology as a mature student herself, she has been passionately interested in the experiences of mature women students – the theme of her recent research – since then. Her research interests are generally in the areas of gender and education and specifically in the area of mature women returners to education and training – a topic on which she hopes soon to do comparative research in both European and South East Asian countries.

Jane Ribbens is a Senior Lecturer in Sociology at Oxford Brookes University, UK, where she is Director of the Centre for Family and Household Research. Her broad research interests concern family lives, especially around parenting, and qualitative research methods, especially the use of autobiography and life histories. Her major publications include *Mothers and Their Children: A Feminist Sociology of Childrearing* (1994); *Mothers and Education: Inside Out?* (with Miriam David, Mary Hughes and Rosalind Edwards, 1993); *Mothers' Intuition? Choosing Secondary Schools* (with Miriam David and Ann West, 1994); and co-editorship (with Rosalind Edwards) of a special edition of *Women's Studies International Forum* (1995, 18 (3)). She is currently researching parenting and step-parenting after divorce/separation, and parents' and teenagers' perspectives on their family lives together. She has a son and a daughter who have left home, and currently lives in a house that is being reconstructed by her partner, together with their three-year-old daughter, and sometimes her stepson.

Miri Song is a Korean–American woman who now lives and works in Britain. She is a Lecturer in Sociology at the University of Kent, UK. Her research interests include theorizing on ethnicity and cultural identity, migration and immigrant family adaptation, young people and dynamics around racism(s).

Kay Standing is a Lecturer in Women's Studies at Liverpool John Moore's University, UK. She is currently undertaking a PhD on lone mothers' involvement in their children's schooling, at South Bank University. The research is interested in how lone mothers negotiate their relationships with various institutions (such as schools) within structural and moral constraints. Originally from a white working-class background in the West Midlands, she has a two-year-old daughter.

PART I

INTRODUCING OUR VOICES

1 Living on the Edges
Public Knowledge, Private Lives, Personal Experience

Rosalind Edwards and Jane Ribbens

Social research is a difficult and perplexing task, whatever its focus and topic. One of its fascinations is that it requires sensitivity to issues on many different levels. On the one hand, we need to think through our theoretical frameworks and assumptions. On the other hand, research is also an intensely practical exercise, requiring us constantly to make detailed, concrete decisions. But these layers within research cannot be distinguished in actuality in quite this way, since theory and nitty-gritty decisions do not occur in different places but are constantly intertwined within the research process.

This edited collection seeks to explore the interplay between theory, ways of knowing about the social world, and methodology and practice in qualitative research projects. This interplay is explored in relation to a particular set of topics, which may be broadly described as concerned with 'private' domestic, intimate, and personal lived experience. We believe that these areas of research highlight particularly sharply some of the intermixed theoretical and practical dilemmas and challenges that arise in carrying out qualitative research, especially where there is a concern with retaining research participants' 'voices' in the production of research accounts.

This integration of theoretical and practical issues is, as we have said, always embedded in the social research process, and raises major dilemmas about the nature of this process. However, some topics of research may allow us to evade these thorny issues more easily than others. In particular, a focus on more 'public' social worlds, and established social science topics, may allow us, as researchers, to avoid confronting and exploring them. As women researchers concerned with domestic and intimate 'private' lives, the contributors to this volume have together explored their shared concerns about how to proceed in academic research when the theoretical, conceptual and formal traditions in which we are located are predominantly 'public' and 'male-stream'. Questions of how to gain access to, interpret, analyse, and theorize research participants' experiences and accounts have formed a concern of qualitative researchers across disciplines and substantive topics for many years. As feminist researchers, we want to highlight the issues involved in doing this when applied to a sphere that has been characterized as 'female' or 'women's matters', and pushed out to the edge of public, mainstream, academic concern. Moreover, in exploring this sphere as researchers, we find ourselves placed at the edges, between public social knowledge and private lived experiences.

Thus, in our research, we have examined 'private' and 'personal' social worlds, which we then make 'public' for academic, and perhaps professional, audiences. Such projects have 'liminal' connotations, in terms of being 'betwixt and between' the dominant social and symbolic classification systems of public knowledge, and less visible and vocal understandings found in the more personalized settings of everyday living. In this way, we find ourselves on the margins between different social worlds.

This liminal position not only applies to the research process and product, but it also concerns us as people with our own personal lived experiences. As researchers we embody and directly experience the dilemma of seeking knowledge and understanding on these edges, even as we seek to explore other people's private lives and translate them into the format of public knowledge. We may thus shift uneasily between the position of participant and observer/listener, constantly reflecting upon how we know about things, and how to view the knowledge we produce. The marginal status of the ethnographer has long been regarded in anthropology as a source of tension and discomfort, as well as a source of insight.

It is the particular topics under consideration – aspects of private, domestic and personal lived experience and understandings – that so clearly draw these issues out and present us with dilemmas. Social researchers concerned with domestic and intimate issues are involved in the social construction and material production of knowledge within the domain of public, and academic, discourses. Ambiguity thus arises when we seek simultaneously to serve an academic audience while also remaining faithful to forms of knowledge gained in domestic, personal and intimate settings.

There is a danger that the voices of particular groups, or particular forms of knowledge, may be drowned out, systematically silenced or misunderstood as research and researchers engage with dominant academic and public concerns and discourses. Both Smith (1987; Griffith and Smith, 1987) and DeVault (1990, 1994) have argued strongly that routine public and disciplinary categories and procedures (in their case, in sociology), insistently pull us towards conventional understandings that reshape, in particular, women's voice and experiences. To counteract this both suggest that, as researchers, we need to ask about, and listen closely to accounts of, 'mundane' everyday domestic activities in detail, and to build more on what we share with our interviewees on a personal level than on disciplinary concepts – although DeVault also warns that we need to be sensitive to differences (see also Riessman, 1987).

In relation to differences, there are perhaps similar dilemmas to be found for researchers exploring lives within non-Western countries, or other social worlds that are marginalized from Western public perspectives (Narayan, 1989). Ong is highly critical of the assumptions based upon a colonial discourse that underlie much feminist research into the lives of non-Western women. Nevertheless, she is hopeful that we can '. . . jettison our conceptual baggage [and] . . . open up the possibilities for mutual but partial, and ambiguous, exchange' (Ong, 1988: 88). Despite this optimism, however, researchers in these areas cannot escape the requirement to take cultures and discourses that are peripheral to predominant Western knowledge forms, and 'translate' them into a discourse recognizable to Western public audiences. Indeed, Ong herself points to this in her reference to 'partial, and ambiguous, exchange'. Mohanty discusses how the term 'colonization' is often used to describe this relation of structural domination. She suggests that these processes operate partly through '. . . the hegemony of the Western scholarly establishment in the production and dissemination of texts', and partly through '. . . the legitimating imperative of humanistic and scientific discourse' (Mohanty, 1991: 74). What is more:

> . . . [this] argument holds for any discourse that sets up its own authorial subjects as the implicit referent, i.e., the yardstick by which to encode and represent cultural Others. It is in this power that power is exercised in discourse. (Ibid.: 55)

We are suggesting that this power in discourse may be seen to be similarly operating when we research private lives in Western societies and then translate them into a representation that is acceptable to public academic audiences.[1]

However hard the researcher tries to position herself within the marginalized culture, she faces a dilemma. As long as she is seeking to be heard by a public academic audience, she cannot evade the necessity to interpret the worlds and understandings of the Other into a discourse or knowledge form that can be understood and accepted within the dominant Western frameworks of knowledge and culture. Such Third World or Other voices cannot be heard by a public Western audience without the researcher as 'interpreter'. This is the inescapable nature of its dominance. Even as the researcher may seek to make herself apparent as the translator, via self-reflexivity, she risks making herself more central to the discourse, again pushing the voice of the Third World narrator out to the edge (Hale, 1991, discussed by Wolf, 1996). Nevertheless, to suggest anything else may be to create an illusion, since in reality the Western researcher is inescapably at the centre of the research account. Patai (1991, discussed by Wolf 1996), thus argues that the relationships between First World feminist researchers and Third World subjects will inevitably be exploitative, whatever the good intentions of the researchers.

To some extent, qualitative research[2] is itself a marginalized methodological discourse in that, in a similar fashion, researchers using this approach cannot escape addressing their position and foundations *vis-à-vis* quantitative and positivist methodologies and traditions. Qualitative research almost inevitably appears 'unconvincing' within this relationship because dominant understandings of concepts of 'validity', 'reliability' and 'representativeness' are posed within a numerical rather than a process framework. In contrast, researchers working within a quantitative framework rarely have to explain the underlying epistemological basis of their work within the terms of qualitative research. Of course, qualitative research can be carried out within a positivist or behavioural science paradigm (see, for example, the debates between Whyte (1992, 1996a, 1996b), Richardson (1996) and Denzin (1996), as well as Pam Alldred's discussion in this volume). For those who have taken the 'reflexive turn' in qualitative research, however – including ourselves and other contributors to this edited collection – the implications are always present, of working on the edges of, and constantly having to engage with, dominant understandings of what constitutes 'proper' research.

As qualitative social researchers reflexively exploring everyday lives, we must continually confront questions of the nature and assumptions of the knowledge we are producing, and who we are producing it for. While we may wish to attain the status of detached and objective observers, producing 'expert' and 'superior' forms of knowledge, such claims are open to doubt. Nevertheless, this does not necessitate taking a totally relativist stance.

> Relativism . . . implies that a person could have knowledge of only the sorts of things she had experienced personally and that she would be totally unable to communicate any of the contents of her knowledge to someone who did not have the same sorts of experiences. (Narayan, 1989: 264)

Narayan suggests, instead, the notion of a perspectival view of knowledge (that is, that who you are, and where you are situated, does make a difference to the knowledge you produce), but that we then have to assess the best ways of seeking to communicate this knowledge to someone else, situated differently.

We suggest that, rather than a relativistic despair, we need high standards of reflexivity and openness about the choices made throughout any empirical study, considering the implications of practical choices for the knowledge being produced. This book explores these implications in detail, for the production of public and academic knowledge within specific qualitative research projects. The projects share the overarching leitmotif of the interplay of voices from 'public' and 'private' social worlds, as well as attending to more personalized experience that struggles to achieve a voice at all. Together, we explore the variability of such voices both within and between public and private settings, including the contributors' own voices as women conducting research.

The Women's Workshop as a setting 'on the edge'

There are two major motivating factors behind this edited collection. The first is our longstanding interest in issues of 'public' and 'private'. We both share a concern (which we explore further below) that what goes on within the private sphere, in family life in particular and especially women's experiences as mothers, has not been well understood or accorded significance within the mainstream of the disciplines in which we were schooled and worked (sociology and social policy). The second is our membership of the Women's Workshop on Qualitative Family/Household Research. The writers in this collection are all current or past members of this Workshop, and while not all members of the Workshop are contributors to this present venture in the sense of authorship, all have had some input to its production in various ways. As with other knowledge outputs, this particular volume is bound up with its social context, and we shall explore here some of the ways in which the social setting of the Workshop is interlinked with the themes of the book.

The Women's Workshop on Qualitative Family/Household Research is an interdisciplinary women's research group centred on domestic and intimate issues. The original members started meeting in 1987 after making contact at a Postgraduate Summer School organized by the British Sociological Association. Since then, the number of members at any one time has fluctuated between three and 15. People have mainly learned about the Workshop by word of mouth, although some connections were made via an advert placed in a postgraduate publication for BSA members. The group did not in fact start out self-consciously as a women's group, but over the years it was women who joined, and this became a valued feature of the Workshop.

All the members of this Workshop have joined at the time of undertaking postgraduate doctoral research, and we think this is significant for the way the group has operated. While doctoral research may sometimes be regarded merely as a 'training ground' for the 'real research' to be undertaken later, we suggest that it may instead sometimes be a highly significant time for research, as the individual is poised at the moment of entry into the public world of academia as an active participant, in transition between different social worlds. In Narayan's (1989) terms, we have had to learn how to belong to, and operate within, two different contexts at the same time, retaining our concerns with private ways of being while also making our voices heard within public ways of being. While this may bring some 'epistemic advantage', it can also be very uncomfortable, '. . . [leading] to a sense of totally lacking any roots or any space where one is at home in a relaxed manner' (Narayan, 1989: 266).

For members of the Workshop, the threshold between these social worlds has been especially difficult because we have often chosen to research topics to which we have a particular personal attachment, based upon our individual experience and knowledge. The Workshop thus contains women with a special type of commitment to their research, which then raises dilemmas for the ways in which its academic production affects the knowledge produced. This carries particular implications (explored further in subsequent chapters) for how we may 'hear' our interviewees, and 'represent' them in our writing up.

The liminal nature of the Workshop, between personal and academic issues, is reflected not only in our topics of research, but also in our interactions with each other. A key significance of the Workshop has been the mutual support it has provided for researchers working with the dilemmas and ambiguities of simultaneously speaking in an academic voice and producing academic, public, knowledge, while retaining research participants' and their own personal, private voices and knowledges. Just at the moment when, as doctoral students, we have been seeking to establish ourselves as academics via accepted and acceptable academic practices, we have also been most in touch with our personal commitment to our topics, and most keen to explore the ambiguities surrounding our knowledge production. Members have been drawn to the group by the need for a setting which recognizes the significance of privately based everyday knowledge and ways of knowing, instead of simply prioritizing the drive towards institutional, public, academic output and credentials.

The Workshop has thus emerged as a space in which to express doubt and admit the possibility of unanswerable questions, rather than falling prey to the certainty of academic rhetoric. As a support group, as well as a place of critical and vigorous debate, the Workshop can be important in helping to think through the dilemmas involved in research, as we consider each member's emerging findings and thoughts, and help to 'pull' each other through the research process. This book, then, is also a celebration of the Workshop's tenth birthday.

Public knowledge and private lives

We both (Rosalind Edwards and Jane Ribbens) first experienced this transition from personal lived experience to public academic output as part of doctoral research projects. Jane chose to study mothers' accounts of their lives and their childrearing, after having been absent from academic work for a period of 10 years while she largely concentrated on caring for her own two children. She found that the doctoral process involved a painful experience of increasing marginalization from the social networks of mothers that had formed the context of her life with her children. When she eventually came to write the thesis for the PhD, she tried to convey some sense of this earlier context:

> I first encountered [women similar to those I studied] in 1975, when I was introduced to my babysitting group when pregnant. In the company of a recent acquaintance who already had two children, I was driven through local side streets that I had never before had reason to use, and entered a room full of women who were mothers and who all seemed to know each other and to organise their lives together. I thus received an overwhelming sense of entering into a whole new social world. (Ribbens, 1990: 1)

The process of doctoral research gradually led her to feel an outsider/insider within these groups, while she also learned different ways of talking about this social world for an academic audience. In particular, it was at this stage that she first became aware of the concepts of public and private, notably through the work of Leonore Davidoff and other feminist historians, which seemed to transform the potential for making such social contexts visible to a sociological audience.[3] The issue of how mothers themselves dealt with, constructed, and mediated public and private boundaries in their children's lives became a major theme for the research. Yet she was still painfully concerned in the final thesis about what was left out, so that her writing barely touched upon, let alone conveyed, the deep emotions that children can evoke in their parents, and that are crucial to their lives together.

Rosalind's doctoral work was, in fact, precisely concerned with these movements between family and academic worlds and forms of knowledge – although she did not explicitly recognize this when embarking on her research. Her interest in exploring the experiences of women combining lives as full-time students in higher education and as mothers and partners was rooted in her own experience of the tensions and dilemmas involved in attempting to mesh the two worlds (see Edwards, 1993: 12–14). Her determination to be a successful student whilst also being a 'good' wife and mother became channelled into attempts to integrate the two aspects of her life, in the face of their increasing disjuncture. In particular, what was valued familialy was not academically, and vice versa. Within the family, as wife and mother, embeddedness in the concrete detail and minutiae of personal relationships was significant and required wholehearted involvement. Within higher education, as a student, the ability to take abstracted and generalized overviews was rewarded, but also required a seemingly boundless commitment to being 'on top' of the work.

In researching the experiences of other mature women students, Rosalind came to understand the nature of these tensions as rooted in the differing socially constructed value bases of 'family' (for women) and 'education', and of what constitutes 'knowledge' and 'being' in each sphere. While Rosalind has extended her concerns with the interaction between personal, social and institutional values and practices to other research topics, the issue of moving between familial and academic worlds and forms of knowledge still remains, both personally and in terms of 'translating' interviewees' 'private' lives and intimate understandings for an academic audience.

Feminist and qualitative epistemologies seemed to provide us with some insight and support in dealing with the transitions and marginalization we describe as so central to our doctoral experiences. Nevertheless, the dilemmas remained. We thus became conscious of how far social theories, concepts and models had been overwhelmingly developed around male activities in the public sphere. But in addition, we also became worried by the tendency within even some feminist work itself uncritically to import and apply these male-stream concepts and theories to discuss the domestic and the intimate within the private sphere. In 1991, a decade after Margaret Stacey's identification of this problem (Stacey, 1981), we noted how we still felt this to be the case (Edwards and Ribbens, 1991), discussing the issue in the context of a debate around the use of the concept of 'strategy' and its application to women's domestic lives. We later went on (Ribbens and Edwards, 1995) to raise the issue of how we might approach and make visible private domestic lives – what is elaborated here as the 'hearing' (Part II of this book) and the 'representing' (Part III).

We have written before, both separately and jointly (Bell and Ribbens, 1994; Edwards, 1993; Ribbens, 1994; Ribbens and Edwards, 1995), about the concepts of 'public' and 'private', their uses, limitations and implications. To restate our position briefly, we believe these concepts are crucial to an understanding of both men's and women's lives in industrialized Western societies. Much feminist attention has been directed towards showing the interaction between public and private spheres at the levels of labour market requirements and state policies. What we believe is key, however, is to explore the meanings of such concepts and distinctions for people themselves, to examine the ways in which they may be invoked or resisted, as well as experienced in a variety of social settings. While recognizing their status as gendered ideological rhetoric, we are also committed to researching their practical implications within particular localities within the context of particular historical moments, and particular contexts of class and ethnicity. As Patricia Hill Collins (1997) has argued so clearly, in relation to public and private spheres and spaces, such locations are 'raced' and 'classed' as well as gendered, and people's perceptions of what constitutes public and private shift according to their social location. Thus the meanings such settings hold, and the ways in which they are experienced, can be quite different for different social groups. In addition, these meanings, and their associated social boundaries, can change constantly over time, to ensure the reproduction of social advantage for particular groups.

Furthermore, we share Stacey's view (1981) that 'public' and 'private' are key concepts for illuminating the history of the social sciences as disciplines rooted within public domains. We would argue that this partiality still continues, such that all students will encounter concepts of macro and micro, action and structure, but they will not all be introduced to the theoretical concerns raised by the concepts of public and private. While some writers have striven to explore the relevance of family and domestic lives for sociological theory, and their integral relevance to key theoretical issues (Morgan, 1975, 1985, 1996), these topics are still not regarded with the same centrality by the social sciences that people accord them in their own lives. And, what is crucial for our concerns here is that when we do study such topics, we may still do so with a theoretical and conceptual framework derived from publicly and institutionally based concerns.

It is also clear, however, that 'public' and 'private' are tricky and ambiguous concepts, which cannot simply be identified by reference to physical locations of home, neighbourhood, workplace, or government, nor can they simply be mapped straight onto gender identities – although they also, of course, have strongly gendered implications. Various writers have sought to identify just what it is that the distinction is about, including Smith's discussion (1987) of different 'modes of organisational consciousness', Cheal's suggestion (1991) of 'contrasting principles of social organisation', and

Ferree's reference (1985) to different 'value systems'. Others have discussed 'gendered cultures' (Dubois et al., 1980; Gullestad, 1984), or 'gendered subjectivities' (Violi, 1992), while we ourselves have suggested that they amount to different 'ways of being' in the world (Edwards, 1993; Ribbens, 1994).

These different 'ways of being' carry gendered implications for a considerable range of issues in people's lives, including orientations to time (Davies, 1990 and Linda Bell, this volume), understandings of the self (Brown and Gilligan, 1992; Gilligan, 1994), variable meanings of rationality (Edwards and Duncan, 1996; Ve, 1989; Waerness, 1989), contrasting moral dimensions (Gilligan, 1982; Ruddick, 1982; Tronto, 1993), different forms of emotional expression (Duncombe and Marsden, 1993), and of language use (Epstein, 1988; Tannen, 1991). All of these may also apply to different ways of relating to people (O'Connor, 1992; Swain, 1989). We have suggested before (Ribbens and Edwards, 1995) that these differences can be summarized to some extent as a contrast in concerns between (1) instrumental and individualized achievement of goals (characteristic of the public) and (2) the concrete details of ongoing processes and connectedness with people (characteristic of the informal and private). Of course, as we observe later, each concern can have negative as well as positive connotations and implications, and there is no strict delineation between the two, with process and connectedness being found in the public sphere, and instrumentality and individualization in the private. Nevertheless, we would argue that, certainly in people's personal understandings and experiences, there is a qualitative difference in orientations, values and 'ways of being' within each sphere.

Some of these themes resonate with longstanding concerns of the 'founding fathers' in sociology, although they do not map onto their discussions exactly. Tönnies' distinction between *Gemeinschaft* and *Gesellschaft* thus particularly focused on differences in types of relationships, with a move from communal, non-transferable and particularistic ties (which were characterized in 'the family'), to individualistic, interchangeable and impersonal ones (characterized in industrial corporations) (discussed by Everingham, 1994; Nisbet, 1970). In addition, Nisbet argues that Weber's distinction, between the ideal types of 'communal' and 'associative' relationships, itself builds strongly upon Tönnies' earlier discussions.

Such distinctions developed from these writers' concerns with major changes in social relationships as Western societies moved from feudal, agrarian economies to industrialized, capitalist economies. Feminist historians and others have drawn attention to the gendered nature of these processes, and have documented and detailed how more traditional values and orientations, rooted in feudal relationships, came to be focused upon the private domain during the course of industrialization and urbanization, and articulated as a domestic ideology (see, for example, Allan and Crow, 1990; Davidoff et al., 1976; Pateman, 1983; Scott and Tilly, 1980; Smith-Rosenberg, 1975). This is one reason that we find such deep debates and agonies within feminism about whether to value the differences of women's lives, based largely upon their family and domestic experiences, or seek an equality based upon a more male experience in the public domain. Are we harking back to traditional values with their feudalistic overtones, or do we want to be part of the project of modernity, even if this entails the loss of relationships and experiences that have been central to women's lives?

Tönnies himself also saw a gender dimension to his distinction, although for him this was likely to be based in nature, rather than socially produced. His actual distinction between *Gemeinschaft* and *Gesellschaft*, however, he clearly regarded as, in effect, ideal types, such that: '. . . [he] is able to show *Gesellschaft* elements in the traditional family as easily as he can *Gemeinschaft* elements in the modern corporation' (Nisbet, 1970: 76). Similarly, we have been at pains to discuss how public and private ways of being may be found in a variety of physical and social settings (elaborated further below).

We would argue that the distinction we have been concerned to explore in our own work, between private and public ways of being, takes a gendered form because women, especially mothers, have a particular social (not biological and essential) positioning within the private domestic sphere of home and family life. Women, of whatever ethnicity or class, are, not always but more frequently, involved in doing housework, in caring for children, the elderly and so on, in both public and private spheres. Women are likely to have a particular location in relation to family life and relationships, in ways that men, of all classes and ethnicities, are less likely to be placed. Like a black identity, for example, this is both an oppressed position and a strength. It is also therefore necessary to stress that this does not imply any rosy glorification of the private over the public. Indeed, members of the Workshop have been as concerned with the tensions and dangers within private lives (e.g. see Barry 1995; Hooper 1995) as they have with the more positive aspects. We endorse suggestions from several writers that contradictions are at the heart of family lives (Ribbens, 1994).

What is significant for the present discussion is the implications of these different ways of being for our forms of knowledge and ways of knowing. In researching these topics, we suggest it requires considerable sensitivity to explore these largely hidden and subordinated private ways of being, with even greater challenges arising as we then seek to represent and translate these into the terms of academic discourses located within public domains. These two aspects of the research process are structured in this book in terms of Part II which concerns the 'fieldwork' process, while Part III discusses various approaches to, and issues arising from, the process of transforming 'the data' for reception by an academic audience (the aspects that Maxine Birch, this volume, refers to as 'being there' and 'being here').

Bringing private lives into public knowledge

Resonating in many ways with some of the distinguishing features of *Gemeinschaft* and *Gesellschaft*, public institutional and academic disciplinary knowledges can be characterized as involving objective, abstract, detached, rational, neutral, broad, institutional epistemologies, which are separated off from, and regarded as superior to, grounded, subjective, involved, emotional, specific, detailed, daily or everyday forms of knowledge. (For discussions from a variety of theoretical and political perspectives, see Apthekar, 1989; Belenky et al., 1986; Collins, 1990; Edwards, 1993; Noddings, 1984; Rose, 1994; Smith, 1987.)

Apthekar, for example, describes the epistemological base of everyday knowledge as manifest in the dailiness of women's lives, and considers how to uncover it:

> By the dailiness of women's lives I mean the patterns women create and the mean-ings women invent each day and over time and in the context of their subordinated status to men. The point is not to describe every aspect of daily life or to represent a schedule of priorities in which some activities are more important or accorded more status than others. The point is to suggest a way of knowing from the mean-ings women give to their labors. The search for dailiness is a method of work that allows us to take the patterns women create and the meanings women invent and learn from them. If we map what we learn, connecting one meaning or invention to another, we begin to lay out a different way of seeing reality . . . dailiness is a process rather than a conclusion; it structures thought. (Apthekar, 1989: 43–4)[4]

This dailiness, its manifestation in fragmented and unspoken ways, and its implications for ways of knowing can, for example, be seen very clearly in DeVault's (1990) discussion of the substantive topic of food.

On the other side of the relationship between public and private knowl-edges, a key issue is the power of public experts, based on disciplinary knowledges, which was also, of course, a central concern in the work of Foucault. We have therefore consulted various interpretations of his work to see what light his own (apparently vast) body of academic knowledge might shed on our discussion here. This has, in itself, constituted an example of some of the dilemmas we are discussing more generally in this chapter. That is, we feel we ought to be seeking to address established mainstream theoriz-ing, in the form of Foucault's work in this case, in order to build bridges with such established theorizing, and to see what we can learn from it, as well as enhancing our own credibility and relevance by linking our work with such writers. Yet we have found it difficult to make any easy link with this writing, since it is focused on a different set of concerns. We have therefore encoun-tered the dilemma here, in this textual production, about whether or not to include discussion of his work.

It is clear that Foucault's writings do have some important points of con-nection with our discussion, but we have been largely unable to find any way into his work that would illuminate our central concern here of the relation-ship between different knowledges based upon public and private ways of being (such as described by Apthekar, above). Almost all of Foucault's work (as well as many of those adopting his particular perspective) was in fact about public discourses, and it is difficult to see a space for introducing our concerns with private discourses, not only as subjective perspectives but as socially located in the dailiness of women's experiences and interactions. At another level, his work could be described as radically undermining distinctions between the public and the personal (see our discussion of these terms, below),[5] with his emphasis upon the ways in which public discourses become inscribed in our subjectivities. However, Apthekar (above) suggests that, for women in the private sphere, it is 'dailiness' that becomes inscribed, in distinction to public discourses.

Maureen Cain's discussion of Foucault's conception of subjugated knowledges does offer some resonance with our own concerns. Subjugated knowledges are '. . . a whole set of knowledges which have been disqualified as inadequate to their task or insufficiently elaborated', (Foucault, 1980, quoted by Cain, 1993: 87). Cain refers to Foucault's writings about the consciousness of 'the masses', whose discourse is rendered illegitimate by dominant discourses. She sees Foucault as arguing that intellectuals (researchers) themselves should be concerned not to utter such '. . . blocking and therefore politically neutralising discourses' (ibid: 87). While such arguments do not directly map onto our interest in 'the private', they do parallel our concerns about the potential damage done by the researcher who, while *appearing* to be speaking on behalf of a group which is subjugated or marginalized, reproduces dominant discourses in an unthinking way.

Thus we find that, while the notion of subjugated knowledges is very relevant to our concerns here, Foucault's own work is now itself a major and powerful element of public, academic knowledge which, as with many earlier, male, classical sociologists, seems to have no place for an explicit consideration of the significance of different knowledges based within private settings in particular, or the ways these may be gendered, 'raced' or 'classed' (or even for any direct acknowledgement of their existence). Furthermore, while Foucault's later work does consider ways in which powerful knowledges might be resisted, and, indeed, suggests that power always entails the possibility of resistance, nevertheless, this resistance is often interpreted in terms of political movements, which are similarly based within the public sphere (see discussion of Foucault's work by Seidman, 1994). In Foucault's genealogical consideration of why particular knowledge claims gain dominance over others, it is unclear whether there is scope for a consideration of something a little different from resistance. We suggest that, at times, public knowledges may not be so much resisted as disregarded, either as irrelevant or unacknowledged. Such disregarding might indeed be seen to occur on the basis of different knowledge forms rooted in more privately oriented social settings and experiences.[6]

These different knowledges can be seen, for example, in Mayall and Forster's discussion (1989) of the different perspectives adopted by mothers and health professionals in considering the needs of children. While the heterogeneous group of mothers they interviewed were concerned with 'now', and with the give and take of daily living with their children, health professionals emphasized children's developmental stages, drawing upon their professionally based, public discourse of developmental psychology. We would argue that, at times, mothers may indeed themselves internalize the psychologistic discourse, but at other times they may resist it, and at other times again, they may also simply operate with a different set of considerations and experiences that disregards the public discourse. Such issues can also be seen in our own work on mothers' mediation with education professionals in relation to their own and their children's education (David et al., 1993).

The central dilemma for us as researchers is that we are seeking to explore such privately based knowledges and personal understandings, but to then reconstitute them within publicly based disciplinary knowledge. In doing so, are we extending the dominance of publicly based knowledge and expertise, and colluding in its intrusion into every nook and cranny of social life? Are we part of the processes of colonization discussed by Mohanty (1991)? Are we contributing to the blocking and politically neutralizing discourse of public power, in Foucault's terms (Cain, 1993)? Perhaps our potential research subjects are right when, and if, they resist us and refuse our endeavours (e.g. see Edwards et al., 1997; Miller, 1995)? Despite such doubts, however, we both persist, on the basis that, without some collective representation, private knowledges are likely to be ever more vulnerable and difficult to sustain. As Violi (1992) argues, we need to produce for ourselves our own social and collective forms of self-representation, in order to transform and modify dominant patriarchal forms of representation, and to make visible a different, alternative, social and cultural order within which to define our identity and subjectivity. In that sense, we are seeking to transform private knowledge into a more publicly based resistance, or at least a diversification and undermining of a hegemony. The challenge is to remain sensitive to the diversity, given the power of the hegemony.

Such sensitivity is likely to require an openness to ambiguity and flux, and a constant concern to re-examine the concepts we are using. In discussing what we mean by 'public' and 'private', we have suggested a coincidence of physical space (as a social construction organized symbolically), psychological space, social networks and activities that produce different 'cultures', 'ways of being', and particular 'ways of knowing'. It is difficult, in practice, to identify unambiguously where exactly we can see the private and where the public. It is easy enough to suggest that the private can be typically characterized as relationship-centred home life, while the public can be typically characterized as the instrumental goal-oriented life of the workplace or government activities. But there are major difficulties beyond this. As we indicated earlier, 'private' ways of being could be occurring at times, perhaps in a subdued way, within the workplace, or could even be subverted into new forms of management style. The public sphere of markets, for example, could not operate without collective social behaviour and connectedness (Hodgson, 1988), and the workplace can be a place of intimacy (Marks, 1994). Similarly, an instrumental goal-oriented attitude can, of course, also be occurring within home life (for examples of one form of this sort of analysis see Carling's discussion, 1991, of rational choice in households). Then there are all the areas that seem not to be clearly public or private anyway, such as caring work within public organizations (Stacey and Davies, 1983), or semi-formal groups such as playgroups operating in local neighbourhood contexts. And how are we to describe the situation when others, such as grandparents, neighbours, or health workers, visit a mother at home? She may then feel that her 'private' space has come under a much more public scrutiny (Ribbens, 1994). In this respect, given the nature of our particular topic concerns, we must also consider how interviewees are likely to regard the research interview, which is itself likely to be occurring within the 'private' home (e.g. see Finch's discussion on this issue, 1984, and Melanie Mauthner's reference to the research interview as semi-public, this volume).

Bringing in the personal

In working with the concepts of public and private and in editing this book, we have come to recognize the importance of another dimension within this conceptualization – that of the 'personal' – and how this is linked to the public and private, and to researching the private in order to make it public. In academic discussion we tend to refer to formal, large-scale organizations (of employment, state, education, etc.) as constituting the public domain, while family, home-centred and informal relationship-centred settings may be described as constituting the private domain. But in their own use of these terms, people may refer to some private settings as 'public' in the sense of exposure to a less intimate and trusted audience, or define some settings within the public sphere as 'private', and thus distinguish a further 'layer' of privacy as personal space.

Figure 1.1 is intended to help clarify some of our thinking on these issues. In our uses of the terms within this diagram, the concepts of both 'public' and 'private' share the fact that they appertain to *social* lives and social settings, in the sense that they refer directly to interactions between people. The public we have already characterized as more goal-oriented and individualistic in its overt value system, and its way of being and knowing. The private we have characterized as more process-oriented and connected in its value system, and its way of being and knowing. Sites that are ideologically constructed as more public include formal organizations, formalized policies and legal systems. Sites that are ideologically constructed as more private include families, kinship, friendship and social networks, and lay knowledges. But the diagram also incorporates the concept of the 'personal', as a way of drawing attention to experiences that are constituted around a sense of self or identity, to do with emotions, intimacy, or the body. We are not suggesting that the personal is not also social, but that it concerns the social as ontologically experienced by the individual; that is, in relation to a person's own sense of being or existence.[7]

The arrows in the diagram refer to the routes by which paths of influence or domination may occur between these different sites. The arrows may thus refer (among other things) to language, actions, the organization of physical space, images and representations, and orientations to time.

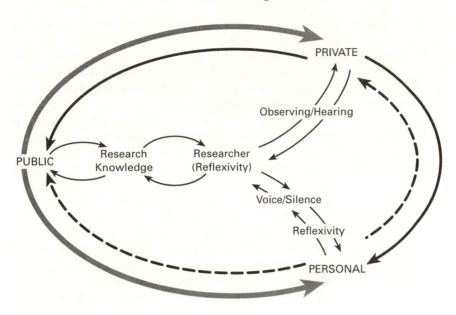

Figure 1.1   *Social settings and the researcher*

Notions of rationality, morality and so on would be expressed via these concrete manifestations. Finally, we have used the diagram to represent the position of the researcher, situated at the interface of the fluid edges between, and the combining of, public, private and personal lives. Before private settings can be represented in public knowledge, they first have to be open to observation, and their 'voices' have to be heard by the researcher, and for personal experience to be heard within academic discourse it first has to be voiced within a research interview, or within other types of material collected from participants, such as diaries (see Linda Bell, this volume). The researcher is thus poised on the threshold between these different experiences and social settings.

Methods, analysis and writing up

Discussions of epistemology and methodology do not always consider the sorts of issues we are addressing in this book – the very particular issues raised by researching the private and personal and seeking to voice it in (the) public. In listening to and representing such subjugated and obscured 'voices' there are issues around data collection methods and techniques of analysis. So far, in feminist and other methodological considerations, far more attention has been paid to the former than the latter, although this is beginning to change. While there is now a significant body of feminist literature devoted to issues of gaining access to research participants and of reflexivity within the data process, far less feminist attention has been paid to the processes underlying the retention of research participants' voices in the phases of data analysis and writing up.

Sometimes also, within examinations of data analysis (whether feminist or not) there is not even a consideration that researchers might not be able just to adopt data collection methods and analysis techniques unproblematically, in much the same way as we have argued that you cannot just import male-based theories and concepts and unproblematically apply them to understanding the private, domestic and personal. Although different analytic methods can be used to examine and provide different perspectives on our interview transcripts (Coffey and Atkinson, 1996), to describe a method in isolation from its theoretical roots is to adopt a 'follow the instructions' or 'technological fix' approach to methodology. Underlying and embedded in all methods and analytic techniques are conceptions of the social world, how it works and how we can understand it. Illustrations of this point within this edited collection include Linda Bell's discussion of the use of diaries, particularly in relation to understandings of time, and Natasha Mauthner and Andrea Doucet's exploration of a 'voice-centred' relational method of analysis. Another example, not addressed within this collection, is the hermeneutic reconstructive model of analysing data (see Chamberlayne and King, 1996; Passerini, 1987; Rosenthal, 1993). Although not explicitly acknowledged within such methodological discussions, the epistemological base of this analytic method has strong similarities with high modernist theories of 'reflexive individuation' (Beck et al., 1994; Giddens, 1991).

Researchers exploring aspects of domestic and intimate lives, and perhaps especially childrearing, will thus need to consider carefully whether or not the tools provided by the method fit with their own epistemological approach to the topic. (And similar points apply to computer analysis packages.) Having made such a point, however, we must not fall into the positivist trap of obscuring the presence and subjectivity of the person using the (analytic) tools. It may be (in a Vygotskian sense) that the intentions and perspective of the user (researcher) are able to transform the 'original' epistemological base of the analytic method. Either way, as we have already stressed, choices have to be carefully and openly reflected upon.

Dilemmas occur at every stage of the research process. From the outset, there is a difficulty in 'letting go' of established academic bodies of knowledge, theories and methodologies (as Janet Parr discusses, this volume). There are dilemmas around needing to be acceptable to others, such as PhD examiners, journal referees, funding bodies, and so on. Yet if we cling to these authoritative ways of knowing, we run the risk of silencing, or shaping in particular ways, private, domestic and intimate ways of knowing, meaning and experience.

The dominance and authority of academic discourses and conventions also extends to how we write up our research. In utilizing and going along with academic conventions we can gain authority and credibility, but again we risk silencing, mutilating or denigrating the voices of the subjects of our research (as Kay Standing discusses, this volume). There is also the issue of whether or not we participate in the dominant discourses and claim academic credibility and status for the knowledge we produce (as Pam Alldred discusses, this volume, in relation to adopting strategies). Equally, becoming aware of how we exercise interpretive authority brings other dilemmas too, in that in our concern for representing the voices of others we may be constrained in developing our own voices as academics and authors, and claiming and asserting our interpretation matters (see DeVault, 1994, and for examples here, see chapters by Melanie Mauthner and Miri Song, as well as Pam Alldred and Maxine Birch).

Introducing our collected voices

The term 'voice' is used in discussions throughout this collection, and its overall structure is organized around 'hearing' (Part II) and 'representing' (Part III). 'Voice' is a concept that can be used with different sets of meanings and antecedents. Jane Ribbens' introductory chapter discusses and explores some of her own personal experience and thoughts on 'voice', particularly in relation to the work of Carol Gilligan on voice, and of Arlie Hochschild on emotions. She considers some of her difficulties in hearing her 'feeling voice' around mothering her youngest child, given the stridency of other voices, from within both public and private domains, which have also become her own personal voices. Given such difficulties, Jane asks how we as researchers can facilitate the vocalization of the more subdued personal voices.

Nevertheless, as editors, and authors of the present chapter, as well as in Jane's own chapter, we have not adopted the term to indicate there is a 'true' or 'authentic' voice to which we can gain access. Rather, we are attempting to signal that there are issues around our ability to hear what is being said about private, domestic and personal lives and then to speak it again (represent it), retaining its meaning and context, in a public forum.

The interplay between epistemology/knowledge and research practice is explored with different emphases in the two main parts of the book. Part II is centred on 'hearing' research participants' 'voices', and is thus concerned with issues of access to research participants and data gathering. Considerations here include the interaction between 'lay', 'grounded' knowledges and practices and 'expert', 'privileged' knowledges and practices, both academic and professional. The various contributors consider whether, and how, people are able to speak – how we obtain the 'private', and personal, voices to which we seek access – and the ways research tools and theoretical orientations can affect how researchers listen to the voices.

This section of the book begins with a chapter by Melanie Mauthner, focused on the data collection stage of the research process. She explores the dilemmas raised when making public the private lived cultures of relationships between sisters, when little in the way of a public or private discourse exists upon which to draw. She describes the advantages and disadvantages of several languages which, in interaction with her research participants and theoretical bodies of knowledge, she used in order to create public knowledge.

These languages included drawing an analogy with other female relationships, a focus on transitions in relationships, and the creation of theoretical
concepts. Tina Miller, in the following chapter, documents how she too
sought to create a space in which women felt able to voice their personal narratives about becoming mothers within the context of an array of public and
lay knowledges that may or may not fit with these personal experiences. She
discusses a number of research dilemmas raised in accessing, gathering and
listening to women's accounts, over time, during a period of uncertain transition, including the potentially pervasive influence of gatekeepers beyond
access, and whether and how women feel able to voice their personal feelings
and experiences. Next, in part continuing the theme of different knowledges,
Linda Bell reveals how she came to realize that the method of gathering data
through solicited diaries may be emphasizing public understandings rather
than other, more personal, voices. She argues that representations of 'time'
and 'activity' observed in diaries need to account for private as well as publicly acknowledged meanings, if we seek to bridge gaps between underlying
concepts of public and private in family or household research. Within this
discussion, as Melanie Mauthner and Tina Miller consider their own location
in their hearing of research participants' voices, Linda Bell also considers her
own field diary in order to shed further light on these issues. Janet Parr's
chapter, too, charts intertwined personal and theoretical shifts, as she discusses the way in which her framework for research into the experiences of
mature women students changed from a positivist to a grounded theory
approach, allowing her research participants', as well as her own, voices to be
heard. She reveals the tensions created between acknowledging a pre-existing
body of theoretical knowledge as required by a PhD and being guided by
research participants' own voices.

Part III focuses on 'representing' research participants' 'voices' – data
analysis and writing up. It examines how we re/construct voices within
research accounts, especially how we make sense of, understand, analyse,
select and re/present narratives or accounts as part of the research process.
Considerations here include whether or not we go 'beyond' the ontology or
understandings of research participants, questions of ethics, how we deal
with competing or contradictory voices, and also the claims we make for the
status of the knowledge we produce.

Miri Song takes us into this section of the book. She discusses the dilemmas
and insights she derived from comparing and interpreting two siblings' interviews, and issues around multiple perception in social research more generally.
Based upon the family stories of siblings in Chinese families running take-
away businesses in Britain, she had to address questions about the relative
credibility and 'truth' of siblings' accounts and questions about reflexivity and
the construction of 'knowledge'. Natasha Mauthner's and Andrea Doucet's
chapter draws further attention to issues in the data analysis stage, tracing the
ways in which they adapted the voice-centred relational method of data analysis in their doctoral research projects and the theoretical and methodological
insights that arose out of their processes of reflecting on the method. They

document how, on the one hand, they sought in their research to transform private concerns into public debates and to voice what might otherwise remain invisible and/or devalued issues pertaining to domestic life, while, on the other hand, being aware that in the process of transformation, private accounts were changed by and infused with their identities as researchers, and became different stories to those originally told by the respondents. They argue that it is not possible to resolve this dilemma but suggest ways of working within it.

Pam Alldred takes us on to examine the epistemological warrants which have conventionally supported ethnographic research and some of its unintended reifications of researchers' power. She then considers how recent discourse analytic research with children and young people presents itself in terms of interpretive authority. The dilemmas she explores revolve around the following questions: if we have lost faith in 'naive' objective-realism and want to avoid placing ourselves centrally in our research accounts at the expense of reinforcing the marginalization of our participants, how might we warrant our knowledge, and what representational claims would we make for our account? She argues that, as long as the discourse of 'hearing children's voices' remains politically persuasive, we might wish to make strategic use of it, even though we may also have theoretical doubts about its conceptual underpinnings and representational claims.

Maxine Birch's chapter documents such decision-making processes in her description of her PhD study as a research journey, from 'going there', and 'being there', to 'being here' in the final analysis and textual reconstruction of the research story. It is this reconstruction of the research narratives that informs Maxine herself of her sociological identity, just as the self-discovery stories informed the participants, in the alternative therapy groups that she researched, of a changed sense of self. A key aspect of the construction of her sociological identity is that the main area of reconstructing the research story is a private, personal experience. Kay Standing also examines issues that arise in the final writing up of research, raising questions about how we write, and who we write for. She explores the differences and power relations between feminist academic language, and the everyday voices of groups of less powerful women. The dilemma she addresses is how we represent the voices of the women in our research (in her example, low-income lone mothers) in a way which is faithful to their experiences and language, but does not position them as 'other' and reproduce hierarchies of power and knowledge.

The division of the book into two main parts – research design and data collection, and analysis and writing up – should not be taken to imply that we see these aspects of the research process as stages that are distinct from each other. Research design, methods of data collection, theoretical and analytic approaches and writing strategies are all part of an overall methodological approach and imply one another, as authors of texts on the subject are now beginning to make clear (see Coffey and Atkinson, 1996; Mason, 1996, for example). This point is also made by the authors here: contributors to Part II of the book, while they may concentrate on the 'hearing' aspects of research, have not confined themselves to this part of the research process alone, and contributors to Part III also raise issues around 'hearing' within their main focus on 'representation'.

While the contributors to this volume may not all agree with the totality of our arguments here about the constitution of, and relationship between, public, private and personal knowledges and ways of being, all acknowledge that theoretical and practical dilemmas and challenges are involved when we are concerned with hearing, retaining and representing research participants' 'voices'. At every point, they reflect on the issues we experience as feminist researchers concerned with the qualitative exploration of intimate, private and domestic lives. Nevertheless, despite our best reflections, the dilemmas remain.

Notes

1 There are, of course, more complex issues behind the parallels we are drawing here between the study of marginalized cultures 'at home' and 'abroad', by researchers working within Western knowledge paradigms. For example, different disciplines have particular histories and variable concerns in dealing with such marginalities. Furthermore, for non-Western women researching women's lives 'at home' (in both senses of the word) there may be multiple forms of marginality involved, with existing powerful (often male-focused) discourses in their own societies, which may or may not parallel powerful Western discourses. (With thanks to Linda Bell for drawing our attention to some of these issues.)

2 Note that we are using the term qualitative research to refer to a broad range of methods, that may in practice not be so neatly dichotomized from quantitative research. For further discussion of the distinction see, for example, David et al., 1994; Hammersley, 1992; Sayer, 1992.

3 Leonore Davidoff ran a masters degree course at Essex University that Jane attended. Examples of Davidoff's written work include Davidoff et al. (1976) and Davidoff (1990).

4 There may well be resonances here with the Marxist notion of praxis, but there is not space to explore this here.

5 We are grateful to Pam Alldred for her discussion of some of these points.

6 There are variable ways of interpreting 'resistance' in Foucault's work, however, some of which might come closer to our notion here of 'disregarding'.

7 We are aware that this diagram, and the distinctions upon which it is based, may have scope for further development and refinement, for example by reference to Albert Hunter's (1995) notion of 'the parochial', which encompasses the grey areas between public and private, of 'community' and 'neighbourhood'. (Thanks to Graham Crow for drawing this to our attention.) Melanie Mauthner's reference to the 'semi-public' (this volume) also constitutes a possible refinement. We are also very conscious that for some writers, 'the private' may be used to refer to experiences that we have here described as 'the personal' (for example, see Bailey, 1997; Hunter, 1995). We would argue, however, that such usage does not allow us to focus on the specific features of experience pertaining to 'the private' that we are concerned with here.

References

Allan, Graham and Crow, Graham (1990) 'Constructing the domestic sphere', in Helen Corr and Lynn Jamieson (eds), *The Politics of Everyday Life: Continuity and Change in Work and the Family*. London: Macmillan.

Apthekar, Bettina (1989) *Tapestries of Life: Women's Work, Women's Consciousness and the Meaning of Daily Experience*. Amherst, MA: University of Massachusetts Press.

Bailey, Joe (1997) 'The private on parade: the private and the public in social thought'. Paper presented to the Annual Conference of the British Sociological Association, University of York, 7–10 April.

Barry, Jacky (1995) 'Care-need and care-receivers: views from the margins', *Women's Studies International Forum*, 18 (3): 361–74.

Beck, Ulrich, Giddens, Anthony and Lash, Scott (1994) *Reflexive Modernisation*. Cambridge: Polity.

Belenky, Mary F., Clinchy, Blythe M., Goldberger, Nancy R. and Tarule, Jill M. (1986) *Women's Ways of Knowing: The Development of Self, Voice and Mind*. New York: Basic Books.

Bell, Linda and Ribbens, Jane (1994) 'Isolated housewives and complex maternal worlds: the significance of social contacts between women with young children in industrial societies', *Sociological Review*, 42 (2): 227–62.

Brown, Lyn Mikel and Gilligan, Carol (1992) *Meeting at the Crossroads: Women's Psychology and Girls' Development*. Cambridge, MA: Harvard University Press.

Cain, Maureen (1993) 'Foucault, feminism and feeling: what Foucault can and cannot contribute to feminist epistemology', in Caroline Ramazanoglu (ed.), *Up against Foucault: Explorations of some Tensions between Foucault and Feminism*. London: Routledge.

Carling, Alan (1991) *Social Divisions*. London: Verso.

Chamberlayne, Prue and King, Annette (1996) 'Biographical approaches in comparative work: the Cultures of Care project', in Linda Hantrais and Stein Mangen (eds), *Cross-National Research Methods in the Social Sciences*. London: Pinter.

Cheal, David (1991) *Family and the State of Theory*. Hemel Hempstead: Harvester Wheatsheaf.

Coffey, Amanda and Atkinson, Paul (1996) *Making Sense of Qualitative Data: Complementary Research Strategies*. London: Sage.

Collins, Patricia Hill (1990) *Black Feminist Thought: Knowledge, Consciousness and the Politics of Empowerment*. London: HarperCollins.

Collins, Patricia Hill (1997) 'The more things change, the more they stay the same: African–American women and the new politics of containment'. Plenary address to the British Sociological Association Annual Conference, University of York, 7–10 April.

David, Miriam, Edwards, Rosalind, Hughes, Mary and Ribbens, Jane (1993) *Mothers and Education: Inside Out? Exploring Family–Education Policy and Experience*. London: Macmillan.

David, Miriam, West, Anne and Ribbens, Jane (1994) *Mothers' Intuition: Choosing Secondary Schools*. London: Falmer.

Davidoff, Leonore (1990) '"Adam spoke first and named the orders of the World": masculine and feminine domains in history and sociology', in Helen Corr and Lynn Jamieson (eds), *The Politics of Everyday Life: Continuity and Change in Work and the Family*. London: Macmillan.

Davidoff, Leonore, L'Esperance, Jean and Newby, Howard (1976) 'Landscape with figures: home and community in English society', in Juliet Mitchell and Ann Oakley (eds), *The Rights and Wrongs of Women*. Harmondsworth: Penguin.

Davies, Karen (1990) *Women, Time and the Weaving of the Strands of Everyday Life*. Aldershot: Gower.

Denzin, Norman K. (1996) 'The facts and fictions of qualitative inquiry', *Qualitative Inquiry*, 2 (2): 230–41.

DeVault, Marjorie (1990) 'Talking and listening from women's standpoint: feminist strategies for interviewing and analysis', *Social Problems*, 37 (1): 96–116.

DeVault, Marjorie (1994) 'Speaking up carefully', *Writing Sociology*, 2 (2): 1–3.

Dubois, Ellen, Buhle, Mari Jo, Kaplan, Temma, Lerner, Gerda and Smith-Rosenberg, Carroll (1980) 'Politics and culture in women's history: a symposium', *Feminist Studies* 6 (1): 26–65.

Duncombe, Jean and Marsden, Dennis (1993) 'Love and intimacy: the gender division of emotion and "emotion work"', *Sociology*, 27 (2): 221–42.

Edwards, Rosalind (1993) *Mature Women Students: Separating or Connecting Family and Education*. London: Taylor and Francis.

Edwards, Rosalind and Duncan, Simon (1996) 'Rational economic man or lone mothers in context? The uptake of paid work', in Elizabeth Bortolaia Silva (ed.), *Good Enough Mothering? Feminist Perspectives on Lone Motherhood*. London: Routledge.

Edwards, Rosalind and Ribbens, Jane (1991) 'Meanderings around "strategy": a research note on strategic discourse in the lives of women', *Sociology*, 25 (3): 477–89.

Edwards, Rosalind and Ribbens, Jane, with Gillies, Val (1997) 'Shifting boundaries and power in the research process: the example of researching "step-families"'. Paper presented to the Annual Conference of the British Sociological Association, University of York, 7–10 April.

Epstein, Cynthia (1988) *Deceptive Distinctions: Sex, Gender and the Social Order*. New Haven, CT: Yale University Press.

Everingham, Christine (1994) *Motherhood and Modernity: An Investigation into the Rational Dimension of Mothering*. Buckingham: Open University Press.

Ferree, Myra Marx (1985) 'Between two worlds: German feminist approaches to working-class women and work', *Signs*, 10 (3): 517–36.

Finch, Janet (1984) '"It's great to have someone to talk to": the ethics and politics of interviewing women', in Colin Bell and Helen Roberts (eds), *Social Researching: Politics, Problems, Practice*. London: Routledge and Kegan Paul.

Giddens, Anthony (1991) *Modernity and Self-Identity*. Cambridge: Polity.

Gilligan, Carol (1982) *In a Different Voice: Psychological Theory and Women's Development*. Cambridge, MA: Harvard University Press.

Gilligan, Carol (1994) 'Listening to a different voice: Celia Kitzinger interviews Carol Gilligan', *Feminism and Psychology*, 4 (3): 408–19.

Griffith, Alison and Smith, Dorothy (1987) 'Constructing cultural knowledge: mothering as discourse', in Jane Gaskell and Arlene McLaren (eds), *Women and Education: A Canadian Perspective*. Calgary: Detselig.

Gullestad, Marianne (1984) *Kitchen-Table Society: A Case Study of the Family Life and Friendships of Young Working-Class Mothers in Urban Norway*. Oslo: Universitetsforlaget.

Hammersley, Martyn (1992) 'Deconstructing the qualitative-quantitative divide', in Julia Brannen (ed.), *Mixing Methods: Qualitative and Quantitative Research*. Aldershot: Avebury.

Hodgson, G. (1988) *Economic Institutions*. Cambridge: Polity Press.

Hooper, Carol-Ann (1995) 'Women's and their children's experiences of sexual violence: rethinking the links', *Women's Studies International Forum*, 18 (3): 349–60.

Hunter, Albert (1995) 'Private, parochial and public social orders', in P. Kasinitz (ed.), *Metropolis: Centre and Symbol of our Times*. Basingstoke: Macmillan.

Marks, S. (1994) 'Intimacy in the public realm: the case of co-workers', *Social Forces*, 72 (3): 845–58.

Mason, Jennifer (1996) *Qualitative Researching*. London: Sage.

Mayall, Berry and Forster, Marie-Claude (1989) *Child Health Care: Living with Children, Working for Children*. Oxford: Heinemann.

Miller, Tina (1995) 'Shifting boundaries: exploring the influence of cultural traditions and religious beliefs of Bangladeshi women on antenatal interactions', *Women's Studies International Forum*, 18 (3): 299–310.

Mohanty, Chandra Talpade (1991) 'Under Western eyes: feminist scholarship and colonial discourses', in Chandra Talpade Mohanty, Ann Russo and Lourdes Torres (eds), *Third World Women and the Politics of Feminism*. Bloomington, IN: Indiana University Press.

Morgan, David H.J. (1975) *Social Theory and the Family*. London: Routledge and Kegan Paul.

Morgan, David H.J. (1985) *The Family, Politics and Social Theory*. London: Routledge and Kegan Paul.

Morgan, David H.J. (1996) *Family Connections: An Introduction to Family Studies*. Cambridge: Polity.

Narayan, Uma (1989) 'The project of feminist epistemology: perspectives from nonwestern feminists', in Alison M. Jaggar and Susan R. Bordo (eds), *Gender/Body/Knowledge: Feminist Reconstructions of Being and Knowing*. New Brunswick, NJ: Rutgers University Press.

Nisbet, R.A. (1970) *The Sociological Tradition*. London: Heinemann.

Noddings, Nell (1984) *Caring*. Berkeley, CA: University of California Press.

O'Connor, Pat (1992) *Friendships between Women: A Critical Review*. London: Harvester Wheatsheaf.

Ong, Aiwa (1988) 'Colonialism and modernity: feminist representations of women in non-Western societies', *Inscriptions*, 3 (4): 79–93.

Passerini, Luisa (1987) *Fascism in Popular Memory*. Cambridge: Cambridge University Press.

Pateman, Carol (1983) 'Feminist critiques of the public/private dichotomy', in S.I. Benn and G.F. Gaus (eds), *Public and Private in Social Life*. Beckenham: Croom Helm.

Ribbens, Jane (1990) 'Accounting for our children: differing perspectives on "family life" in middle-income households'. Unpublished PhD dissertation, CNAA/South Bank Polytechnic, London.

Ribbens, Jane (1994) *Mothers and their Children: A Feminist Sociology of Childrearing*. London: Sage.

Ribbens, Jane and Edwards, Rosalind (1995) 'Introducing qualitative research on women in families and households', *Women's Studies International Forum*, 18 (3): 247–58.

Richardson, Lauren (1996) 'Ethnographic trouble', *Qualitative Inquiry*, 2 (2): 227–9.

Riessman, Catherine K. (1987) 'When gender is not enough: women interviewing women', *Gender and Society*, 1 (2): 172–207.

Rose, Hilary (1994) *Love, Power and Knowledge: Towards a Feminist Transformation of the Sciences*. Cambridge: Polity Press.

Rosenthal, Gabrielle (1993) 'Resconstruction of life stories', in R. Josselson and A. Leiblich (eds), *The Narrative Study of Lives*. London: Sage.

Ruddick, Sara (1982) 'Maternal thinking', in Barry Thorne and Marilyn Yalom (eds), *Rethinking the Family: Some Feminist Questions*. New York: Longman.

Sayer, Andrew (1992) *Method in Social Science: A Realist Approach*. London: Hutchinson.

Scott, J.W. and Tilly, L.A. (1980) 'Women's work and the family in nineteenth century Europe', in Michael Anderson (ed.), *Sociology of the Family* (2nd edition). Harmondsworth: Penguin.

Seidman, Steven (1994) *Contested Knowledge: Social Theory in the Postmodern Era*. Oxford: Blackwell.

Smith, Dorothy E. (1987) *The Everyday World as Problematic: A Feminist Sociology*. Boston: Northeastern University.

Smith-Rosenberg, Carroll (1975) 'The female world of love and ritual: relations between women in nineteenth century America', *Signs*, 1 (1): 1–29.

Stacey, Margaret (1981) 'The division of labour revisited, or overcoming the two Adams', in Philip Abrams, Rosemary Deem, Janet Finch and Paul Rock (eds), *Practice and Progress: British Sociology 1950–1980*. London: George Allen and Unwin.

Stacey, Margaret and Davies, Celia (1983) *Division of Labour in Health Care: Final Report to the SSRC 1983*. Warwick: University of Warwick.

Swain, Scott (1989) 'Covert intimacy: closeness in men's friendships', in Barbara Risman and Pepper Schwartz (eds), *Gender in Intimate Relationships: A Micro-Structuralist Approach*. Belmont, CA: Wadsworth.

Tannen, Deborah (1991) *You Just Don't Understand: Women and Men in Conversation*. London: Virago.

Tronto, Joan (1993) *Moral Boundaries: A Political Argument for an Ethic of Care*. London: Routledge.

Ve, Hildur (1989) 'The male gender role and responsibility for childcare', in Katya Boh, Maren Bak, Cristine Clason, Maja Pankratova, Jens Qvortrup, Giovanni B. Sgritta and Kari Waerness (eds), *Changing Patterns of European Family Life: A Comparative Analysis of 14 European Countries*. London: Routledge.

Violi, Patrizia (1992) 'Gender, subjectivity and language', in Gisela Bock and Susan James (eds), *Beyond Equality and Difference: Citizenship, Feminist Politics and Female Subjectivity*. London: Routledge.

Waerness, Kari (1989) 'Caring', in Katya Boh, Maren Bak, Cristine Clason, Maja Pankratova, Jens Qvortrup, Giovanni B. Sgritta and Kari Waerness (eds), *Changing Patterns of European Family Life: A Comparative Analysis of 14 European Countries*. London: Routledge.

Whyte, W.F. (1992) 'In defense of *Street Corner Society*', *Journal of Contemporary Ethnography*, 21: 52–68.

Whyte, William F. (1996a) 'Qualitative sociology and deconstruction', *Qualitative Inquiry*, 2 (2): 220–6.

Whyte, William F. (1996b) 'Facts, interpretations and ethics in qualitative inquiry', *Qualitative Inquiry*, 2 (2): 242–4.

Wolf, Diane L. (1996) 'Situating feminist dilemmas in fieldwork', in Diane L. Wolf (ed.), *Feminist Dilemmas in Fieldwork*. Oxford: Westview Press.

2   Hearing my Feeling Voice?

An Autobiographical Discussion of Motherhood

Jane Ribbens

Evoking and listening to research voices raises issues about the contingency and precariousness of the perspectives being voiced. For private perspectives and understandings to be communicated, and formulated as public knowledge, they first have to be articulated in a personal voice. Yet, given the power of public bodies of knowledge, we may struggle to find a voice that can express more private ways of being. In this introductory discussion, I want to consider the difficulties I have found in hearing my own voice amidst the multitude of voices that occur around mothering. Over the years, I have moved, in various ways, in and out of the academic forum, and I have also moved in and out of the intense preoccupation of mothering a small child. I want to consider how this mothering has been interlinked with more public academic work, and in particular, how my most recent experience of mothering has been affected by various thoughts and experiences from both public and private domains. As a result, I have come to want to hear my own voice about my mothering more clearly, but have also become aware of how hard I find it at times to do this. A continual self-monitoring occurs, raising issues about the sociology of emotions, and the nature of our internal 'self', or 'voice', in contemporary living. I shall examine these issues particularly in relation to the work of Arlie Hochschild, and of Lyn Brown and Carol Gilligan, exploring some of the areas that lie between their different foci of concern. The struggle to hear my own voice about how to mother my small child raises general issues about how to distinguish, and theorize, the various voices we may hear in research interviews, how to hear the more muted voices of those we research, and how the awareness of audience may shape what is spoken.

My motherhood in differing contexts

I first became a mother when my son was born in 1975, followed by my daughter in 1978. There was never the slightest question of doing anything other than becoming a full-time mother. I had never personally known a 'working mother', either in my childhood or my adult life. Employment simply was not an issue. I recall being phoned, when Jonathan was about 10 months old, by a colleague from my previous job, who asked me to undertake some work for him. I was amazed and puzzled. I had a small baby to look after – how could I possibly be involved in any sort of daytime paid employment?   .

This arrangement also suited me. I had found work life difficult, I enjoyed my life at home as a mother, and was already building up quite a framework of friends, acquaintances and activities with Jonathan. I had also previously studied some psychology while at university, and was well aware of psychological theories that suggested children need their mothers with them during the 'vital early years'. This theory made me feel good about being at home with small children, and I did not question it. After all, it would only be a few short years before my children started playgroups and schools, and I could then think about returning to work.

I was probably fairly confident as a new mother. I had expected the early months to be hell. I could not *imagine* how on earth one got up in the middle of the night to see to a small baby. I did not know what the middle of the night looked like! (My profound sleep patterns of pre-motherhood have in fact never returned.) When Jonathan arrived, I was overwhelmed by the joy of new motherhood. The earth seemed to have shifted on its axis, and I was the lucky surprised inhabitant of a new planet. He cried a lot, but I did not care. He was wonderful.

I went along to mother and baby groups run by the local health visitors, and talks put on by the local National Childbirth Trust group. An older friend had given us a well-worn copy of Dr Spock (1958), and I bought a copy of Penelope Leach (1974). I looked at these sometimes, and found tips which seemed quite useful. I don't think they changed my underlying approach in any way, though. And the books I liked very much the best were the research reports from the work of John and Elizabeth Newson (1965, 1968, 1978), in which they had asked mothers what they actually *did* with their young children. I found it wonderful to get some sense of other mothers' experiences, rather than reading what I was *supposed* to be doing. It was such a comfort to read about the numbers of boys still in nappies at night at the age of four!

It was the Newsons' work that formed the starting point for my own research, many years later, when I decided to undertake a PhD study of mothers and their children. I had spent more than ten years away from the formal academic study of sociology, and one of the first new names I came across on my return was that of Foucault, with the notion that modern life has seen new forms of surveillance of our personal lives, a surveillance increasingly internalized and carried out as self-monitoring. I also, of course, came across a burgeoning feminist literature, which at that time (early 1980s) was primarily oriented to the view that motherhood is oppressive (Rich, 1977, being a notable exception), and that women had been duped into accepting ideologies of domesticity that led to their exploitation and imprisonment within the confines of the home. I was also aware of more 'classic' sociological work investigating social class patterns in childrearing, which suggested that women's behaviour and attitudes with their children were derived from the social class experiences of their husbands.

I did not find any of these accounts very convincing, since they did not seem to correspond to the experiences and views of the mothers I knew. It seemed to me that many/most mothers were highly committed to being with their children, that motherhood was a very powerful experience for women, and that it was bound up with very strong feelings indeed, both joyful and, at times, difficult (the complexities being so eloquently portrayed by Jane Lazarre, 1987). It also seemed to me that women are individuals in their own right, with personal histories and social class experiences of their own. Furthermore, I saw women as exercising some agency in their lives, actively developing their understandings of the world based on their everyday life activities (as Rosalind Edwards and I discuss in Chapter 1), not simply accepting some ideology or surveillance imposed from the top down. As Porter (1996) points out in discussing the relevance of Foucault's framework to an analysis of the power of nurses, people have the capacity to resist surveillance and keep their lives 'private' even against the authoritative questioning of caring professionals. What were probably more significant in our childrearing views were the expectations and assumptions of other mothers in the various networks and activities that occurred around childrearing (Bell and Ribbens, 1994). While I was aware that women like myself did read childrearing books, and did listen to 'expert' advice, I felt that we did so critically, and purposefully sought out the information we felt we needed (Jamieson and Toynbee, 1990; Kohn, 1963; Stolz, 1967; Urwin, 1985). These are still the views I hold today, and I continue to reject any simplistic notion that women as mothers are, somehow, cultural dupes, or the victims of false consciousness. Nevertheless, we clearly do not stand 'above' or 'outside' culture, in its broadest sense, and I want to explore here the complexities of my own childrearing views and feelings in relation to a range of particular, individual, and more generalized cultural contexts.

My PhD study was completed by 1990 and I started working as an academic, teaching courses about gender, and about families. Then in 1992 my first marriage broke up, over quite a short period of time. I was divorced early in 1993, and started living with a new partner. He and I had both always yearned for another child within our earlier marriages, but were amazed and delighted when I became pregnant in my forties, giving birth to Suzannah in 1994. The personal circumstances of motherhood this time round are very different from my earlier experiences. My position as a mother is different for a start. I am not a full-time mother, but only a very part-time mother. My life does not revolve around my motherhood, but rather Suzannah's life has to revolve more around my work commitments, and numbers of significant other people in my life with whom I want to spend time. In turn, I have to be prepared to 'share' Suzannah's delightful company with a greater number of other carers. And I am not as involved in the networks and activities of other, younger, and more full-time mothers as I was before.

It has felt very special, and a great privilege, to have another beautiful daughter so unexpectedly, in my middle age. I believe that I have also changed, as a person, since I first became a mother. I have been through years of considerable self-examination and self-exploration, leading me to review many of my family patterns and experiences, and reconsider the ways in which I relate to others. It has also felt more relaxing this time around, and there seems to be less to worry about in terms of how to look after her. I have been more prepared to 'go with the flow', more prepared to compromise, and to modify my views of childrearing according to circumstances, although there are limits to this too.

Before having Suzannah, I had also become more aware of my own taken-for-granted assumptions and behaviours around childrearing as a result of experiences with my new partner, Peter. I want to explore some of the class and gender differences between Peter and myself, first, because they have profoundly challenged some of my assumptions about childrearing at a very personal level, and, secondly, because they also relate to much wider issues of how class and gender may be significant in the management of emotions (Hochschild 1979, 1990). Hochschild suggests that working-class occupations are much less concerned with the management of emotions than are middle-class jobs, which are more concerned with '. . . the on-the-job task of creating and sustaining appropriate meanings . . . an appreciation of display rules, feeling rules and a capacity for deep acting' (1979: 570). Working-class jobs, by contrast, '. . . more often call for the individual's external behaviour and the products of it', so that '. . . the creation and sustaining of meanings . . . is not such an important aspect of work' (ibid). Hochschild also points out the feminine dimension of occupations requiring emotion management. Tancred-Sheriff (1989) similarly points to the significance of women's emotional management skills as a source of 'adjunct control' for business enterprises.

These issues come to life very vividly in my relationship with Peter, the class and gender differences both being quite marked between us. The latter are rather too complex (being sometimes sharply defined and at times contradictory) to unravel easily here, but the class difference is simpler to describe. Although my parents were from quite working-class and lower middle-class backgrounds, my own life has always been unequivocally middle-class. My father did well in his working life as an electrical engineer, and I experienced a comfortable middle-class childhood. I went to university, entered professional occupations, and married a college lecturer. Although our finances were never particularly easy, there is no doubt we lived a middle-class family life in terms of our attitudes and values, and friendship networks. Peter, on the other hand, regards himself, and is regarded by others, as unequivocally working-class, in terms of his upbringing, his lifestyle, and his adult working life in the building trade. He is also, of course, a particular individual, as well as a working-class male, a parent and grandparent. I hope I am not in danger here of stereotyping the differences between our experiences by reference to our gender and/or our class positions, although we often discuss such issues between ourselves.

Peter has always loved small children, and already had close, very loving, relationships with his two small granddaughters before I met him. Watching him with his granddaughters, I was amazed, and envious, to observe his way of relating to them. It all seemed to be so much simpler, and more straight-forward, than my own assumptions of how to care for children. When left with them in his care, he would incorporate them into his own life with con-siderable easiness, rather than tailoring his activities around them. He would take them into settings where I would not have thought it possible to take them (pubs, workplaces, social events). And when it was really not possible to include them, he would look around among his network of acquaintances for childminding help, which seemed to be quite easily available and readily given. When he was with them at home, I saw that he took such enormous delight in their company, playing with them in all sorts of silly ways, for the delight of the game and of the moment. But also, when he really wanted something for himself that conflicted with their desires, he would simply assert his own wishes without any sign of 'guilt' or ambivalence. When it came to basic childcare tasks, he seemed quite prepared to do what came most easily, rather than be bound by any preconceived ideas of what was 'cor-rect'. And the children, in turn, took immense delight in his company and in his warm and relaxed physical contact.

In Hochschild's terms, Peter seemed to be expressing fewer framing/feeling rules about childcare than I was used to, or at least, he seemed not to share *my* framing/feeling rules (although I was not aware of his being constrained by other rules instead, except perhaps an overriding one to protect small children, and not to display anger to them). As a result, my own rules became more visible to me, and more open to conscious reflection, without necessar-ily regarding them as less desirable than Peter's.

Another way of describing the difference I felt between us is to suggest that Peter seemed to be quite largely free from the images of what a parent should be that I had observed in research with mothers. My own research involved mothers who had not identified themselves as problematic (Ribbens, 1990). I was also familiar with Natasha Mauthner's (1994) study of mothers who identified themselves as suffering from severe postnatal depression. In com-paring these two groups of women, it was striking how all these mothers seemed to hold images of what motherhood, and childhood, should be like. With the depressed mothers, these images seemed to be so oppressive they became a major factor in the depression itself. With my sample of mothers, the images were less obviously oppressive, and I described them as 'typifica-tions' of children (Schutz, 1954). Nevertheless, they were very significant in providing a framework for the ways in which mothers talked about their childrearing. Yet, in both Natasha's sample and my own, there were also the one or two women whose accounts of motherhood and childrearing did *not* seem to draw on such images, or clear typifications. These women seemed instead simply to discuss 'what came most easily', and what 'suited' them to do, and, in that sense, to have more freedom to be the active agents and creators of their own childrearing.

These experiences, both from research based in the public knowledge domain, and from relationships in my private life, have been quite an insight for me, as a mother second time around. Furthermore, I have the confidence of knowing my feelings better, of believing that I have 'dealt with' some of my childhood issues, and of experiencing my own inner source of wisdom. I also see my older children grown into people that I love and admire. I feel overwhelming love for my new daughter, and have no doubt that she will receive an abundance of love and caring from both her parents – even if she will experience some feeling of being different from other children whose parents are younger than we are. In addition, in my academic work I have been very concerned to critique the status of child development 'knowledge' and to re-examine assertions about what constitutes 'correct' childrearing. I have wanted to give greater priority to the voices of mothers themselves, and the view that each woman brings up her child/ren in ways that make sense to her. I have argued that differences of childrearing cannot be regarded as right or wrong in any straightforward way, but relate to much more fundamental values about the nature of social life, and of individuality (Ribbens, 1994).

Then one day, not long after Suzannah was born, someone (I cannot now remember who) asked me what difference it made to my mothering that I have been so involved in researching and teaching about mothering as an academic topic in the years since my older two children were born. I readily replied that this time around I wanted to feel more able just to do what I *wanted* to do, to be less concerned about being a 'good mother', and to accept that my feelings could be a legitimate basis for making decisions. I was happy to have articulated this reply, and went home contemplating its significance and ramifications. But over time, I have come to realize that, even when I try to 'listen' to my own voice and to 'know' my own feelings and wants, other images and voices intervene.

Finding my 'feeling voice'

This has raised numerous questions. What do I mean by these various 'voices' and where do they come from? Might some of them be 'imposed' upon me, and is there one voice which is more 'authentic' or 'truer' to 'myself'? Are some voices external while others are internal? Which of these voices is actually verbalized and under what circumstances (a major question for research)? Are some voices silenced even before I hear them myself?

I do not find it helpful to think about some voices as being 'out there' while other voices are 'inside my head'. I see the boundaries between outside and inside as more permeable and contingent than that. Some voices may literally be expressed by others around me, 'out there' in my current life, but some voices may also be voices from my past, which were 'out there' but which I have incorporated and reshaped, and now echo in my mind, even below my conscious awareness.

Burkitt offers us a sustained discussion that seeks to challenge the inner/outer divide of psychological discourse, suggesting that emotions are an indissoluble complex, 'irreducible to social structures, discourses or physiology' (1997: 52), and rooted in relationships: '. . . there is no "inner" world of feelings separated from "outer" cultural norms or values' (ibid.: 48). However, while this may be a crucial point to consider at a theoretical level, at the experiential level this inner/outer divide may be highly significant for the ways in which people think about their lives.[1] As Burkitt himself argues, the relationships or emotional habitus in which we learn our emotions may be rooted in our childhoods, and I suggest that they are thus *experienced* as *internal*ized. Furthermore, while Burkitt at times argues strongly for an action component as integral to emotion, he also at times suggests that emotion may be expressed in action *or thought*. If the latter is the case, it will be experienced as an internal phenomenon. While Burkitt does suggest that individuals do have a psychological or physiological life, he also argues that this is '. . . fragmentary and intermittent . . . held together in a meaningful way only in the "weave of behaviours" that compose the practices of everyday life' (ibid.: 44). Building on the work of Elias, he goes on to argue that emotional habitus is linked to power and status structures, and that post-Renaissance Europe has required the open expression of certain emotions to become taboo. Yet this itself hints at our contemporary concern with knowing what a person is 'really' feeling. I find therefore that Burkitt overstates his argument when he asserts that, '*Emotion only exists in action, contained as it is in relations of power, interdependence and communication*' (ibid.: 53; original emphasis). Indeed, I will argue that, at an experiential level, I am seeking to shift the balance of power towards paying attention to, and hearing, my feeling voice more consistently.

Nevertheless, I do not believe I have a 'true' or 'authentic' voice, that could be heard if only it was not drowned out by others. I agree with Burkitt that any voice I have will be a socially constructed voice (as Maxine Birch has shown so clearly in her empirical study of the practices of alternative therapy groups for the exploration of the 'self', 1997).

In a different direction, Carol Gilligan appears, at least at times, to state her commitment to the concept of an 'authentic' voice (1994; Brown and Gilligan, 1992), and to distinguish this voice from the 'moral voice' (Brown and Gilligan, 1992: 29). Yet I would prefer to distinguish between a moral (socially constrained?) voice(s), and a more creative voice(s), that constitutes the author-ity of the speaker. In Brown and Gilligan's framework, it seems to be just a short step from their discussion of authentic voices, to their evaluation of authentic relationships (ibid.: 49). Furthermore, the voicing of the '. . . full range of feelings and thoughts' is then taken to indicate psychological 'health' (ibid.: 52), with all the potential this concept has for obscuring the judgements of the more powerful behind an apparently scientific and neutral knowledge base. There is clearly scope for differing interpretations of Carol Gilligan's work, and the understanding of *self* with which discussions of *voice* are connected is quite explicitly relational: 'Within this framework of interpretation, the central metaphor for identity formation becomes dialogue rather than mirroring; the self is defined by gaining voice and perspective and known in the experience of engagement with others' (Gilligan, 1988: 17). But rather than hesitate over the ontological or theoretical dilemma of how to speak of my own 'voice', I am seeking here to sidestep the issue by emphasizing that some of my voices *feel* more empowering to me as an individual, and seem to give greater expression to my feelings and creativity. Indeed, in Natasha Mauthner's (1994) study of depressed mothers, the recovery of 'voice' could serve as a route out of depression. I am thus making a personal, experiential exploration and statement here, although it then has implications for how, and which, voices might be expressed and heard in research interviews. (For a rather different discussion of the politics of 'voice', see Pam Alldred, this volume.)

Paying attention to my feeling voice(s) may thus give me a sense of greater empowerment or author-ity, while on the other hand, by implication, it also feels as though some of my own voices are more concerned with pleasing other people, or particular audiences (including myself as an audience making moral judgements upon myself). What I have wanted to do in my motherhood this time around is to find a voice that enables me to please myself in my relationship with Suzannah.[2] (Although, reading this sentence, another (moral) voice wants to monitor it, and amend it to take account of pleasing Suzannah as well as me – is that not right as a mother?) I want to create a space in which I can know my own feelings and desires as a mother, but I seem instead to hear a cacophony of voices. Some of these voices are so effective and powerful that they close up any space I may have for knowing my feelings, and they accomplish this without any stridency. It does not seem so much a psychological suppression, as a silent and stealthy subversion.

In seeking to examine the implications of these issues, I have turned to the work of Arlie Hochschild on the management of emotions. In her earlier work, Hochschild (1979) suggests that 'emotion work' can be distinguished from ego defence mechanisms, the former being more conscious and open to active 'evocation' and 'shaping'. She thus makes quite a sharp distinction between 'emotion work' and 'suppression'. Emotion work, she suggests, is concerned with the management (via display/expression, with or without corresponding 'deep acting') of feelings that she seems, on the whole, to regard as *unproblematically already known* by the individual concerned. Although she does suggest in her later work that, 'In managing feeling, we contribute to the creation of it' (1990: 120), her conceptual framework, and her questions of concern, do not focus on the processes by which the 'ongoing stream of experience' becomes articulated and known as particular feelings to be managed. There thus seems to be a lacuna between the work of Hochschild (the sociologist) and Brown and Gilligan (the psychologists). Brown and Gilligan assume that, once regained, voice is unproblematic, whereas Hochschild's focus of concern assumes that emotion is already known, but its expression, and sometimes the feeling itself, is then managed.

Nevertheless, in her later work, Hochschild explicitly raises a greater variety of questions about feelings, distinguishing between: '. . . the way we wish we felt, the way we try to feel, the way we feel, the way we show what we feel, and the way we pay attention to, label and make sense of what we feel' (1990: 117). In this extract, the most significant question for me in my personal quest, and for us as researchers of private and personal lives, is the last one – how *do* any of us attend to, and give meaning to, *and voice*, our feelings (a question that raises further issues about the relationship between cognition and feeling)? What I am suggesting, from my own reflections on my maternal voice, is that I do not so much suppress my own voice as allow these various strands that Hochschild distinguishes to become fused together in a sort of internal hegemony,[3] shaping my feelings accordingly. What I would like to do, instead, is to bring my feeling rules under more conscious scrutiny, so that I can then 'get past' them, to bring my feelings to voice. The difficulty of doing so, I believe, is not so much an issue of unconscious repression, as of the struggle to produce an identity for myself (and others) that I find morally acceptable, i.e. where the feelings, the feeling rules and the situation do coincide. By trying to get past the feeling rules, I am trying to create more space to hear my feeling voice.

Again, as I stated earlier, I do not believe that this internal hegemony represents any straightforward internalization of an external surveillance emanating from powerful bodies of knowledge. But who I am is clearly bound up with the culture, social structure, and associations I have experienced in my life – what Jon Bernardes has referred to as 'structured beingness' (1986). And I believe that my gender, my class background, and my wider socio-historical heritage (including my maternal grandmother's Methodist affiliations), as well as my particular history of family relationships, have all led me to attend particularly closely to the voices of others, and have made it much more difficult for me to know my own feelings and wants, and bring them to a voice – albeit, that this 'feeling voice' would itself be shaped and constructed via social contexts, including the 'bringing to language'. Until articulated and voiced (at least to myself), my feelings, as with those we research, have no shape or form, nor any socially meaningful reality even for myself (maybe resonating with Burkitt's (1997) discussion after all).

Furthermore, it is within the intensely moral space of my mothering that I am seeking this time around to listen explicitly to my own wants and feelings. What I have found, however, is that my voice concerning my moral obligations towards my child subverts, or drowns out, my feeling voice as a basis for my mothering. Further, these moral voices may well monitor and reshape the feeling voices, so that I may only experience the correct feelings appropriate for a good mother. Indeed, the moral voice instructs me in the imperative that there are certain feelings that I *should* have as a mother. It is not enough just to do the right things with my child; I am also supposed to have the right feelings to go with the actions, and this is a central part of motherhood as I have experienced it in this society at this period of time. Thus Mary, whom I interviewed for my earlier research, regarded playing board games as an important maternal responsibility, but it was important to bring her feelings into line with the activity: 'I made myself enjoy it and now I really do enjoy it. Because I thought, it's no good unless I enjoy it, so I forced myself to enjoy the games' (Ribbens, 1994: 62). I find this an amazing statement, but what do we make of it? While Mary's comment may sound rather extreme, it may be striking only because she has articulated particularly clearly something that we all tend to do as mothers, but perhaps do not like to admit we do. Feelings are thus monitored, silenced or shaped, as Brown and Gilligan have explored in detail with their studies of adolescent girls, showing how a girl may '. . . disconnect from her feelings and knowledge in an attempt to connect to what others want' (1992: 110). Yet, in Hochschild's terms, Mary seems to have accomplished the ultimate, successful 'deep acting':

> The most generous gesture of all is the act of successful self-presentation, of genuine feeling and frame change, a deep acting that jells, that works, that in the end is not phony (since it is what the emotion *is*) though it is none the less not a 'natural' gift. (Hochschild, 1979: 569; original emphasis)

What is perhaps remarkable in Mary's comment is that this emotional production continues to be recognized by Mary as a self-conscious act, yet I would also hesitate to describe Mary's voice as 'inauthentic' in Brown and Gilligan's terms.

At most, my maternal feeling voices *may* be allowed space to be heard, as long as they exist under the control of the moral voices, without any direct link with maternal actions. While some such control may of course be necessary in caring for small children, for myself I feel that it has gone too far, and I would like to redress the balance. Again, this is not because I regard my feelings as constituting my 'authentic' voice (authenticity, Trilling suggests, being the 'new moral virtue' – discussed by Hochschild, 1979: 271). What I am more concerned with is my sense of loss of power and agency in my life, through this well-rehearsed subversion and management of my feeling voices.

However, as a basis for making decisions about how to care for Suzannah, the moral voices proclaim that the feeling voices are not relevant, and have no legitimacy. I cease to *have* a feeling voice other than through the moral monitoring. And this monitoring occurs so automatically, I have very little awareness that it is happening at all. And if I am doing this in relation to myself as my own moral audience, how much does this happen for our interviewees, who may well be simultaneously acting as moral audience for their own feeling voices concerning sensitive private issues, as well as attending to us as researchers, as moral audience (see Melanie Mauthner, and Tina Miller, this volume)? Women as mothers, for example, frequently find themselves being subjected to unsolicited and unexpected advice and judgements by others. It is clear that many areas of 'personal choice' and 'private lives' evoke very strong feelings in others. Research with various groups of mothers (David et al., 1996) testifies to women's extensive and automatic assumption of obligation and responsibility as mothers, such that as a researcher, even questions that are carefully thought out to be value neutral will be heard as carrying moral overtones. Mothers may well have difficulty in believing that researchers will not make judgements, and beyond the researcher, there is also the eventual possible public readership to be considered.

One immediate area where all this became apparent for me as a mother this time around was in relation to our sleeping arrangements for Suzannah – sleeping arrangements being a very significant issue in the care of small babies. I am aware of theories that suggest that it is good for small babies to have the close physical contact and security of sleeping with their parents. Indeed, in some cultures, putting a baby to sleep by itself in a separate room would almost be regarded as child abuse. I am also aware of other views that suggest that having a baby in your own bed is the start of a very difficult habit that may not be broken for years. Furthermore, it is a habit that is detrimental to the mother's capacity to cope, and the child's need for clear boundaries and routines. These various views were put to me quite explicitly by health professionals and (kind and caring) friends and neighbours, even when they knew I have already brought up two children to adulthood, and might be expected to know my own mind.

But there is the rub. How to know my own mind? It has taken real attention and concentration at times to create a space where my feeling voices may come into being. Thus at times, I overwhelmingly loved having Suzannah's small body nestled into mine in bed at night, to feel her breathing and be close to her little noises. It felt very precious to be able to offer her my breast without any rearrangement, and sometimes even without my conscious awareness, in my sleep. This may have felt all the more important because her care has been shared with others during the daytime, and furthermore, I had never expected to experience the joys of breastfeeding in my life again, especially with such a sweet, contented baby. But at other times, I so much wanted to be able to move about restlessly without any concern for her, and to switch off my attention completely. The tiredness became totally debilitating, and in addition, I was aware of other people's surprise that I was still breastfeeding her at 10 months. I remember one particularly poignant night after she had stopped breastfeeding during the day at all, so that the feed in the middle of the night was the last one left. As she started to stir and I offered her a dummy in place of the breast, I lay and waited to know whether or not she would waken fully and feed after all. Part of me longed for it not to end, for her to continue to wake and nestle into me, demanding for this special closeness to continue. Another part of me was simply desperate for undisturbed sleep. I just did not have the energy for the concentration necessary to elucidate *what* I wanted or felt!

As I struggled to find a space to attend to these feelings, other voices asked what all this might say about my mothering (other than that I was confused and ambivalent!) Did it mean that I was overprotective, that I could not bear to allow her to separate from me, as the much-loved child of a middle-aged love affair? Or did it mean that I was tense and unyielding, needing to create an unnecessary and premature space between us? (Now that she sleeps in her own bed in a separate room I still suffer the same wrench at parting from her each night, while still valuing the security of knowing that she has consistently 'slept through the night' (i.e. given me an undisturbed night) since being parted from us.)

There are numerous monitoring voices discernible here, including a variety of moral voices. One is quite pragmatic, another is quite puritanical. Another again is idealistic in its vision of a secure and protected childhood. A particularly difficult one to confront is the voice that assumes that childhood involves laying down patterns for the future, so that I must always be oriented to future time, and the possibility that what I do now may have consequences for my child for years to come. Indeed, this orientation is fundamental to our contemporary understandings of childhood and child 'development'. Thus I have been regaled with warning stories of how Suzannah might carry on waking and feeding at night for several years if I did not end it before a year. I could not just please myself in the here and now. The significance of the time orientation is also related to the notion that I must be consistent, such that I should not behave one way one day, according to how I feel, and another way another day. I must build up routines and habitual expectations in order to provide security and develop a child who can fit into 'normal' social expectations.

The importance of paying Suzannah attention is another theme that is voiced effectively in my mothering. I recall taking her to a research meeting one day, when she was a few months old. I had left the meeting early to give her some lunch in a friend's office. When she had finished and was happy, I laid her on the floor while I read the local newspaper. As other people walked into the office, I was aware of a guilty startle in front of this new audience, that I should be seen to be sitting with my baby, ignoring her, leaving her unstimulated while I was preoccupied with trivial news.

I am also now uncomfortably aware of the gaze of others when she has her dummy (soother) in her mouth, as a toddler. My own feeling is quite strongly in favour of giving small babies a dummy to satisfy what I see as their need for comfort sucking. But as she gets older, it becomes more and more difficult to resist the subtle communications that I should be discouraging this habit. I may go to a group of mothers and toddlers where she is conspicuous for being the only child with a dummy. Her childminder has also discouraged her from using the dummy during the day (and I have gone along with this, encouraging Suzannah to put it on one side as she goes in to play). Recent research on the use of dummies has received widespread media coverage, suggesting that the use of dummies retards the child's development. Perhaps her 'language development' will be hindered by daytime use of the dummy? Perhaps her teeth will be malformed by its prolonged use? All of this means that I feel much more comfortable when she is happy without the dummy (so that she resolves the conflict for me). But what do *I* actually *want* to do about her use of the dummy? I do not know. It is only now, as I sit here and consider the issue, that I am aware of a vague feeling that I want her to be comforted, secure and happy. Indeed, if I had not committed myself to writing this chapter, perhaps I would have given up any attempt to attend to my feeling voice months ago, under the pressures of everyday life as a mother. And what message am I conveying to Suzannah in all this, about her ability (her right?) to know and pursue her own wants?

A further example of my awareness of sensitive audiences for my mothering occurred in a teaching context, without Suzannah being present. During the course of an undergraduate seminar on the experience of motherhood, several younger students expressed very positive anticipations of motherhood, while an older student (already a mother) spoke of her life with her young child in very negative terms. The younger students appeared considerably discouraged and appalled by this account, and I sat silently wondering whether to voice my own more positive experiences of motherhood. I am aware in such discussions that students are tentatively exploring, in a public setting, some very sensitive issues and feelings, and that my own input as the lecturer can be quite powerful – although my personal experience and feelings are, of course, neither more nor less relevant than anyone else's. I believe it is probably very helpful for younger students to hear about the more negative experiences of motherhood, but I would also prefer them to hear a mixture of views. Should I let them know that my own experience does more closely resemble their own anticipations of the joy of motherhood? But even then, perhaps the voicing of my joy might reveal some deep deficiency in my own make-up, exposing a lack of wholeness in myself, and a fundamental need to have a sense of purpose and self-esteem based outside of my own being? As I sat and mused on these permutations, evaluations and guilt seemed possible in every direction. I kept my mouth shut.

And what of my sense of audience here and now: how have I decided what to include in my writing here, and how to present it to you? How have I arranged the pieces to develop an overall story? And what do you, dear reader, make of this present discussion? Does it resonate with Brown and Gilligan's arguments (1992) about the suppression of women's authentic (albeit 'polyphonic and complex', 1992: 23) voices, and Mauthner's (1994) linking of this with depression in mothers? Or does it resonate more with Davis's suggestion (1994), *contra* Brown and Gilligan, that women deal with multitudinous, contradictory and fragmented voices? Perhaps you think I am neurotic and anxiety-ridden, deeply lacking in self-confidence as a mother. Perhaps you think just the opposite, that I must be quite fundamentally confident to be able to write all of this down for a public audience, or that I am a wise fool who knows she's one. I sit here at my computer in my bedroom in suburban England, quietly typing, constructing and refining this textual version of my voice at this period in time, but very aware that, once written and published, this account will take on a life of its own, quite separate from me. I hope you will hear me kindly, and make of this what you will.

Research implications

In this autobiographical discussion, I have sought to pay attention to the 'internal' processes of voice, while also recognizing their fundamentally cultural construction. But I am not only seeking to find my own voice in my mothering. I am also committed to hearing the voices of others (women and men), rooted in their own experiences and understandings, about their lives with their children. I want these voices to be heard within the public domain, to contribute to the contestation of public 'expert' bodies of knowledge and to the empowerment of women and men in their own lives. Doubtless, the two quests (personal and academic) are connected. I am not seeking to hear an 'authentic voice' in myself or others, but to shift the balance of power, away from a moral self-monitoring and towards a greater sense of agency and personal control over the definition of our feelings. After all, what Burkitt, Hochschild, and Brown and Gilligan clearly share is a concern with the power dimensions (particularly around gender) of feelings and their voice/expression.

I have thus suggested that not only does it require much attention and care to hear my own voice, but it requires even more attentiveness to hear and represent the voices of others. How should we regard what is being said, as our interviewees talk to us, as researchers and as the (potentially moral) audience? Are we hearing them articulate the feeling rules they hold, and/or do we interpret what is said to us as examples of 'deep acting' (whether explicitly recognized or not) (Hochschild)? Or can we, as researchers, provide a space to enable others to bring their 'authentic' voice to language (Brown and Gilligan)? Can the research process foster empowerment, via the articulation and wider communication of people's own understandings of their lives, just as I seek self-empowerment by listening to my own maternal voice? Or will our presence as researchers in relationships with interviewees, acting as the personalized interface between the expression of private meanings and their ultimate reception by the powerful audience of public knowledge production, mean that we can only offer a semblance of hearing, contributing in the end to an even more subtle subversion of private understandings? These are the processes and dilemmas to be explored in subsequent chapters in this book.

Notes

I am particularly grateful to Natasha Mauthner for her comments on this chapter.

1 This point parallels in some ways the discussion of the experiential significance, as distinct from the theoretical adequacy, of the concepts of public and private, as discussed in Chapter 1.

2 I am thus tending here to place my feelings, and knowledge of my feelings, as a central part of 'myself'. The significance of emotions for a sense of 'self' is also discussed by Maxine Birch (1997) in her empirical study of alternative therapy groups.

3 I am grateful to Rosalind Edwards for suggesting this concept to me.

References

Bell, Linda and Ribbens, Jane (1994) 'Isolated housewives and complex maternal worlds: the significance of social contacts between women with young children in industrial societies', *Sociological Review*, 42 (2): 227–62.

Bernardes, Jon (1986) 'Multi-dimensional developmental pathways: a proposal to facilitate the conceptualisation of "family diversity"', *Sociological Review*, 33 (2): 679–702.

Birch, Maxine (1997) 'The quest for self-discovery: the reconstruction of self-identity stories in alternative therapy groups'. Unpublished PhD dissertation, Oxford Brookes University, Oxford.

Brown, Lyn Mikel and Gilligan, Carol (1992) *Meeting at the Crossroads: Women's Psychology and Girls' Development*. Cambridge, MA: Harvard University Press.

Burkitt, Ian (1997) 'Social relationships and emotions', *Sociology*, 31 (1): 37–57.

David, Miriam, Davies, Jacky, Edwards, Rosalind, Reay, Diane and Standing, Kay (1996) 'Mothering and education: reflexivity and feminist methodology', in Louise Morley and Val Walsh (eds), *Breaking Boundaries: Women in Higher Education*. London: Taylor and Francis.

Davis, Kathy (1994) 'What's in a voice? Methods and metaphors', *Feminism and Psychology*, 4 (3): 353–61.

Gilligan, Carol (1988) 'Remapping the moral domain: new images of self in relationship', in Carol Gilligan, Janie Victoria Ward and Jill McLean Taylor, with Betty Bardige (eds), *Mapping the Moral Domain: A Contribution of Women's Thinking to Psychological Theory and Education*. Cambridge, MA: Harvard University Press.

Gilligan, Carol (1994) 'Listening to a different voice: Celia Kitzinger interviews Carol Gilligan', *Feminism and Psychology*, 4 (3): 408–19.

Hochschild, Arlie Russell (1979) 'Emotion work, feeling rules, and social structure', *American Journal of Sociology*, 85: 551–75.

Hochschild, Arlie Russell (1990) 'Ideology and emotion management: a perspective and path for future research', in Theodore D. Kemper (ed.), *Research Agenda in the Sociology of the Emotions*. New York: State University of New York Press.

Jamieson, Lynn and Toynbee, Claire (1990) 'Shifting patterns of parental control 1900–1980', in Helen Corr and Lynn Jamieson (eds), *The Politics of Everyday Life: Continuity and Change in Work and the Family*. London: Macmillan.

Kohn, M.L. (1963) 'Social class and parent–child relationships: an interpretation', *American Journal of Sociology*, 58 (4): 471–80.

Lazarre, Jane (1987) *The Mother Knot*. London: Virago Press.

Leach, Penelope (1974) *Babyhood*. Harmondsworth: Penguin.

Mauthner, Natasha (1994) 'Postnatal depression: a relational perspective'. Unpublished PhD dissertation, University of Cambridge, Cambridge.

Newson, John and Newson, Elizabeth (1965) *Patterns of Infant Care in an Urban Community*. Harmondsworth: Pelican.

Newson, John and Newson, Elizabeth (1968) *Four Years Old in an Urban Community*. London: George Allen and Unwin.

Newson, John and Newson, Elizabeth (1978) *Seven Years Old in the Home Environment*. Harmondsworth: Pelican.

Porter, Sam (1996) 'Contra-Foucault: soldiers, nurses and power', *Sociology* 30 (1): 59–78.

Ribbens, Jane (1990) 'Accounting for our children: differing perspectives on "family life" in middle-income households'. Unpublished PhD dissertation, CNAA/South Bank Polytechnic, London.

Ribbens, Jane (1994) *Mothers and their Children: a Feminist Sociology of Childrearing*. London: Sage.

Rich, Adrienne (1977) *Of Woman Born*. London: Virago.

Schutz, Alfred (1954) 'Concept and theory formation in the social sciences', *Journal of Philosophy*, 51: 257–73.

Spock, B. (1958) *Baby and Child Care*. London: Bodley Head.

Stolz, Lois Meek (1967) *Influences on Parent Behavior*. Stanford, CA: Stanford University Press.

Tancred-Sheriff, Peta (1989) 'Gender, sexuality and the labour process', in Jeff Hearn, Deborah Sheppard, Peta Tancred-Sheriff and Gibson Burrell (eds), *The Sexuality of Organisations*. London: Sage.

Urwin, Cathy (1985) 'Constructing motherhood: the persuasion of normal development', in C. Steedman, C. Urwin and V. Walkerdine (eds), *Language, Gender and Childhood*. London: Routledge and Kegan Paul

PART II

SPEAKING AND LISTENING: REFLECTING MULTILAYERED VOICES

3   Bringing Silent Voices into a Public Discourse

Researching Accounts of Sister Relationships

Melanie Mauthner

How does a researcher explore a socially invisible personal relationship? Unlike motherhood and marriage (and 'the family') (Clark and Haldane, 1990; Rich, 1984), relationships between biological sisters lack their own social institutions or representations in the public sphere. This chapter considers some of the difficulties of researching a topic that exists primarily in the private realm of domestic and family life with no language, public discourse, institution or images of its own (Mason, 1989). This reflexive and retrospective account draws on data collected from 37 women in an exploratory qualitative study.

First, I document the absence of representations of sister relationships in *public knowledges* in general and in social research in particular. Second, I examine the *lived culture* of sister relationships in the private sphere (Johnson, 1986). Third, I describe the various languages I developed in order to gather data and represent these relationships during the research process: through analogy with other female relationships, a focus on transitions in relationships, and the creation of theoretical concepts. Fourth, I examine the appropriateness of these methods in the field and the way I located myself as a researcher. Finally, I provide some interpretations of the different types of representations these languages produced.

These dilemmas can illuminate other invisible ties without their own social institutions – relationships between lesbians and gays, adopted children and birth parents and other family bonds where voluntary negotiation of responsibilities and 'contracting'[1] – instead of duty – is becoming the prevailing ethos (Clarke and Haldane, 1990; Finch and Mason, 1993; Giddens, 1992; Weeks et al., 1997).

An invisible relationship in the public sphere

One of the absences around sister relationships occurs in both the public sphere and the research literature itself. By public sphere, I mean the formal organizations, formalized politics, law, media and academia, discourses on high culture and politics that form public knowledges (Johnson, 1986: 287). Sister relationships are unrepresented here in contrast with the mother-in-law/daughter-in-law tie, for instance, which exists through a long tradition of parody (Cotterill, 1992). There are, however, some exceptions in three specific sites. Sibling rivalry is addressed in childcare manuals for parents (Fabera and Mazlish, 1987; Reit, 1985); images of the sister bond flourish in the media, film and fiction – the recent screen adaptations of Jane Austen's novels are a good illustration of this (Cahill, 1989; Mackay, 1993; McNaron, 1985); and sisterhood has provided a metaphor and political rallying point for women coming together in the nineteenth and twentieth centuries to build communities and campaign for their rights (Fox-Genovese, 1991; Morgan, 1984).

Nevertheless these public representations remain marginalized and fail to provide substantial knowledge of the private lived cultures of sister relationships or a language for experiencing this private world as a lived culture. Johnson (1986: 287) offers some useful explanations for understanding why this knowledge is not available: power, he says, operates in a way that ignores salient issues for subordinated groups – in this case women – and privatizes the secrecies of the oppressed; moreover, public representations of private forms can distort these when they are male-defined and middle-class; they can also universalize, stigmatize or pathologize. Hence, the absence of representations of sister relationships from wider public life explains the lack of a language for sisters themselves to speak about this aspect of their lives 'in public'. A private language, however, does exist which sisters use to voice their relationship either with each other 'in private' and/or with the researcher – a language of emotions and power relations (see Mauthner, 1997).

This absence of public representations is echoed in the research literature where studies in development psychology and medicine outnumber sociological work (Allan, 1977; O'Connor, 1987). What little is known about sister relationships concerns psychological rather than social or cultural aspects of this tie, childhood and old age rather than adolescence and adulthood (Lamb and Sutton-Smith, 1982; Murphy, 1992). In addition, the sibling bond or 'sibships' (Hudson, 1992; Powell and Steelman, 1990),[2] relationships between brothers and other family ties between parents and children have received more attention than sister relationships (Apter, 1990; Dunn, 1984; Mendelson, 1990; Sharpe, 1994; Warman, 1986). In-law relationships, step-families, gay families and family negotiation and communication have also been explored (Burgoyne and Clark, 1984; Cotterill, 1994; Holland et al., 1996; Weeks et al., 1997; Weston, 1991).

How can this neglect be explained? Relationships between biological sisters remain a taken-for-granted aspect of women's lives compared with their role and identities as mothers, wives, daughters and even mothers/daughters-in-law (Brannen and Collard, 1982; Cotterill, 1994; Doucet, 1995; Mason, 1987; Ribbens, 1994; Sharpe, 1994). Changes in kin relationships are little researched apart from transitions in marital relationships and the evolution of notions of family responsibility (Edwards, 1993b; Finch and Mason, 1993; Mason, 1989, 1996; Vaughan, 1987). Relationships between sisters have been the subject of popular psychology and autobiography rather than sociological enquiry (Dowdeswell, 1988; Downing, 1988; Spender and Spender, 1984). While these texts do construct a form of public language about the sister bond, this language is descriptive rather than analytical and focuses on individual rather than social aspects of the bond.

There are a number of reasons why adult sister relationships remain underexplored compared with other female relationships between mothers and daughters and female friends. Sociology's neglect of private and personal relationships reflects its traditional concern with public, institutional and structural forms of social life and lack of interest in women's relationships with each other in general (Rosalind Edwards and Jane Ribbens, Chapter 1 of this volume; O'Connor, 1992). In particular, the continuing preoccupation with women's gendered servicing and caring role overshadows other possible identities, as friend, for instance – a tie where pleasure rather than meeting physical dependency needs may be primary (O'Connor, 1992).

Secondly, greater attention has been paid to a critique of romantic love than to an exploration of friendship between women apart from historical accounts and recent studies of girls' and married women's friendships (Faderman, 1981; Hey, 1997; Lasser, 1988; O'Connor, 1991; Oliker, 1989; Raymond, 1986; Smith-Rosenberg, 1975). Friendship, equally ignored, is similarly not institutionalized in our society and is difficult to define (Allan, 1989). There is also the taboo surrounding the underexplored issue of friendship and lesbianism, especially physical intimacy between female friends (Griffin, 1994; O'Connor, 1992).

A third reason for this neglect, suggested by my own study, is the gap between the idealized and politicized myths of sisterhood as solidarity and similarity upheld by the women's movement (Fox-Genovese, 1991; Morgan, 1984) and women's personal experiences with a sister, which can include conflict and arouse painful and ambivalent emotions about what is often a sensitive relationship (Fishel, 1994; Mathias, 1992; Sandmaier, 1995). As political ideal, sisterhood '. . . has drawn upon a familial metaphor to evoke an image of nonauthoritarian bonding among female peers. It thus sought to retain notions of attachment and loyalty associated with noncontractual family relations' (Fox-Genovese, 1991: 15–16). While sisterhood has come under scrutiny for ignoring class and race differences between women, part of its strength and appeal as a political rallying-point lies in its vision of collective experience and creation of new knowledge about previously invisible aspects of women's lives. In the next section I examine some of the difficulties involved in collecting these experiences and creating this knowledge for both the research process and the sisters who spoke to me.

Sisters in private

One of the implications of researching a publicly invisible relationship which exists primarily in the private realm is that the research process is located midway between each world. This process is about making '. . . explicit what we know already implicitly as participants in a culture' (Johnson, 1986: 301). The tension between entering the private world of lived cultures made up of moments '. . . embedded in every day social intercourse in very specific sites and occasions' and representing the more hidden aspects of relationships in a semi-public way appears in the interview situation (Johnson, 1986: 287). By semi-public I mean the space between the existence of sister ties as 'private' forms and their absence in the public institutionalized sphere – a space where the relationship becomes visible to participant(s) and researcher as sisters.

The act of describing and representing these relationships relies on revealing aspects of experience in a very personal and emotional way. I use 'personal' to refer to the individual 'I' as distinct from 'private', although these four definitions – public, semi-public, private and personal – permeate each other and cannot be neatly separated (Rosalind Edwards and Jane Ribbens, Chapter 1 of this volume; Griffiths and Seller, 1996). Exposing private and personal experience in this way, through events and emotions, is a sensitive process where participants and researcher can feel cautious and vulnerable. Perhaps this approach is necessary, as Adrienne Rich suggests, in order to create a new collective and public knowledge: 'I believe increasingly that only the willingness to share private and sometimes painful experience can enable women to create a collective description of the world which will be truly ours' (1984: 16).

However, this process of describing private lived cultures and creating new knowledge is not without its costs. I briefly outline my research before looking in detail at these difficulties. I carried out 29 interviews, individual and paired, with women aged between six and 50 from a range of class and ethnic backgrounds in the UK. I sampled across five decades, from the pre-teenage years to the fifties. I accessed the sample principally through snowballing and used several techniques to gather the data including an ecomap of kin and friendship networks, a flowchart of life events and turning-points, and a semi-structured depth interview (Department of Health, 1988). I collected narratives of sister relationships in order to document the different types of tie and contact patterns that exist between them, the factors that affect their relationships, the differences and similarities with other female friendships, and changes in these ties over time.

One difficulty was the feelings of ambivalence experienced by the women I spoke to about the impact of taking part in the research. Many felt disloyal in talking about a personal relationship to a stranger, although others felt positive about acknowledging an important relationship and talking to me as researcher and 'sister'. Another was the challenge of remembering past events. However, one woman in her twenties said after the interview that it made her want to find out more about their early teens from her sister, who did not participate in the study.

Attempts to represent elements of a private relationship are reflected in some of the tensions between talk and silence, verbal and physical behaviour, distance and intimacy in an interview with two young sisters. Hilda, aged nine, and Adrienne, aged 12, sitting on a couch while they spoke to me, moved closer together and further apart throughout the interview as they laughed, giggled and quibbled about different aspects of their relationship. Their physical intimacy was apparent in these 'couch dynamics'. But for most of the interview, they talked about each other in the third person as 'she' rather than 'you', which distanced them from each other. Another way that Adrienne distanced herself from Hilda and, implicitly, the intimacy of their relationship, was her repeated use of the term 'annoying'.

> *Adrienne*: We, I mean, I find her totally annoying most of the time, and that, I mean, you know but we're not, you know, we get on sometimes but . . . you know, I just find little, I mean . . .
> *Hilda*: [under Adrienne's voice] Yeah.
> *Adrienne*: I'm like that with everybody really.
> *Hilda*: [under Adrienne's voice, talks more slowly than Adrienne] I think so really, yeah an' it's . . .
> *Adrienne*: [talks more haltingly than Hilda] I mean I get annoyed the way she speaks you know and everything . . .
> *Hilda*: [Laughs]

What is striking about this semi-public account of the relationship is the assertion of having little in common. These reasons were offered by Adrienne and agreed by Hilda:

> *Adrienne*: We both go to very different schools, we did go to very different schools anyway and so . . . we don't have much in common to talk about really.
> *Hilda*: No, we couldn't . . .
> *Adrienne*: And as there's an age gap, you know we don't, we don't have much to talk about really, I mean.

This oscillation between distance and intimacy, through their words and their body movements on the couch, the emphasis on their differences as well as the issues on which they see eye to eye, pervades their dialogue. Their discussion of the ethics of friendship, for example, reveals a shared understanding of their social world, when Adrienne first condemns Hilda's practice of 'dumping' best friends before acknowledging that she too is familiar with this practice:

> *Adrienne*: Hilda goes through her friends like, just amazing, how many best friends she has.
> *Hilda*: I've got one best friend.
> *Adrienne*: You had, she just goes through them, you know.
> *Hilda*: I've got one best friend and lots of special friends.
> *Adrienne*: Yeah, but you, first it was Juliette, then it was Rhonda, then it was Gwen.
> *Hilda*: It wasn't Rhonda.

> *Adrienne*: It was Rhonda.
> *Hilda*: It was not Rhonda, I never . . .
> *Adrienne*: It was Rhonda.
> *Hilda*: It was not Rhonda.
> *Adrienne*: It was Rhonda.
> *MM*: But why, why's that not OK?
> *Adrienne*: Because, because she just dumps them, like they're little . . .
> *Hilda*: I do not. I've only . . .
> *Adrienne*: . . . little pieces of rubbish or something . . .
> *Hilda*: No, it's, I do not. The only person I've ever kind of said, I've kind of gone off, 'cos I do not like her, was Juliette that's the only person [. . .] I didn't kind of, I didn't become her best friend because um she was really nice and stuff, and . . .
> *Adrienne*: Because there was no one else to be your best friend. [Laughs.]
> *Hilda*: Yeah, I mean I just got attached to her and then she just became it and I tried to work off her. And then she's got lots of other friends now.
> *Adrienne*: Yeah. No, I mean I don't think it's bad, I mean I've done it tons of times but . . . [Laughs.]

Hilda and Adrienne's detailed analysis of the 'dumping' and 'working her off' phenomenon highlights their implicit shared understanding of the intricacies of best friendship and the appreciation they have of each other, their actions and motives. Indeed talk in friendship generates and maintains a social world through 'shared knowledge structures' (Coates, 1996; Duck, 1990; Morgan, 1990).

The sisters do not express their understanding and appreciation of each other explicitly; this could be due to their age. Instead, it is visible through their body language as they both sit on the sofa in the privacy of their home: this forms the private experience of their relationship, only accessible in the social interview situation. Here is another example of Hilda and Adrienne affirming their sibship:

> *Hilda*: [whispering] Well, I'd rather have Adrienne than any other sister.
> *Adrienne*: So would I.
> *Hilda*: Just because I mean like . . .
> *Adrienne*: I mean I'd rather have Hilda . . . [Laughs.]
> *Hilda*: [laughs] I'd rather have me than anybody else, I mean I . . .
> *Adrienne*: I'd rather have Hilda.

In this semi-public account of their relationship the pair's affection is implicit and embedded in the way they finish each other's sentences, return to a topic following a digression, sit next to each other, and possess intimate knowledge of each other's lives. This knowledge is exemplified by their grasp of the ups and downs of each of their various friendships: their affection creates a space where they can complain, listen and comment about friends or 'stupid cows', discuss arguments with friends together and ask each other for advice:

> *MM*: If you have an argument with a friend, do you tell each other?
> *Hilda*: We don't do it kind of personally. But we do it kind of. We're always listening to each other. When we're telling Mum about something, we're always commenting and talking.
> *Adrienne*: Yeah.
> *Hilda*: . . . we're always commenting and . . .

Adrienne: Yeah.

Hilda: . . . and talking.

Adrienne: You know, we'll say, 'Oh, I had a really awful day today, I had a really horrible, you know stupid cow sitting next to me', you know or, when we will say. I mean we, we'll . . .

Hilda: And we'll kind of ask, 'Now who's she?' . . .

Adrienne: Yeah.

Hilda: . . . like that.

Adrienne: I mean we'll just, we won't really sort of . . .

Hilda: . . . kind of sit down at a table . . .

Adrienne: Normally we . . .

Hilda: . . . and kind of say, 'Guess what's happened at school?' and then we go and talk about it . . .

Adrienne: I mean . . .

Hilda: . . . but I mean then just kind of overhear a conversation and she's telling everything . . .

Hilda and Adrienne's sense of their relationship as not having a lot in common contrasts with their intimacy and understanding of each other: one interpretation of this is to view their semi-public account during the interview of their private experience as a narrative of tensions and contradictions, differences and pleasures of intimate relationships, in this case between sisters. This narrative embraces both emotions and power relations found in other female relationships (Cotterill, 1994; Hey, 1997) and reflects the absence of a specific language to make this particular relationship visible.

The absence of a specific language to describe the sister relationship

One of the aims of my study is to create a new language for representing the tie between sisters, a language as yet undeveloped. One woman I interviewed describes her difficulty with putting her feelings into words about her changing relationship with her younger sister:

> Um, what was I going to say. It's hard to sort of explain it all logically or say eloquently but . . . it's fine now, I mean it's good. I mean it was fine, it was good before, it was just this one you know these couple of issues kept on coming up.
>
> (Rae, 30, speaking about Bukhi, 25)

This new language draws on three different sources: first, analogy with discourses of other female relationships – between friends, and mothers and daughters; second, life events and turning-points in sister relationships which foster both intimacy and distance; and third, theoretical concepts to do with power relations and subjectivity.

Representing sister relationships through analogy with other female relationships occurred frequently among the women I spoke to. Several compared their relationship with their sister to that with a best friend or mother figure.

> *Zoe*: . . . it's like um you have best friends, yeah, but . . . you know that you've got that secret from your best friend as well that you can only tell your sister . . . so it's like, it's like a second best friend where you, so, I don't know, she is.

MM: So . . .
Zoe: She is like one of my best friends.

(Zoe, 17, speaking about Sofia, 16)

I like her in a way that um, if I'm with her, I can eh, try . . . I try to be sisterly but I
end up to be motherly in that sense. And um, when she's in a good mood we could
have a giggle.

(Carmen, 46 speaking about Rita, 32)

Both the women and I appropriated discourses about mothers and friends
in order to explore and describe sister relationships. These discourses hinted
at areas of similarity and difference and enabled us to make the invisible
accessible. Mother–daughter relationships, female friendship and 'best friendship' which touches on sisters as 'best friends' suggest several relevant themes
for understanding sister relationships: confiding, changes in power, interdependence, separation and change over time (Apter, 1990; Cohler and
Grunebaum, 1981; Fischer, 1986; Hey, 1997; Nice, 1992; O'Connor, 1987;
Oliker, 1989). Adrienne Rich's poem *Sibling Mysteries* contains images of
mothers, best friends, even lovers:

> The daughters never were
> true brides of the father
>
> the daughters were to begin with
> brides of the mother
>
> then brides of each other
> under a different law
>
> Let me hold and tell you
> (Rich, 1978)

A second way of representing sister relationships during the research
process is by focusing on life events and turning-points in the women's lives as
sisters. This approach stems from work on the life-course, family histories and
auto/biography (Burgoyne and Clark, 1984; Stanley and Morgan, 1993;
Vaughan, 1987; Weiss and Lowenthal, 1975). A sociological approach to
auto/biography allows the complex webs of relationships in which women's
lives as sisters are enmeshed to be traced. It also highlights the difficulties that
ensue for participants *and* researcher when attempting to both 'tell their stories' and interpret them (Hamson, 1995; Plummer, 1995).

Significant turning-points include changing schools, moving, leaving home,
getting married, 'coming out' and becoming a mother, in relationship/s with
sister/s and other members of wider kin groups – fathers, brothers, cousins,
aunts. The importance of these events lies in the emotional and physical intimacy and distance which they create. Here Anne, aged 38, describes a change
in her relationship with one of her younger sisters, Hailey, aged 33, when they
were teenagers, brought about by the family's move abroad. Anne remained
in England and lived with some relatives while Hailey moved with her parents.

Anne: my sister Hailey and I had a terrible relationship when we were much younger. I mean I think I was very sort of weak willed and she would bully me. Well no not physically bully me but she could just irritate me beyond belief and for a long time we had quite a distant relationship but in fact now I get on extremely well with her [. . .]

MM: When did that change then?

Anne: I think probably by her going off to Vienna was quite a major move. I remember being in the kitchen with my mother and I can't remember what age now. But they'd certainly been in Vienna three or four years and my mother was complaining about something that Hailey had done and I was actually defending her behaviour. I really can't remember the details but I do remember was my mother turning round and saying . . . you know that's extraordinary to find you actually defending something that Hailey's done. I mean that must be the first time in your life. And I suddenly realized that I think I probably distance . . . um had a lot to do with it.

A third way of representing sister relationships in order to make this tie visible is to develop a theoretical language: theory can prove useful for setting lives and relationships in a wider context than that of the individual by relating the experience of the individual to social structures or historical time (Miller, 1995; Steedman, 1992). The theoretical language employed in my study stems from two sources. The first is empirical sociological research on kinship and female friendship (Allan, 1977; Fishel, 1994; Hey, 1997; Mathias, 1992; O'Connor, 1987; Oliker, 1989; Sandmaier, 1995). The second is from a 'tool-box' approach, currently utilizing three theories (Ball, 1994: 14): feminist standpoint theory, feminist postmodernism and post-structuralism, and sociological work in auto/biography. Several concepts derive from these sources: power and negotiation, gendered talk, subjectivity and emotions.

Feminist theories allow women's gendered subjectivity and the sister relationship to be placed at the centre of women's lives (Maynard, 1995). Feminist research on women's lives highlights a number of methodological concerns to do with researching a family relationship and a sensitive issue, as well as the issue of power relations between participant and researcher (Brannen, 1988; Edwards, 1993a; Holland and Ramazanoglu, 1994). It has also pointed to the importance of making the subjectivity of both participants and researcher visible in the research process, something which more traditional objective and masculine methodologies ignore (Maynard, 1994).

Feminist postmodernism and post-structuralism enable particular moments in stories of a relationship to be captured – a shift or a turning-point – while locating these in the fluid, flowing and changing aspects of relationships (Alcoff, 1988; Bloom and Munro, 1995; Griffiths, 1995): they have influenced my attempts to collect 'stories' about contradictory forms of gendered subjectivity in researching private experience (Steedman, 1989; Walkerdine, 1990).

In addition I have drawn on recent sociological work on auto/biography and the life and oral history traditions in order to develop: a *method* of data collection, a quasi-ethnographic style in the field and a reflexive approach to locating myself in the research (Geiger, 1986; Stanley, 1993; Troyna, 1994). Combining ideas from these three different theories which do not necessarily coexist together forms an 'eclectic project' (Maynard, 1995) and a creative process which is in itself a post-structuralist notion.

These three attempts to create a new language for representing sister relationships – through analogy with other female relationships; a focus on life events and turning-points; and developing theoretical concepts such as power relations and subjectivity – provided a framework for outlining the research questions, design and method of analysis. How useful is this language for talking to and about sisters in the field?

In the field: talking about sisters

Fieldwork raised issues which I had not foreseen about the intersections between the personal, private and semi-public in interviews. I adopted a feminist methodology during fieldwork and collected data according to five relevant principles: I paid attention to reflexivity, power relationships, participants' voices, the researcher's voice, and emotions in the research process. Applying these principles, however, raised several dilemmas for me as researcher which the language I developed for representing sister relationships did not address. This language – of analogy, life events and turning-points, and theoretical concepts – while useful for designing the study, selecting appropriate methods with which to gather the data, and encouraging the women to 'tell their stories', presented several difficulties for myself and the women I spoke to in terms of the five feminist principles. I present a retrospective and reflexive account of my struggle with these principles in the field, especially my attempt to maintain a balance between participants' voices and my own voice or location in the research process, and between accounts of personal and private experience in the semi-public space of the interview.

I began fieldwork with a clear mission to gather accounts of private experience from participants and in this endeavour, the language I developed for representing and elucidating women's accounts of their relationships with their sisters was successful. For example, I devised a series of topics rather than questions covering life events and relationship transitions. Some of these topics included: contact patterns, changes in your relationship/s, school years, the age gap, significant events in your life and in your relationship/s with your sister/s, sisters and friends.

These topics allowed us, researcher and interviewee, to meander our way through the pleasures and tensions of the sister bond in an open exploratory way rather than a standard chronological or linear fashion. Using the topics as a guide created a conducive atmosphere for talking about the 'sister experience', 'sistering' and other relevant issues. In the early stages of fieldwork I was concerned with gathering these accounts and accessing women to talk to me, and felt satisfied with my technique. Gradually I felt the emotional exhaustion of listening to the women's stories and eventually, in the middle of fieldwork, I puzzled over how I, as researcher and sister, was going to locate myself and my personal experience in the research. I return to this later.

I adopted several measures central to a feminist methodology for carrying out research in an ethical and sensitive manner with the women I spoke to (Stanley and Wise, 1990). I explained the research to potential participants, negotiated access and consent with women and some of their sisters, attempted to manage the interview as a social interaction rather than 'therapy', respected privacy during interviews about women's personal experiences and their confidentiality from one interview to the next with related sisters. Throughout I adopted a flexible approach: some women offered to contact their sisters on my behalf to request their participation, others preferred me to contact them directly. I listened to their feedback at the end of the interview and contracted to send them a summary of the findings when the study is finished.

Moreover, during the interview itself, I adhered to several tenets of the technique to listen to the women attentively and let the interaction follow the themes the women raised (Brannen, 1988; DeVault, 1990).

> We talked about what cropped up, what was relevant for her: like being single for instance [. . .] (Field notes)

> I was so taken by her powerful narrative, her style and her forceful personality that I let myself be carried by her. (Field notes)

My style became quasi-ethnographic as I collected forms of life histories. At the outset I refined the questions after every couple of interviews. I discovered that some private experiences were far too personal to discuss in an interview: certain childhood experiences and aspects of sexual relationships were off-limits. Some women remained silent and teenagers found the whole area of the body and sexuality far too salient and personal. The longer I spent in the field the more I moved away from my original set of questions to the topics mentioned above (see p. 48). The interview had a loose structure and so the order in which the topics were covered varied. My interviewing style became looser and I learned to ask fewer questions.

These ethical concerns and practical techniques ensured respect and sensitivity for the voices or subjectivities of the women with whom I spoke. They also provided me with complex, detailed, rich and 'messy' accounts of private experience (Clandinin and Connelly, 1994). The language that influenced the interview topics enabled the women and me to represent moments and events in their relationships. These ethics, techniques and new language of representation, however, ignored another feminist principle, reflexivity, with which I grappled and only felt comfortable with towards the end of my fieldwork. Reflexivity is a central tenet of a feminist methodology whereby the researcher documents the production of knowledge and locates herself in this process for '. . . the subjectivity of the researcher herself is part of research production' (Stanley, 1987).

Placing myself in the research required me to consider the place of personal experience in the accounts of private lived cultures that we – the women and I – produced and represented in the semi-public space of the interview. This was a fraught, taxing and shifting process. I experimented with several attempts to locate myself as researcher. Initially I detached myself from the research because of its personal nature for me in order to maintain the privacy of my own relationship with my sister. I too am a sister and I found it difficult to keep the two realms of personal life and research in the semi-public domain separate (as did Miri Song in her work about siblings, this volume). I addressed this issue in the field notes I wrote after each interview. Here is one example:

> I do want to establish more distance with the participants [. . .] Their experience felt close to mine. Maybe that was why I want to distance myself from it. (Field notes)

Sometimes I veered to another extreme of degrees of disclosure during interviews which made me feel vulnerable afterwards.

> They asked me some questions too and I answered, I figured they had told me so much. They were curious about my own relationship with my sister so I told them in a nutshell. (Field notes)

My ambivalence about wanting to preserve my own privacy while asking others to make semi-public parts of their private experience was a dilemma throughout the research. (Linda Bell writes about this issue in relation to keeping diaries, this volume.) Only gradually did I find a position where I felt comfortable enough to disclose some personal information, engage with participants about the content of the research including its 'political' or feminist nature (Thorne, 1980), and address the draining emotional effect of the research on me as researcher:

> I think it's the most exploratory interview so far. Also one where there is more of myself in terms of the kinds of questions I asked though I did not actually say anything specific or explicit about myself. Perhaps this is me letting go a bit more. Also she did not ask me anything about me or the research . . . (Field notes)

> So I said that it was also hard for me to listen and I have learned to become better at this myself only recently, i.e. how to go away from it all and not carry it all inside me. I did not talk at all about myself this time except in this way to say what the research process was like for me. I felt I struck the right note at last after the 22nd interview! I said to her that I have a sister and it has been hard to keep me separate from the 'work'. So I was talking about me, me as researcher, rather than me as private person which I was doing before although I hadn't wanted to. This felt right, comfortable, some reflexivity and sensitivity but no disclosure of the personal on my part. (Field notes)

I alternated between distancing and disclosure regarding the women I interviewed before I found a middle-ground position that took account of my own subjectivity. My position shifted and the research process reflects my ambivalence (see Tina Miller's chapter for an example of her attitude to talking about her experience of giving birth with her interviewees, this volume). Asked about myself and the research I usually answered. Next time I would follow suit with other researchers who adopt controlled self-disclosure and reveal little information about the self unless the participants ask and then keep it to a minimum (Edwards, 1993b). This is the position I felt most comfortable with as it allowed me to talk about myself as researcher with the women and maintain my own privacy as sister.

Narratives of sister relationships

Some of the contradictions of applying feminist principles in the field for both the women I spoke to and myself as researcher stem from collecting narratives of private experience in the semi-public space of the interview. Managing the interview as a social event when researching an invisible relationship was difficult for two reasons. The act of making public private facets of life raised problems for both participants and myself to do with exposing personal, contradictory and taboo aspects of an idealized and significant bond – emotions and power relations (see Mauthner, 1997). Risks are involved for all when representing hidden experience in order to produce collective and new knowledge, reflected in the oscillation between distancing and disclosure during interviews.

Another reason is the challenge of separating out one relationship from many other more prominent ones in the public eye and attempting to focus on it alone. The interviewees and I veered between enthusiasm and delight at this initiative, and caution and vulnerability about personal disclosure and possibly 'betraying loyalties' to family members. This ambivalence reflects the social position of the sister relationship itself, intertwined with other intimate ties between mothers and daughters and sexual partners: '. . . "a life", whether of one's own self or another, is never composed of one decorticated person alone. Lives are composed by a variety of social networks of others that the subject of "a life" moves between . . .' (Stanley, 1993: 50).

Just as the women's emotions about taking part in the research varied so did the form of their narratives during the interview. The interview is a privileged space where a specific form of interaction takes place allowing both participant and researcher to construct meanings and interpretations about the sister relationship. It is this process which makes this common though taken-for-granted and socially 'invisible' family relationship accessible.

In the interviews, the narratives of sister relationships constructed between participants and researcher ranged from interpretation and exploration to resistance and silence. The women's accounts of their lives and relationships with their sisters were represented in three different forms: first, in a monologue or stream of consciousness where a thought-out interpretation was presented to me; second, in a joint exploration between participant and researcher; and third, through resistance and silence. These positions illustrate some of the dilemmas involved for women as sisters in representing a hidden relationship.

Some of the women I spoke to had pondered over their relationship with their sister/s at length. They had developed a reflexive and analytical perspective, a language in a sense, to depict this changing tie. For some of them, painful emotions of sadness and regret were often intertwined in their stories. Hazel, aged 34, told her tale with hardly any prompting. Towards the end of the interview she meditates on this:

> *Hazel*: I'm saying things I know but you must have actually had conversations with people who've realized things as they're talking.
> *MM*: Yes yes I was thinking that er . . . you are quite different in that way, a lot of people at the end'll say you know . . . I hadn't really thought about this much whereas . . .
> *Hazel*: No but I am very analytical . . .
> *MM*: You've thought of it all in quite a lot of depth and complexity and I'm always amazed when people say that to me and I sort of think well yes but these are your sisters or this is your sister and I'm always quite shocked that you know, that they haven't and it's actually quite hard work for them to . . .
> *Hazel*: Sit and think it through as a . . .
> *MM*: Yes and I mean I've got all these questions here and themes but with you it's just like I haven't really had to ask you that much because . . . you . . . [Laughs.]
> *Hazel*: [laughs] I've done the analysis already.

Other women had also given this aspect of their lives considerable thought and the interview provided an opportunity to explore this relationship further. The marked difference is that these women did not have an overall viewpoint or interpretation and were mainly still struggling to understand it. Some of the women who had puzzled it over with a friend or their sister offered a very fluent narrative.

> I find it very interesting actually, I find it very interesting . . . er . . . I don't find it difficult to be open. And I suppose maybe it's . . . well it's . . . a form in which I've said things that I haven't said to my sister at all and why is that? It's probably because I've never sat down for two hours with an agenda to talk about er . . . but also you can't talk about something objectively, if we talked about [the] relationship she would always pick out things from the past, . . . oh I remember the time when you did this . . . you know and all the emotions sort of flood back in . . . oh yes . . . that was the time when you tried to pinch my boyfriend wasn't it . . . I suppose we have talked but she has the ability to make things into . . . she always talks in a jocular way about things so . . . (Rowena 37, speaking about Grace, 34)

In other cases, the narrative was more hesitant:

> *Eliza* (aged 38): . . . you feel well . . . strange, . . . I don't know whether I've told you anything I just feel well . . . I sort of warbled on really. I wouldn't say anything that I felt that might sort of betray them . . . so I feel strange about that . . . is that what you actually want to know, all these deep inner secrets, but I wouldn't tell you [laughs] . . . well certainly not on a first meeting anyway not knowing you very . . . I don't know you at all [laughs]. So I think well . . . I'm not quite sure what you actually really do want to know. I mean I know . . .
> *MM*: You mean in the study or by talking to you?
> *Eliza*: What are you looking for?
> *MM*: In the study?
> *Eliza*: Mm.

And some women drew clear lines around topics that they were unwilling to discuss and resisted the researcher through their silences. Here Suzanne, aged 29, encapsulates the distinction between experiences she shares with her sister Collette, aged 25, and wants to keep personal and other elements of private life that can be voiced in the interview:

> *Suzanne*: If we need comfort we can, we do get comfort from each other. You know if I've if I've got a problem or anything that I need to discuss, even there's a few

things that I I've thought I would never be able to tell anyone and I've been able to tell her. You know she, and once I told her I found it easier to tell a few other people because we'd discussed it together.

MM: What sort of things are you thinking of?

Suzanne: Just these are just personal things that you know I just really couldn't tell anyone but I and I was really amazed that I could tell her, it was quite, I want, I needed to tell her and yeah so it's really changed, our relationship.

MM: And does she talk to you the same way?

Suzanne: I think so, yeah.

Conclusion

A number of difficulties surface when researching and gathering data on a socially invisible relationship: first the absence from public institutions and the research literature; and secondly, the tensions between voicing and silencing private and personal experiences in the semi-public space of the interview situation. Participants and researcher may feel reluctant and vulnerable to exposing emotional aspects of intimate relationships, in this case between sisters. Reasons for this include the very personal and possibly subordinated position of the private world in relation to the semi-public interview context and wider public institutional sphere (Johnson, 1986). These dilemmas appear throughout the research process, require a sensitive approach and maybe are essentially irresolvable.

Several strategies allow participants and researcher to construct narratives of a taken-for-granted relationship. First, the creation of an appropriate language – through analogy with other female relationships between best friends, mothers and daughters; by reviewing changes and turning-points in individual lives and relationships; and by elaborating concepts derived from different relevant bodies of theoretical knowledge – all can facilitate representation of the research topic during the access and data collection stages.

A second strategy is to adopt a flexible approach when applying principles of feminist research to do with power relationships and reflexivity in the field. In this case experimenting with a range of positions between distancing and disclosure enabled me as researcher to locate myself at a middle-ground point. Third, there is an opportunity in the interview situation for participants and researcher to create new public knowledge and represent previously hidden facets of a relationship in the construction of unique narratives: the specific status of each account – from fluent interpretation and exploration to resistance and silence – shows the women's ease and difficulty in voicing and silencing both the personal and the private.

Notes

I would like to thank Rosalind Edwards, Valerie Hey, Janet Holland, Natasha Mauthner and Jane Ribbens for their insights, helpful discussions and comments on these ideas and earlier versions of this chapter.

1 Giddens (1992: 155, 158) uses this term as a synonym for negotiation in the context of the 'pure relationship . . . entered into for its own sake, for what can be derived by each person from a sustained association with another'.

2 Hudson (1992: 2) defines 'sibships' as fraternities (or sororities) in a literary context: 'Based on mutual respect, individual worth, and shared beliefs and concerns, they herald a new dimension in the English novel to the extent that they are relatively egalitarian societies.'

References

Alcoff, L. (1988) 'Cultural feminism versus post-structuralism: the identity crisis in feminist theory', *Signs*, 13 (3): 405–36.

Allan, G. (1977) 'Sibling solidarity', *Journal of Marriage and the Family*, 39 (February): 177–84.

Allan, G. (1989) *Friendship: Developing a Sociological Perspective*. Hemel Hempstead: Harvester Wheatsheaf.

Apter, T. (1990) *Altered Loves: Mothers and Daughters during Adolescence*. Hemel Hempstead: Harvester Wheatsheaf.

Ball, S. (1994) *Education Reform: A Critical and Post-structural Approach*. Buckingham: Open University Press.

Bloom, L.R. and Munro, P. (1995) 'Conflicts of selves: nonunitary subjectivity in women administrators' life history narratives', in J.A. Hatch and R. Wisnieswski (eds), *Life History and Narrative*. London: Falmer Press.

Brannen, J. (1988) 'Research note: the study of sensitive subjects', *Sociological Review*, 36 (3): 552–63.

Brannen, J. and Collard, C. (1982) *Marriages in Trouble: The Process of Seeking Help*. London: Tavistock.

Burgoyne, J. and Clark, D. (1984) *Making a Go of It: A Study of Stepfamilies in Sheffield*. London: Routledge.

Cahill, S. (ed.) (1989) *Among Sisters: Short Stories by Women Writers*. New York: Mentor/Penguin.

Clandinin, D.J. and Connelly, F.M. (1994) 'Personal experience methods', in N.K. Denzin and Y.S. Lincoln (eds), *Handbook of Qualitative Research*. London: Sage.

Clark, D. and Haldane, D. (1990) *Wedlocked? Intervention and Research in Marriage*. Cambridge: Polity Press.

Coates, J. (1996) *Woman Talk*. Oxford: Blackwell.

Cohler, B.J. and Grunebaum, H.U. (1981) *Mothers, Grandmothers and Daughters*. New York: John Wiley.

Cotterill, P. (1992) 'Interviewing women: issues of friendship, vulnerability and power', *Women's Studies International Forum*, 15 (5/6): 593–606.

Cotterill, P. (1994) *Friendly Relations? A Study of Mothers-in-law and Daughters-in-law*. London: Taylor and Francis.

Department of Health (1988) *Protecting Children: A Guide for Social Workers Undertaking a Comprehensive Assessment*. London: HMSO.

DeVault, M.L. (1990) 'Talking and listening from women's standpoint: feminist strategies for interviewing and analysis', *Social Problems*, 37 (1): 96–116.

Doucet, A. (1995) 'Gender equality, gender differences and care: towards understanding gendered labour in British dual earner households'. PhD dissertation, University of Cambridge, Cambridge.

Dowdeswell, J. (1988) *Sisters on Sisters: A Fascinating Look at their Special Relationship*. Northampton: Grapevine.

Downing, C. (1988) *Psyche's Sisters: Re-imagining the Meaning of Sisterhood*. San Francisco: Harper and Row.

Duck, S. (1990) 'Relationships as unfinished business: out of the frying pan and into the 1990s', *Journal of Social and Personal Relationships*, 7 (1): 5–29.

Dunn, J. (1984) *Sisters and Brothers*. London: Fontana.

Edwards, R. (1993a) 'An education in interviewing: placing the researcher and the research', in C.M. Renzetti and R.M. Lee. *Researching Sensitive Topics*. London: Sage.

Edwards, R. (1993b) *Mature Women Students: Separating or Connecting Family and Education*. London: Taylor and Francis.

Fabera, A. and Mazlish, E. (1987) *Siblings without Rivalry: How to Help your Children Live Together so You Can Live Too*. New York: Avon Books.

Faderman, L. (1981) *Surpassing the Love of Men: Romantic Friendship and Love between Women from the Renaissance to the Present*. London: The Women's Press.

Finch, J. and Mason, J. (1993) *Negotiating Family Responsibilities*. London: Routledge.

Fischer, L.R. (1986) *Linked Lives: Adult Daughters and their Mothers*. New York: Harper and Row.

Fishel, E. (1994) *Sisters: Shared Histories, Lifelong Ties*. Berkeley, CA: Conari Press (First published 1979).

Fox-Genovese, Elizabeth (1991) *Feminism without Illusions: A Critique of Individualism*. Chapel Hill, NC, and London: University of North Carolina Press.

Geiger, S.N.G. (1986) 'Women's life histories: method and content', *Signs*, 11 (2): 334–51.

Giddens, A. (1992) *The Transformation of Intimacy: Sexuality, Love and Eroticism in Modern Societies*. Cambridge: Polity.

Griffin, C. (1994) 'Absences that matter: constructions of sexuality in studies of young women's friendship groups'. Paper presented at the BSA Conference on Sexualities in Social Contexts, University of Central Lancashire, Preston, 28–31 March.

Griffiths, M. (1995) 'Making a difference: feminism, post-modernism and the methodology of educational research', *British Educational Research Journal*, 21 (2): 219–35.

Griffiths, M. and Seller, A. (1996) 'Hannah Arendt and the world of schoolgirls: rethinking the public, private, political and personal'. Paper presented at the Rethinking Identities Conference, Nene College of Higher Education, Northampton, 11 May.

Hamson, R. (1995) 'Writing women's friendship: an intimate experience?', in M. Maynard and J. Purvis (eds), *(Hetero)sexual Politics*. London: Taylor and Francis.

Hey, V. (1997) *The Company She Keeps: An Ethnographic Study of Girls' Friendships*. Buckingham: Open University Press.

Holland, J. and Ramazanoglu, C. (1994) 'Coming to conclusions: power and interpretation in researching young women's sexuality', in M. Maynard and J. Purvis (eds), *Researching Women's Lives from a Feminist Perspective*. London: Taylor and Francis.

Holland, J., Mauthner, M. and Sharpe, S. (1996) *Family Matters: Communicating Health Messages in the Family*, *HEA Family Health Reports*. London: Health Education Authority.

Hudson, G.A. (1992) *Sibling Love and Incest in Jane Austen's Fiction*. Basingstoke: Macmillan.

Johnson, R. (1986) 'The story so far: and further transformations?', in D. Punter (ed.), *Introduction to Contemporary Cultural Studies*. London: Longman.

Lamb, M.E. and Sutton-Smith, B. (eds) (1982) *Sibling Relationships: Their Nature and Significance across the Lifespan*. London/Hillsdale, New Jersey: Lawrence Erlbaum Associates.

Lasser, C. (1988) '"Let us be sisters forever": the sororal model of nineteenth-century female friendship', *Signs*, 14 (11): 158–81.

Mackay, S. (ed.) (1993) *Such Devoted Sisters: An Anthology of Stories*. London: Virago.

McNaron, T.A.H. (1985) *The Sister Bond: A Feminist View of a Timeless Connection*. Oxford: Pergamon.

Mason, J. (1987) 'Gender inequality in long-term marriages'. PhD dissertation, University of Kent, Canterbury.

Mason, J. (1989) 'Reconstructing the public and the private: the home and marriage in later life', in G. Allan and A. Crow (eds), *Home and Family: Creating the Domestic Sphere*. Basingstoke/London: Macmillan.

Mason, J. (1996) 'Gender, care and sensibility in family and kin relationships', in J. Holland and L. Adkins (eds), *Sex, Sensibility and the Gendered Self*. London: Macmillan.

Mathias, B. (1992) *Between Sisters: Secret Rivals, Intimate Friends*. New York: Delta.

Mauthner, M. (1997) '"I'm just the kid sister": power, pleasure and emotion in sister relationships'. Paper presented at the BSA Annual Conference on Power/Resistance, University of York, York, 7–10 April.

Maynard, M. (1994) 'Methods, practice and epistemology: the debate about feminism and research', in M. Maynard and J. Purvis (eds), *Researching Women's Lives from a Feminist Perspective*. London: Taylor and Francis.

Maynard, M. (1995) 'Beyond the "Big Three": the development of feminist theory into the 1990s', *Women's History Review*, 4 (3): 259–81.

Mendelson, M.J. (1990) *Becoming a Brother: A Child Learns about Life, Family and Self.* Cambridge, MA: MIT Press.

Miller, J. (1995) 'Trick or treat? The autobiography of the question', *English Quarterly*, 27 (3): 22–6.

Morgan, D.L. (1990) 'Combining the strengths of social networks, social support and personal relationships', in S. Duck with R.C. Silver (eds), *Personal Relationships and Social Support*. London: Sage.

Morgan, R. (1984) *Sisterhood is Powerful: An Anthology of Writings from the Women's Liberation Movement*. New York: Vintage Books.

Murphy, S.O. (1992) 'Using multiple forms of data: identifying pattern and meaning in sibling–infant relationships', in J.F. Gilgun, K. Daly and G. Handel (eds), *Qualitative Methods in Family Research*. London: Sage.

Nice, V. (1992) *Mothers and Daughters: The Distortion of a Relationship*. Basingstoke and London: Macmillan.

O'Connor, P. (1987) 'Very close relationships'. PhD dissertation, University of London, London.

O'Connor, P. (1991) 'Women's confidants outside marriage: shared or competing sources of intimacy', *Sociology*, 25 (2): 241–54.

O'Connor, P. (1992) *Friendships between Women: A Critical Review*. London: Harvester Wheatsheaf.

Oliker, S.J. (1989) *Best Friends and Marriage: Exchange among Women*. Berkeley and Los Angeles, CA: University of California Press.

Plummer, K. (1995) *Telling Sexual Stories: Power, Change and Social Worlds*. London: Routledge.

Powell, B. and Steelman, L.C. (1990) 'Beyond sibship size: sibling density, sex composition, and educational outcomes', *Social Forces'*, 69 (1): 181–206.

Raymond, J. (1986) *A Passion for Friends*. London: The Women's Press.

Reit, S.V. (1985) *Sibling Rivalry*. New York: Ballantine.

Ribbens, J. (1994) *Mothers and their Children: A Feminist Sociology of Childrearing*. London: Sage.

Rich, A. (1978) 'Sibling Mysteries', *The Dream of a Common Language: Poems 1971–1977*. New York/London: W.W. Norton.

Rich, A. (1984) *Of Woman Born: Motherhood as Experience and Institution*. London: Virago.

Sandmaier, M. (1995) *Original Kin: The Search for Connection among Adult Sisters and Brothers*. New York: Plume/Penguin.

Sharpe, S. (1994) *Fathers and Daughters*. London: Routledge.

Smith-Rosenberg, C. (1975) 'The female world of love and ritual: relations between women in nineteenth-century America', *Signs*, 1 (1): 1–29.

Spender, D. and Spender, L. (1984) *Scribbling Sisters*. Sydney: Hale and Iremonger.

Stanley, L. (1987) 'Biography as microscope or kaleidoscope? The case of "power" in Hannah Cullwick's relationship with Arthur Munby', *Women's Studies International Forum*, 10 (1): 19–37.

Stanley, L. (1993) 'On auto/biographies in sociology', *Sociology*, 27 (1): 41–52.

Stanley, L. and Morgan, D. (eds) (1993) Special Issue: 'Auto/biography in Sociology', *Sociology*, 27 (1).

Stanley, L. and Wise, S. (1990) 'Method, methodology and epistemology in feminist research processes', in L. Stanley (ed.), *Feminist Praxis: Research, Theory and Epistemology in Feminist Sociology*. London, Routledge.

Steedman, C. (1989) *Landscape for a Good Woman: A Story of Two Lives*. London: Virago.

Steedman, C. (1992) *Past Tenses: Essays on Writing, Autobiography and History*. London: Rivers Oram Press.

Thorne, B. (1980) '"You still takin' notes?" Fieldwork and problems of informed consent', *Social Problems*, 27 (3): 284–97.

Troyna, B. (1994) 'Reforms, research and being reflexive and about being reflective', in D. Halpin and B. Troyna (eds), *Researching Education Policy: Ethical and Methodological Issues* London: Falmer Press.

Vaughan, D. (1987) *Uncoupling: Turning-Points in Intimate Relationships*. London: Methuen.

Walkerdine, V. (1990) *Schoolgirl Fictions*. London: Verso.

Warman, D.W. (1986) 'Father–adolescent son communication about sexuality'. Unpublished PhD dissertation, Syracuse University, New York.

Weiss, L. and Lowenthal, M.F. (1975) 'Life courses perspectives on friendship', in M.F. Lowenthal, M. Thurnher and D. Chiriboga et al. (eds), *Four Stages of Life*. San Francisco, CA, and London: Jossey-Bass.

Weeks, J., Donovan, C. and Heaphy, B. (1997) 'Families of choice: narratives of non-heterosexual relationships'. Paper presented at the Thomas Coram Research Unit, Institute of Education, London University, 18 February.

Weston, K. (1991) *Families We Choose: Lesbians, Gays, Kinship*. New York: Columbia University Press.

4 Shifting Layers of Professional, Lay and Personal Narratives

Longitudinal Childbirth Research

Tina Miller

Some events that are highly significant for private lives and personal biographies are also very publicly defined affairs, for example marriage. The event of childbirth and the process of women becoming mothers similarly has major significance for individual biographies and is also publicly defined. Yet unlike many other life events, transition to motherhood is surrounded by pervasive ideologies – both biologically determined and socially constructed – which can be clearly discerned before and long after a child is born. It sits at the interface between the biological and the social. The period of transition to motherhood, from confirmation of pregnancy to identification with the role of mother, is then both a public event and a very personal experience. During this process, women becoming mothers are confronted with an array of public (medically/professionally defined) and lay (informal) knowledges, which at times are discernible as distinct and separate, whilst at others appear inter-woven and multi-layered.

In exploring how individuals develop and construct meanings around a professionally defined, but personally experienced transition – how women make sense of becoming mothers for the first time – the research process itself becomes a major focus. In seeking to gather individuals' private and personal experiences and place them in the academic, and therefore public, arena, questions around how women are accessed and listened to, and how their narratives are analysed and re/presented in the final research account become paramount. In this chapter the dilemma of creating a space in which women feel able to voice their personal narratives – which may not resonate with public and lay accounts and may therefore be difficult to voice – will be explored. Listening to, and privileging, personal narratives then becomes a major focus in the research process. My current research, which involves a qualitative, longitudinal study of women's experiences of becoming mothers for the first time, will be referred to throughout.

The focus on 'public' and 'private' areas of our lives has continued to interest feminist writers who have challenged the authority of 'scientific' knowledge and particular ways of knowing (Stanley, 1990a; Stanley 1990b; Stanley and Wise 1983). The importance of autobiography in research and research writing is now acknowledged and increasingly practised (see Maxine

Birch, this volume; Aldridge, 1993; Cotterill and Letherby, 1993; Ribbens, 1993). Yet in research which involves the very individual experience of becoming a mother a further distinction alongside 'public' and 'private' is needed. In my research the term 'public' refers to the professional definitions of childbirth maintained and practised by medical and health professionals, and the term 'private' to lay knowledges of childbirth made up of informal interactions between women and their families, mothers, sisters and friends, but a finer focus is also needed. The term 'personal' is introduced here to represent the sense of self in an individual's account which does not fit with either the public or private account and which may challenge or contradict both these professionally defined and/or lay 'knowledges' (see Rosalind Edwards and Jane Ribbens, Chapter 1 of this volume).

Voicing the 'personal' then can involve self-disclosure in a way that may be felt by some to incur too much risk. Voicing experiences which are not thought to be commonly shared, to a researcher, may be perceived as risky. The presence of a personal narrative in a research account, distinct from those emanating from the public or private knowledges surrounding childbirth, raises questions about whether and how women feel able to voice their own personal experiences. If an aim within research is to create a space in which women feel able to voice personal narratives, then the research process itself becomes a point of focus. I will argue that factors which can affect whether and how women feel able to 'voice' their own experiences include issues around research design, access through 'snowballing', gatekeeping and re-access, and trust in the researcher and her assurances of confidentiality and anonymity. These are the issues I will be exploring further in this chapter.

The idea to focus a piece of research on women's experiences of becoming mothers in the mid-1990s arose from links that emerged between my own private and public 'lives'. Following the birth of my third daughter and several years at home with young children and intermittent studying for a further degree, I re-entered the public sphere with a job as a university lecturer. In that role I teach, amongst others, groups of midwifery degree students. It was a combination of their questions, linked to my own and other friends' experiences of motherhood, which led to my present piece of research. The midwives, returning from periods of practice, often shared their frustration at having to leave the women with whom they had formed relationships, 10 days after the birth of a new baby. Private feelings led these midwives to question their professional roles: it was just at this time that they felt they could offer most practical and emotional support, and at this time too that they perceived that mothers most seemed to need it. I, however, had felt in turns frustrated at the intervention by various health professionals and grateful for the safe delivery of each of my children. I had experienced feelings of elation and desperation, but the overriding feeling was that no one had said it would be like this: the lived experience of becoming a mother did not resonate with the 'public' account of what it would be like. And it was not only me; other new mothers I met spoke of the unacknowledged hard work of being a mother, of the disparity between what they had thought it would be like, and had been led to believe it would be like during antenatal 'preparation' classes, and their experiences of motherhood.

My autobiography then led to my current research – exploring women's transition to motherhood through their narrative accounts – and as a researcher the private and the personal in my autobiography led to my desire to privilege women's personal narratives. The researcher's autobiography can be discerned as a continuous and dynamic thread running through all stages of the research process in qualitative research. Decisions taken throughout the various stages of the process, from areas for exploration in interview schedules, presentation of self in accessing and interviewing participants – which will be considered in this chapter – to analysis and final write up, will all be influenced by the invisible presence of the researcher's autobiography. This should not only be acknowledged, but necessitates high standards of reflexivity throughout the research process and openness about the choices that are made.

Research design

In order to gather women's accounts of their experiences of becoming mothers it was necessary to choose a research method which would enable the women's voices to be distinct and discernible (Edwards and Ribbens, 1995). I decided to use qualitative methods, specifically in the form of depth interviews using a semi-structured interview schedule. As the focus of the research is on the process of, what is publicly defined as, becoming a mother (i.e. a process spanning both antenatal and postnatal periods defined by the medical profession), I needed to design the research so that the interviews could capture episodes as the stories of women's experiences unfolded. A longitudinal component would mirror the period of transition, giving the data collection period a fluidity not usually achieved in one-off interviews.

I decided to interview participants on three separate occasions: once antenatally at seven to eight months pregnant, and twice postnatally, at six to eight weeks following the birth and finally when the baby was between eight and nine months old. The rationale behind the timing of the interviews was that antenatally it was important that the pregnancy was well established and that participants had been exposed to routinized antenatal care. Postnatally the first interview was timed to coincide with the routine six-week postnatal check-up of the new mother by her general practitioner and the final interview was timed to elicit as late an episode of the participant's story as possible within the imposed timescale of PhD research. In effect the research has been largely defined by reference to the public events in the childbirth process. Similarly, descriptions of the different phases of childbirth rely on public (usually medically defined) language. So whilst I wish to privilege, where possible, women's personal accounts, there is some irony in the fact that I will be accessing them at stages through their transition which are publicly defined.

Whilst 'research design' is often presented as static, designed before 'entering the field' and then subject to change after a 'pilot phase', carrying out research into a sensitive area, such as that of childbearing, can call for continual review of the design. It is because the process of becoming a mother is uncertain and unexpected confusion may be experienced between the public, private and personal versions of the event, that the research design must be adapted. The semi-structured interview schedule I use was compiled from a combination of findings from other studies and areas I, and participants in the pilot study, identified as potentially relevant. The longitudinal aspect of the research has involved the development of three separate interview schedules, and issues arising from previous interviews are incorporated into these, prior to subsequent interviews. At the end of each interview, I ask participants if there is anything they would like to add.

The public concept of research, as ordered, academic and rational, does not fit with the disorder of private and/or personal experiences. Participants who may willingly enter the research during the antenatal phase, perceiving their transition as unproblematic (and isn't that the public story of motherhood? It's natural isn't it?), may wish to reassess their participation postnatally, or may feel reluctant to talk about certain issues. It is not easy to give an account of experiencing something which does not resonate with the public story of becoming a mother, especially when a public assumption exists that all women *naturally* know how to mother.

Participants may find their stories are difficult to tell, or over time are different to what they had anticipated, and this needs to be acknowledged by the researcher. The establishment of a relationship between the researcher and participant, and the importance of participants being able to place the researcher (Edwards, 1993; Finch, 1984) become crucial factors in whether and how participants feel able to speak.

As I have said, whilst I am aware that multi-layered knowledges surround childbirth and mothering I am seeking in this research to privilege, where discernible, women's personal narratives. Yet in creating a space in which women feel secure and able to voice their own account of becoming a mother I sometimes feel uncomfortable. I think this relates to two issues. Firstly, disclosure of a personal sense of *self* by a participant may be in some way linked to how comfortable and trusting they are made to feel. The interaction between the participant and me as the researcher may produce a situation in which it is felt to be 'safe' to disclose 'personal' thoughts. And yet I am not always sure I will know how to deal with the disclosure of personal trauma or unhappiness that such an approach can invite. Similarly, I am unsure of the ramifications of disclosure on the participant once I have left the interview situation.

Secondly, interpretation and representation of women's accounts also becomes an issue – how faithful to their accounts will I be able to remain? I am explicit about my research when I first meet the women in the study, and tell them that I wish to gather women's *own* accounts of *their* experiences of becoming mothers, which will form part of my PhD thesis and eventually may be published. Yet the intention of making public, through production in the academic arena, what is essentially private and/or personal accounts does, at times, concern me (see Linda Bell, this volume). Whilst these concerns, and others, are discussed in Part II of this collection (see Maxine Birch, this volume), it is apparent that they exert an influence long before the writing up of research voices, but during the fieldwork phase of the research too. I think my concerns are related to the different audiences I anticipate my work may eventually reach, and the ways in which it may be (mis)represented: once in the public arena I feel I will have lost control over my findings. The dilemma of retaining control over research findings is not new (Sieber, 1993), but the potential risk involved in disclosure of experiences which do not fit those pub- licly defined is heightened in research around sensitive topics such as childbirth. Childbirth and motherhood are closely bound up with ideas around 'morality' and publicly defined ways of being. Research findings which challenge such notions could be used in counter-productive ways, blaming women for perceived 'inadequacies'.

It is also necessary for the researcher to consider how disclosure about oneself might affect both how comfortable a participant feels and what she may feel able to voice during an interview. Feminist researchers have written of the different practical ways in which they have approached this problem (Edwards, 1993; Finch, 1984; Ribbens, 1989). I resolved at the outset to inform all the participants that I was a mother of three daughters who were now all at school and that I worked part-time outside the home. Yet I have found that my self-disclosure increases in relation to the phase of the research, so that whilst I am careful to make only neutral comments if asked about my experiences of giving birth during antenatal interviews ('everyone seems to experience it differently'), when I return to interview participants postna- tally I reveal more about my own experiences if asked (see Melanie Mauthner, this volume). In my research then, I have decided that informing women antenatally of the potential pain of childbirth is not part of my role as researcher.

In some ways my decisions about how and what to disclose of my own experiences mirror the public wall of silence which seems to shroud discus- sions about pain in childbirth. During one early postnatal interview, I was confronted by the new mother. 'To be honest', she said, 'even you didn't tell me what it would be like.' Clearly she felt that I had let her down. This illus- trates the complex interweaving of boundaries that can arise in research, between the public and private in the lives of the researcher and participant. I had clearly colluded with the publicly held silence around pain in child- birth, and in so doing had myself contributed to the multi-layered knowledges which surround childbirth. Indeed in this case it appeared that *I* had become part of the public/lay knowledge/s surrounding this woman's transition to motherhood. So, whilst I have felt comfortable in sharing cer- tain information about myself, it has also been important that I continually reflect on the potential effect of this disclosure. For example, when returning to interview a new mother six to eight weeks after the birth of her child, I am aware that I may appear to be, as one participant put it, 'superwoman', because I am a mother and working and, perhaps more importantly, appear to be coping. I am always quick to respond that it has not always been like that and that my children are now at school. But in research focusing on aspects of motherhood it is important to consider how advancement in terms of a 'mothering career' may affect the researcher–participant relationship (Ribbens, 1989: 585), and the ways in which women feel able to voice their experiences.

Access and the role of the gatekeeper

As the focus of the research is on exploring how women make sense of becoming mothers within the context of an array of public and lay knowledges and personal experiences, the way in which potential participants are accessed becomes an important consideration. I used informal snowballing techniques to locate potential participants. This decision was based on the principles of not wanting to advertise and so recruit a self-selected sample, nor to recruit through health professional contacts. My concern was that women recruited through antenatal clinics by midwives/ health visitors might perceive the research as in some way linked to the delivery of health care services and feel inhibited in the ways in which they felt able to talk about their experiences, and similarly, that women accessed in this way might feel obliged to present their experiences in a way that mirrored public accounts given by health and medical professionals.

The use of 'snowballing' is a widely recognized technique in qualitative research concerned with accessing stigmatized groups. It is less often used as a method to access 'socially acceptable' and 'visible' groups and yet in my research appeared an appropriate technique for the reasons outlined above. What is not generally acknowledged in research texts, and what I had not foreseen, was the potentially problematic nature of snowballing. At the outset I took a decision not to approach potential participants directly and so intermediaries ('gatekeepers') were sought. I made this choice because I did not want participants to feel coerced into participating in my research. Initially I experienced unexpected difficulties in finding participants, and because of the *non*-snowballing of the snowballing technique this led to several gatekeepers being sought. Later the type of sample reached and the relationship between 'gatekeeper' and participant became problematic, affecting both whether and how women felt able to speak about their experiences.

As a starting point for the snowballing I used my own social network, asking other mothers at my children's school if they knew of anyone who was expecting a first child. Two mothers, both acquaintances of mine, responded to this request and eventually acted as 'gatekeepers' to three participants. What I had not foreseen was how slow the process of snowballing could be and how important the gatekeepers would be in the type of sample located. In this research the participants are predominately professional, working women, reflecting my own social network. Having made contact with the first three participants and arranged convenient times for interviewing, I was dismayed to find that far from belonging to a network of other expectant mothers as I had naively assumed/hoped, they knew of no-one else who was expecting a first child. Other entry points had to be explored and further 'gatekeepers' had to be recruited. A year later, following sporadic success with 'snowballing', I had located 18 women who were expecting their first child. These difficulties have raised interesting questions about the boundaries of professional working women's networks – that they don't encompass particular groups, also that working women appear to choose to make public their pregnancy only once it is well advanced.

The ability of 'gatekeepers' to exert leverage in the research setting has previously been documented (Miller, 1995: 303). But the ways in which gatekeepers, through their relationships with participants, can *continue* to exert an influence over whether and how a participant feels able to speak is less well documented. The potentially inhibiting influence of the relationship between gatekeeper and participant was clearly illustrated in one particular case in the research. Two of the participants were related by marriage and both had been located through an acquaintance of mine who lives in the same locality. Once initial contact had been made, the gatekeeper arranged that both interviews should take place in her home as both participants lived some distance away, although I had made clear my willingness to travel to their homes. Whilst the two antenatal interviews went well, by the time the first postnatal interviews were due, one of the participants was clearly experiencing difficulties (as she later commented), not in coping with the new baby, but with the effect the birth had had on her marriage – to the brother of the gatekeeper. This participant initially 'chose' (at least, she told me that her health visitor and husband instructed her) not to be interviewed when the first postnatal interview was due. This action raised several important issues. The need to renegotiate access at each stage in longitudinal research was highlighted. So too was the dilemma of how to respond to a participant who is clearly, by her own account, experiencing unhappiness and appears to be 'silenced' by others. Another awkward issue for me concerned being in a position of having gathered data on aspects of the participant's life and subsequently experiencing pressure from the gatekeeper (her sister-in-law) to let her know 'what was going on', as I relate below.

Renegotiating access

As I have noted, the importance of renegotiating access at each stage of a longitudinal study must be acknowledged. I informed all the women in my study that they could withdraw from the research at any time, and negotiated re-access by telephone shortly before the second and third interviews. But it is only retrospectively that I have recognized the importance of *re*negotiation. The dilemma I faced of participants feeling unable to continue with the study because they are experiencing, paradoxically, the very thing that the research is about – the potential disjunction between public and lay knowledges and personal experiences – is less easily resolved. In the case I referred to earlier, I contacted the woman by telephone to talk about her second interview. Telephone contact was made on several occasions over a period of weeks during which times she spoke at length about feeling angry at having been diagnosed as having 'postnatal depression', and lonely being 'stuck out here' and 'isolated'. I made notes of our telephone conversations for my fieldwork diary but felt uneasy about whether this was 'legitimate' data gathering, and how and whether I should use it. Eventually the participant agreed to a second interview, to take place at her home and not that of the gatekeeper (her sister-in-law) where the first interview had taken place. However, shortly before the interview was due to take place, she phoned to say she was visiting her parents and so was unable to be interviewed. Feelings of professional frustration ('This is just what the research is all about and I want to capture her account') mixed with personal sympathy ('I hope it isn't my research which is causing her to be reflexive and find her situation difficult to cope with') led to my deciding to write to the participant to invite her to contact me if she wished to rejoin the study for the third interview when her baby was nine months old. Several months later she did telephone me and a final interview was arranged and carried out.

The participant's anxiety that the gatekeeper (her sister-in-law) might find out what she had said in her interviews was apparent. She was concerned because she said she had sounded 'negative' during the interviews (revealed her personal sense of *self* in her account which did not fit with the public and/or her sister-in-law's account of becoming a mother). I reassured her that I was ethically and professionally bound to observe confidentiality and could not relate anything she had said to her sister-in-law. In fact her sister-in-law had expressed a keen desire to find out the contents of the tape, even telling my children that I had a tape recording she would like them to help her get her hands on! The interweaving of private lives and public research threads were all too apparent at this point.

This participant had continually referred to 'her tape' when we had spoken on the telephone and so when I met with her to carry out the final interview I returned her tape to her, although reminding her that it had been transcribed verbatim. Her relief at being given the tape was obvious and, having initially requested that this interview not be tape recorded, she changed her mind and said that the tape recorder could be used after all. The inhibiting influence of the gatekeeper's relationship with this participant was apparent throughout.

The ways in which participants are initially accessed then becomes crucially important in research which attempts to collect individuals' accounts of periods of transition. The potential power of the gatekeeper, to influence whether and how women feel able to voice their experiences (or whether self-disclosure is perceived as too risky), needs to be considered throughout the research process. Renegotiating access in longitudinal research is also necessary, but may be problematic where accounts of transition do not fit with the publicly defined version of the event.

Listening to women's voices

The issues of whether and how women are able to speak are fundamental to the data-gathering process. At one level, asking women to speak about their experiences of becoming mothers, and listening to their accounts, seems straightforward. Yet it is because the event of childbirth and becoming a mother is both highly significant for private lives and personal biographies and, simultaneously, a very publicly defined affair that collecting and listening to women's accounts is a complex enterprise. The distinctions made earlier in this chapter between 'public' (professional/medical knowledges and practices), 'private' (informal, lay knowledges) and 'personal' (a sense of *self* in an individual's account) provide markers for the researcher when listening to women's voices. However, the contradictions in and between individual accounts adds a further dimension to the complexities of this process. In the accounts I have collected so far, over the course of 42 interviews, the 'personal' is, at times, clearly discernible – women begin to express *their* feelings and experiences which may not fit with more public accounts. In others, the women's experiences have either apparently resonated with the predominant public discourse, or have been supported by lay accounts (from mothers, sisters, friends, etc.), or the women perhaps have not felt comfortable enough with me to share their personal experiences and voice their feelings.

Time may also be a factor affecting whether and how women feel able to voice their thoughts and experiences. It is important to acknowledge that the women in this study are all first-time mothers and could be regarded as still developing or trying out their version of themselves as 'mothers'. In her account of motherhood and hearing her own voice, Jane Ribbens considers the difficulties of hearing her 'own voice amidst the multitude of voices that occur around mothering' (this volume, p. 24). Yet Jane Ribbens is also writing with the experience and confidence born of time; as she says '*this time around* I wanted to feel more able just to do what I wanted to do' (this volume, p. 29; emphasis added). For first-time mothers this may be even more difficult to achieve. This clearly has implications for listening to women's voices. When and if women find that aspects of their own experiences do not fit with the public or even private 'knowledges' that surround and shape perceptions of childbirth and motherhood, the pressure for conformity may be so great that they perceive disclosure as too risky. Childbirth and becoming a mother lie also at the interface between the biological and the social. Public definitions of these events often revolve around biologically determinist rhetoric – that women *naturally* know how to, and want to, be mothers. The stakes then can be high for those who admit to personally experiencing something other than this public account. *Self*-disclosure may be perceived as too risky in a society where motherhood and family life are all about being a moral person.

The issues I have discussed here – research design, access, gatekeeping and renegotiating access – are all crucially important in creating a space in which women feel able to voice their personal narratives. The ways in which the research is presented to, and perceived by, participants will also have an impact on what is voiced during an interview. Using the very public language of research, the establishment of 'rapport', and the effect of 'researcher reactivity' will also be significant factors in how experiences are voiced. Yet the public language of research should not obscure the private and/or personal experiences and feelings that the researcher takes into the interview, and with which she leaves it, and which may affect the ways in which women's voices are listened to. I acknowledge that in my current research I have liked some of the participants more than others (sometimes where an aspect of their biography resonates with my own), and that my public (professional) researcher role and private and personal life are interwoven. Similarly some of the women in the study will have liked me more than others, and this will almost certainly have affected the ways in which they have felt able to voice their experiences, the ways in which they have constructed *their* story. Collecting and listening to women's accounts of their experiences of becoming mothers is then a complex process requiring continual reflection. By learning from these complexities, the research process itself is enhanced.

In listening to women articulate their experiences of becoming mothers, 'multi-layered' voices can be discerned. The 'multi-layers' as I earlier noted, comprised public, private and sometimes personal narratives (narratives of a personal sense of *self*) and are often complex and interwoven, but at times are distinct. So, whilst I am wishing to privilege personal narratives, where discernible in this research, this is not a straightforward enterprise. The following extract, taken from an antenatal interview, illustrates how the public, private and the personal are both interwoven and, in places, distinct:

> . . . the thing about something else actually taking over your body, out of control . . . because I got pregnant, in some people's eyes, quite late in my life [participant is 29 years old], because I've had that independence, that way of life, I could just please myself as and when, then you become pregnant, your whole body is taken over . . . you feel very sensitive to things, you know, you could just sit down and cry sometimes, ehm . . . and the fact of becoming so large, not obscene, but . . . I mean, I never knew that, *I suppose I shouldn't say this*, I never knew that your backside could actually increase, double the size just through being pregnant, because it has happened to mine! But I know that there's going to be a bundle of joy at the end of the day and that's what I'm looking for . . . but I wouldn't go straight into being pregnant again. (Emphasis added)

This participant acknowledges the existence of public and lay definitions around what are perceived to be appropriate periods in a life when pregnancy is anticipated/expected, and that her pregnancy does not 'fit' with these. Her experiences of being pregnant have not been as she had anticipated and she looks to her age and the 'independence' of her previous way of life to try to understand the changes she is experiencing. She seems aware that the way in which she is describing pregnancy does not resonate with the public account and is tentative in voicing her personal experiences which do not fit, 'I suppose I shouldn't say this'. Yet having risked disclosure, she quickly returns to the 'acceptable' language of public and lay knowledge and asserts that she knows 'that there's going to be a bundle of joy at the end'. When this participant was finally interviewed postnatally, having disclosed to me that she had been diagnosed as postnatally depressed, she made little attempt to describe her experiences of becoming a mother in 'acceptable' public language. Being interviewed gave this participant the opportunity to reveal her personal sense of 'self' and in so doing question the ways in which other people reveal or conceal their experiences:

> . . . and when you see other people, you see them for face value, but when they go home is it a different story and do they actually tell you? And no, I don't think they do and that annoys me because I think to myself I know what we've been through, or we as a family have been through, and I'd love other people not to know that it's us, but to know that it's not all hunky dory and *you've not failed if something has gone wrong*. (Emphasis added)

This extract not only raises questions about whether and how people feel able to voice their experiences (that which lies behind the 'face value'), but also the acceptability of particular accounts in the different public and private spheres of our lives. Clearly there are perceived moral dimensions to public accounts which this participant wishes to contest, 'and you've not failed if something has gone wrong'. What is also interesting on looking back over the verbatim transcript of this interview is my extensive contribution to the dialogue. I remember that I had wanted to reassure the participant that it was acceptable to me for her to give an account which did not resonate with other, apparently more acceptable accounts. In effect I was attempting to create a space in which the participant felt able to voice her personal narrative.

The complexity and apparent contradiction of multi-layered voices in longitudinal accounts is demonstrated in the following extracts. During an antenatal interview this participant (a health professional herself) said,

> [Y]ou're going to be stuck with the medical way of doing things, but then I'm quite happy to do that. I don't know what to do if I have problems, I want them to tell me what to do.

Yet, postnatally she contradicts this and appears to voice what she had really felt when anticipating the birth (perhaps self-disclosure is perceived as less risky after the event),

> I thought my birth was going to be easy, I don't know why, I just thought that . . . I was expecting sort of a four-hour labour, I didn't expect stitches or anything like that, I thought, I just thought my body would be very good at that, but it wasn't . . . it let me down, it wasn't as good as I thought it was going to be.

Antenatally this participant had clearly voiced an acceptance of the public (medical) account of childbirth. This endorsement may well be linked to, amongst other things, her occupation. Yet, when interviewed postnatally she uses a different, contradictory voice. Following the birth it is apparent that although acceptance and endorsement of the 'medical way of doing things' was voiced at one level, at a personal level this participant did not think her birth experience would require medical intervention. Postnatally then she reveals that she had expected her birth to be different. She had apparently not felt able to disclose her 'personal' voice antenatally, or may have felt it was 'tempting fate' to do so. This retrospective use of the personal narrative has been echoed across several of the antenatal and postnatal interviews, and it may be that disclosure of the self *retrospectively* is not perceived as such a risky enterprise – after all a live birth has been achieved and the public and biological transition to motherhood fulfilled. It may also be that participants feel more comfortable talking to me postnatally; they have already met me and they know what to expect from the interview situation.

The multi-layered narratives running through women's antenatal and postnatal accounts are then complex and at times contradictory. The complexity and contradiction, at times discernible in and across women's accounts, appear to be linked to their perceptions of 'acceptable' ways of voicing their experiences. What becomes clear is that an 'epistemological struggle' is experienced by some women, the privileging of different ways of knowing, of different (private, public and personal) knowledges over others. Antenatally the public (medical) account is often the most dominant. This should not be surprising in a society where doctors and health professionals hold 'the privileged stories' (Fox, 1993: 113). Voicing a public account does not appear to involve risk; women are perceived to be preparing 'appropriately' for motherhood. Moral 'sanctions' are avoided. Postnatally women's narratives become more complex. An experience of birth which may not have resonated with the public (medical) account leads to the greater use of private (lay) accounts and sometimes personal disclosure. Personal experience can then lead to the *reordering* of 'knowledges', with the privileging of private and personal knowledges.

Conclusion

The period of transition from conception to motherhood is then both a very publicly defined affair and simultaneously a very private experience. In my research I am seeking to gather and listen to women's personal narratives through transition and to privilege their accounts. Yet in seeking to create a space in which women feel able to voice personal experiences and feelings – which they may not have anticipated and may find difficult to voice – dilemmas in research design and practice have had to be continually confronted. Issues affecting whether and how women feel able to voice their experiences have included research design, access, the 'pervasive' influence of gatekeepers, negotiating re-access and the researcher–participant relationship. It has become clear that in longitudinal research which aims to mirror a period of (uncertain) transition, the ways and times at which accounts are collected cannot be cast in stone, but must be flexible enough to accommodate the *shifting* nature of private and personal experiences of transition.

Similarly, in research which is attempting to capture stories *through* periods of transition the need to *re*negotiate access becomes crucially important. In seeking to create a space in which women can voice their experiences and feelings the potentially 'pervasive' influence of the gatekeeper has to be acknowledged. In my research the perceived and continued influence of one gatekeeper contributed to the self-silencing of one participant for part of the study, and it was clear that the relationships between other participants and gatekeepers had an impact on the ways in which some women felt able to voice their experiences.

The relationship between the researcher and participant is also brought into focus in longitudinal research which follows women through a period of transition *already* experienced by the researcher. Whilst I have sought to establish an interview situation in which women can place me, and feel able to voice their experiences without fear of 'judgement' from me, I am also aware that I am already a mother and that what I choose to reveal during the interviews about my own experiences actually reinforces much of the silence which exists around childbearing. So, whilst endorsing notions of reciprocity and equality within interviews I find that in reality these aims are only sometimes achieved.

Collecting and listening to women's accounts then requires continual and systematic reflection in order that, where present, multi-layered voices can be distinguished, and personal narratives privileged. Through the process of listening to women voicing their experiences the complex and contradictory nature of individual accounts becomes clearer. Whilst layers of professional, private and (sometimes) personal narratives can be discerned throughout the period of transition, it is apparent that the experience of childbearing can lead to a privileging of private and personal accounts.

References.

Aldridge, J. (1993) 'The textual disembodiment of knowledge in research account writing', *Sociology*, 27 (1): 53–66.

Cotterill, P. and Letherby, G. (1993) 'Weaving stories: personal auto/biographies in feminist research', *Sociology*, 27 (1): 67–79.

Edwards, R. (1993). 'An education in interviewing: placing the researcher and the research', in C.M. Renzetti and R.M. Lee (eds), *Researching Sensitive Topics*. London: Sage.

Edwards, R. and Ribbens, J. (1995) 'Introducing qualitative research on women in families and households', *Women's Studies International Forum*, 18 (3): 247–58.

Finch, J. (1984) '"It's great to have someone to talk to": the ethics and politics of interviewing women', in C. Bell and H. Roberts (eds), *Social Researching: Politics, Problems, Practice*. London: Routledge and Kegan Paul.

Fox, N.J. (1993) *Postmodernism, Sociology and Health*. Buckingham: Open University Press.

Miller, T.A. (1995) 'Shifting boundaries: exploring the influence of cultural traditions and religious beliefs of Bangladeshi women on antenatal interactions', *Women's Studies International Forum*, 18 (3): 299–309.

Ribbens, J. (1989) 'Interviewing: an "unnatural situation"?', *Women's Studies International Forum*, 12 (6): 579–92.

Ribbens, J. (1993) 'Facts or fictions? Aspects of the use of autobiographical writing in undergraduate sociology', *Sociology*, 27 (1): 81–92.

Sieber, J. (1993) 'The ethics and politics of sensitive research', in C.M. Renzetti and R.M. Lee (eds), *Researching Sensitive Topics*. London: Sage.

Stanley, L. (1990a) 'Feminist auto/biography and feminist epistemology', in J. Aaron and S. Walby (eds), *Out of the Margins: Women's Studies in the Nineties.* Lewes: Falmer Press.

Stanley, L. (1990b) *Feminist Praxis: Research, Theory and Epistemology in Feminist Sociology.* London: Routledge.

Stanley, L. and Wise, S. (1983) *Breaking Out: Feminist Consciousness and Feminist Research.* London: Routledge and Kegan Paul.

5 Public and Private Meanings in Diaries
Researching Family and Childcare

Linda Bell

'Today is a one-off. It has never happened like this before, when I've seen so many people in one day.'

I've interviewed 'Linda', talked to her many times, to me she always seemed busy and cheerful. Yet here she is, in her diary account (written at my request) appearing to say, 'I may be telling you what happened today, but my life is not *really* like this at all.' Linda's account echoes voices of other women, who, whilst describing personally significant events and activities to me, repeatedly insisted their lives were *in reality* 'nothing special'. Viewing me as a researcher and 'public' spectator in some sense, how were these women then attempting to present their lives for me?

I aim in this chapter to consider the use of diaries (in particular those which are 'solicited') in family or household research. By 'solicited diary', I mean an account produced specifically at the researcher's request, by an informant or informants. Initially I identify some themes underlying examples of substantive social research using diary methods. In particular, notions of time, of public and private, and inter-relationships between these themes, have emerged as relevant to research using diaries. My own understandings about using solicited diaries changed while conducting a piece of research on women's support networks and child care (Bell, 1994). I began to realize how solicited diaries could be presenting public understandings of these notions, but thereby suppressing other voices. Using my own research project as an example, I discuss implications of using diaries when trying to bridge gaps between concepts of public and private in family or household research, and alternatively where such use(s) could be problematic.

I initially identified several different research approaches and methods involving use of diaries (for reviews, see Gibson, 1995; Plummer, 1990). These include data collection and analysis through personal diary accounts, 'logs', 'time budgets', and what has been called the 'diary-diary interview method' (Zimmerman and Wieder, 1977). Auto/biography (which can also draw explicitly upon diary accounts) is another approach increasingly identified as significant to sociological (including feminist) research. Significant autobiographical work may occur within a 'historical' frame (e.g. Evans, 1993), and editors of some historical diaries (e.g. Gates, 1991) may even present their own account of involvement written up in an archaic diary format. Full consideration of wider auto/biographical forms of data collection is beyond the scope of this chapter. However, analysis of pre-existing ('literary') diaries (e.g. Gates, 1991; Stanley, 1984, 1987, 1995) raises some relevant issues for my purposes, including questions about the nature of self and identity; issues of time and narrative; or using diaries to include the emotions and concerns of the researcher her/himself within the research frame (Cotterill and Letherby, 1993).

Research approaches and substantive topics involving diary methods

However diary material is used in social research, some attempt (often explicit) is usually being made by the researcher to tap into material recorded by the diarist which may be regarded as private or personal (for the purposes of this chapter, I would interpret 'personal' as the individualized aspect of the private). However, this immediately raises as a significant theme issues around our notion of what is considered personal or private, and connections to more public forms of account, or wider forms of discourse. Secondly, diary accounts of various kinds crucially relate, as Plummer points out, to the issue of *time*: '. . . each diary entry – unlike life histories – is sedimented into a particular moment in time: they do not emerge "all at once" as reflections on the past, but day by day strive to record an ever-changing present' (Plummer, 1990: 17–18).

Time appears significant in a number of ways. In health research, several studies have used diary methods to examine individual (or perhaps 'family') reactions to particular illnesses or treatments, often over a period of time (see, e.g., Killien and Brown, 1987; Rosner et al., 1992; Stoller, 1995). In 'family' and 'household' research involving diaries, researchers often consider the significance of time, as in studies of *individual or household time use* (Gershuny, 1983; Gershuny and Robinson, 1988; Marini and Shelton, 1993; Robinson 1987); *diet* (Charles and Kerr, 1986); *consumer behaviour* (Jackson-Beeck and Robinson, 1981); *childcare* (Hill 1987; Lucca 1991; Tietze and Rossbach, 1991); and *time spent with children* (Bryant and Zick, 1996; Nock and Kingston, 1988).

Time has also been considered as significant in the *social construction of therapeutic discourses*; these may connect private or personal issues concerning family or household with more 'public' issues such as the socially constructed idea of mental health (see Boscolo and Bertrando, 1993, who describe attempts to synchronize differing individualized times during therapeutic work with families).

Many studies using diaries have had a *focus on gender* (Berheide, 1984; Sandelowski et al., 1991; Tivers, 1985), although not necessarily from a 'feminist' research perspective (see also Elchardus and Glorieux, 1994). Burt (1994) also suggests that diary-keeping itself may be seen as a kind of coping behaviour, more prevalent amongst females. In addition, gender has, for some time, been a significant concept in wider sociological discussions around issues of public and private (e.g. Gamarnikow et al., 1983).

As discussed elsewhere (Bell, 1995; Ribbens, 1994), public and private may be seen on one level as actual locations, and the foci of specific kinds of activities. Some research using diaries has tapped into this idea, for example research on the *links between 'home' and 'work'* (Meiners and Olson, 1987; Nock and Kingston, 1989), or on *leisure* (Harvey, 1990; Shaw, 1991). But public and private are also much more than this, and have wide implications (see Rosalind Edwards and Jane Ribbens, this volume, for a more detailed examination of the complexities of bringing private lives and ways of being into public knowledge). Complex links between the apparently simplistic dichotomy of public/private, involving different time spheres and localities, are suggested by some research (Bell, 1994), and clearly the social construction of the concepts of public and private has meanings both for researchers and for those they research. As Ribbens points out, these concepts have considerable sociological potential in drawing our attention to a dichotomy which is a significant feature of contemporary Western societies (Ribbens, 1994: 206).

The way in which time is woven into ideas around private or public can in itself be an important reflection of the way private and public are constructed in individual accounts, especially in relation to gender. Davies (1990) for example introduces the notion of 'process time' operating *alongside* 'clock time'; 'process time' can be associated with letting things such as caring for others take the amount of time they need to take, thus being hard to schedule or measure (unlike 'clock time' with its linear framework). Davies does not intend to set up a false dichotomy between two kinds of time. But she suggests 'process time' offers more space than 'clock time' for a person's own, private judgements and activities, and that gender may influence how 'process' and 'clock' time are managed in parallel in everyday life.

These various themes, of private and public, aspects of time, space, locality and gender, in differing combinations, have been the concern of much existing family and household research which has employed diary methods. These underlying themes should be considered more closely as we examine how 'diaries' are drawn into research as a method of data collection.

Uses made of diary accounts in research

I suggest that even when we focus on solicited diaries, fundamentally differing methodological approaches can underlie what are seen and glossed over as 'diary methods' in social research. This suggests researchers are taking different approaches to the private and public construction and nature of the accounts they analyse. We should note that some studies may draw directly upon *personalized diary accounts* which reveal emotions and attitudes as well as activities, changing day to day. The *interpretation* of private meanings then becomes an explicit and crucial research issue. Other researchers seem to be soliciting and using informants' diaries mainly in the sense of actively solicited but essentially *depersonalized* records of publicly measured time use or activity patterns. These patterns are often linked to particular locations as well as timetables (Bell, 1995), and implicit private meanings associated with them may then be considered unproblematic (e.g. a classification of women's activities as taking place simply 'inside' or 'outside' the home).

In understanding how diary accounts have been used in research, it is therefore crucial to acknowledge any shifting approaches to private and public construction of accounts within research projects. Furthermore, diaries need to be acknowledged as constructed by both the writer and, through research and analysis, by the soliciting researcher. In auto/biography, the focus may be on research into the emotions or self-expression which the auto/biographer her/himself wishes to present. The power of such construction might be seen initially as lying more with the diarist than with the researcher; but the researcher may try to assert her/his own construction reflexively, for example by chronicling in detail the timetable of steps taken in editing and publishing the diarist's account (e.g. Gates, 1991).

Actively soliciting diary accounts from participants, however, may be used explicitly by social researchers to attempt to bring in the auto/biographical, to 'let people be heard on their own terms'. This may happen even where it is clear the research focus is mainly on the construction and analysis of depersonalized, publicly recognizable categories, rather than on personal meanings. Jonathan Smith (1994) draws heavily on a small number of women's own accounts of pregnancy, and compares these with their retrospective accounts of pregnancy made during early motherhood; the apparent focus throughout this research might therefore appear to be on private and personal understandings. However, the study is intended as 'an empirical investigation of the notion of self-reconstruction'. Smith uses diary accounts and other data such as interview material to reveal a number of 'reconstructive narratives'. He suggests that, in their later narratives, women were inclined to gloss over difficulties originally presented during their 'real-time pregnancy' accounts, and that (with hindsight) they emphasized personal growth and continuity of self apparently lacking (from an *observer's* perspective) in their earlier accounts. Intent mainly on revealing glaring inconsistencies between the narratives over time, rather than on the 'current' personal spirit of each diarist's account, Smith observes that individuals may modify their biographical presentations retrospectively to produce 'self-enhancing personal accounts'. (But see Tina Miller, this volume, for a different understanding of women's self-disclosure antenatally and postnatally.)

The use of diary-keeping in research now begins to raise significant issues concerning research participants' personal identity, their agency or instrumentality: their power both to act and to construct private meanings which will be conveyed into the researcher's account. What exactly, we might ask, is the link between this instrumentality and identity, which diary accounts could reveal?

When we consider formats that researchers may consider suitable for recording diary accounts, examination of the literature reveals that although diary methods are increasingly used, some researchers (for example in health) may be counselled *against* using 'unstructured' diaries with informants. Gibson (1995), for example, recommends precise instructions be given to informants when asking them to 'make public' the activities, time budgeting or even (sometimes) the personal thoughts the researcher wants to read. Once again, like Smith, Gibson seems to feel that the personal account needs to be clearly modified and shaped by the researcher, or else it will be useless for research purposes.

Although these issues are relevant to all researchers in their use of diary materials, I feel they are of particular significance for researchers attempting to take a feminist perspective. To illustrate this, I will use my own research project on the social networks of mothers with young children, which employed diary accounts to collect material on their everyday experiences.

Diary accounts used as a research instrument might (as it seemed initially to me) appear relatively unproblematic, for example in the context of seeking to explore women's own accounts and experiences of substantive topics such as childcare arrangements. However, I found a number of issues of particular concern as I progressed with my study; I suggest we need to examine the following:

1　implications of using the diary as a quasi-observational method, raising issues of public and private understandings;
2　how diary methods of data collection and analysis conceptualize the issues of time and activity, the public representation of these and the links to privately represented, personal accounts;
3　what connections there may be between diaries solicited from informants and researchers' own 'field' diaries.

Diaries used as 'unobtrusive observation'

Making use of the apparently private representation and personal data that diaries contain, the researcher may, explicitly or implicitly, be attempting to uncover and examine further the personal context of what people 'say' to the researcher, elsewhere in the research process (particularly in interviews). This can be done by attempting to observe 'what they really do' on a day-to-day basis. This may seem particularly vital where observation is considered necessary to the research but deemed practically 'impossible'; for example Coxon (1988) made a study of detailed sexual behaviours which relies entirely on personal accounts, presented publicly and then indexed by the researcher into a standardized format which codes active, passive and mutual elements. Diary collection methods may thus be used, as in this example, specifically as a way of trying to avoid ethical or epistemological difficulties which would be involved in direct observation of such intimate situations (see review in Gibson, 1995). This emphasis on observation by the researcher immediately raises questions for feminists, I would suggest, through the attempt to represent something through the researcher's observation of another's viewpoint.

Anthropological research has a long tradition of attempting to record in parallel 'what people say, what people do and what people say they do'. As an anthropologist and feminist I am interested in the tensions between an apparently publicly accepted research formula, such as ' say/do/say they do' and the privately represented thoughts and activities which the use of diary methods attempts to unravel. Earlier 'functionalist' versions of social research were less clearly concerned with individuals' own expressions of actual lived experiences; however, more recently the intention has also been to encourage people to both speak and act their own version(s) of reality, and to record these thoughts and activities for themselves. In shaping these thoughts, researchers might attempt, for example, a family 'biography' in which time and the passing of events significant to the informants rather than only to the observer can play a crucial part (Werbner, 1991).

In seeking to explore my own informants' opportunities for 'instrumental' activity in relation to their own children, I asked 10 main informants to keep a diary for me for a period of one month. There were a number of implications lying behind my decision to allow them to 'collect their own data' as I saw it. For me, I suppose, taking a 'feminist approach' entailed revealing the instrumentality or agency I felt I had identified in the initial interviews with the informants (see Jane Ribbens, this volume). I felt the women I interviewed 'knew what they were doing' in their work as mothers, they were not just 'dupes' of the environment or social context in which they found themselves. I felt they had serious concerns reflecting the (presumed) significance they attached to their mothering. I think that I began with a fairly simplistic view of how to represent these various points, by showing how these women planned ahead and co-operated with 'colleagues' who were involved in the same type of mothering work. However, I would suggest that in not wishing to view mothering as *entirely* circumscribed by emotion and private concerns, perhaps I went too far in tacitly *leaving out* these aspects when soliciting the diaries. Even where researchers have, however, been more aware of the implications of leaving out emotions, this can still reflect a dilemma, as Ribbens (1994) notes: '[S]omewhere along the line the emotion has not been expressed, and has become obscured by the requirement of a rational discussion for a more public audience' (Ribbens, 1994: 37).

I was therefore convinced that my informants would *prefer* to be told that they should record for me the times of their various activities, the childcare arrangements they made, at what time their partner left the house and when 'he' returned; I took so much for granted that these would be the significant events of the day, because they were factors which appeared significant to my research. They were, I suppose, the 'events' (in a *publicly recognizable* sense) which I would have observed and taken note of in a field diary account, had I been with them. I also think that at the time I was preparing my PhD thesis (mid-1980s onwards), debates around the idea of mothering seen as 'work' were a very powerful influence (e.g. Boulton, 1983; Oakley, 1986; O'Donnell, 1985), and like Jane Ribbens (this volume) I had encountered feminist literature suggesting motherhood is oppressive.

My informants complied with my request to keep diaries and so presented these *public* accounts of their 'working lives' in a broad sense. But their own concerns are fortunately also evident in their accounts; those accounts are in themselves more varied than perhaps I expected, given the apparently similar lifestyles of these informants. Ribbens (1994) usefully points out that with her own informants, particular sets of personal constructs or 'leitmotifs' occurred throughout the interview-based accounts, which revealed meanings that certain ideas or actions held for that particular informant: for example, 'being one's own person'. It is this aspect of personal meaning which, I feel, is revealed in some of my own informants' diary entries, which are not just about the measuring of time or activity – although this is what they seem to record.

> *Tuesday*: Took [son] with me to school [where informant works] 12.50–1.30 pm. Son looked after by girls at the school. I noted that he went with the girls very willingly . . .
> *Wednesday*: 12.40. Left home with [son] to go to school (arrangements as yesterday). Several members of staff noted how happy and outward going [son] is becoming the more I take him to school and the more he meets other people . . . (Rose)

A central theme in Rose's interview and diary accounts, as well as in her activities, was that her (single) child should 'fit in' with the parents' lifestyle, and particularly with her own paid employment. She also took great trouble to present herself publicly as a competent and caring mother, with a united and well-organized family life. Rose's comments were very much her own, but she certainly seemed to take to heart my own theme of 'mothering as work'. Her diary was thus a way of communicating to me the recognition she sought as a mother, and the significance she attached to her career, as well as to the instrumental (and therefore, she suggests, significant) uses on which she spent her time. For example, she clearly measured her time carefully and did not spend as much time visiting other local mothers as some of my other informants; similarly she 'hadn't time' to attend babysitting circle coffee mornings, saw little point in joining the circle as she 'couldn't help others much' with babysitting. The combination of her public responsibility as a mother and as a teacher locally being presented alongside Rose's own private/family and personal/individual motives was very striking throughout her diary account.

Another informant, Jane, firmly believed in the importance of the 'individual', whether adult or child, and a thread running through her diary, interviews and activities was the difficulty (and less frequently the positive side) of managing the demands of different individuals, including her own needs.

> *Tuesday*: 3.50 pm. Arrived at C's, en route home, for a 'cuppa'. [The two children] played somewhat haphazardly. Departed 4.35 pm. 4.50 pm arrived home, started tea for [son]. [Husband] rang and cancelled his evening meal, so I ate with [son]. 5.05 pm. M called round with [her son] to return my cake tin, but didn't stay. 6.05 pm. Husband home. 6.10 pm. [Son] in bed – he was shattered after this morning's play and could really have done with a quiet afternoon at home. [Jane]

Jane had decided that she was not prepared to take on paid employment until her children were of school age (although some time after the initial interview with me when she and her husband purchased a larger house, she did do this). She clearly found and expressed the tensions in her situation at times, particularly over other people's expectations of her. Where these expectations came from other local mothers – for example, through her membership of a local babysitting circle – we would be right to question whether these are public expectations (as presented by Rose, through reference to her paid employment) or private concerns, since the locus of interaction between Jane and other local mothers occupies a space neither clearly public, nor private (see Bell and Ribbens, 1994: 255–6). Jane felt some of these expectations were 'public' to the extent that they took place outside her home, but also 'private' since they impinged very clearly on her own family life. This illustrates the difficulties of trying to guess from what is 'observed' through diary accounts and then 'classify' whether people are carrying out 'public' or 'private' activities.

Drawing on these two case examples, I suggest that using diary material as unobtrusive observation by itself does little to unravel the private meanings applicable to each woman, which were generally made visible to me quite slowly, through both formal interviewing and further participant observation. Furthermore, although any research method must surely affect the ways in which research participants express themselves and the issues which, given the opportunity, they decide to make public, I suggest that different issues are involved with respect to interviews, and to written communications like diaries. Talking confidentially to a researcher may be viewed differently from setting words down on the page for others to read; public explanation of private experience may be thought necessary (as in Linda's comment at the beginning of this chapter). From the researcher's point of view, diary accounts may only seem to reveal their private meanings fully if the researcher has also 'called the informant to account' through conducting interviews with informants in which these issues can be discussed. We need to ask whether diaries, for example, potentially offer more or less *control* for the informant, or for the researcher, than interviews may do. This has important implications for researchers, but especially for feminist researchers concerned about power relations between themselves and those they research.

Diaries, time and activity

As noted initially, time is significant in almost all diary-related methods, and a particular focus in my observations was on the idea of mothers' personal 'agency'/'instrumentality'. Through the diary records of everyday activities within localized social networks, I discovered that time seemed to have variable meanings and value, particularly between weekday-times, evenings and weekends in this local setting. But did the diary research method itself- which inevitably involved collecting material presented in accounts which I then tended to analyse as 'publicly' measured time use or activity patterns – mean that women unnecessarily 'depersonalized' their accounts for me, emphasizing 'public' meanings firstly for their actions, and secondly in their approaches to time?

We can appreciate that one of the main reasons for using time budget diaries as a method for data collection, especially with large numbers of informants, is to show some kind of 'representative' activity and time use patterning (representative perhaps in a statistical sense) of a particular population. In relation to health research, for example, whilst Gibson points out that as a data collection method 'diaries seem to be most useful in intimate situations . . .' (1995: 72), at the same time she is heavily concerned, like some other researchers, with questions of representativeness (see also Rosner et al., 1992). Gibson suggests that one of the main problems with the diary collection method concerns 'authenticity of [diary] entries' (1995: 72). She cites various examples of studies where attempts were made to check for 'accuracy and bias' in accounts. In other words, accounts were checked against some other measurable criterion which was supposed to show what *really* happened; an example she cites is how many times the diarist actually received or made a phone call, as expressed in diaries, which was then measured against telephone company records (ibid.: 71). She also suggests the diary collection method is very time-consuming for researchers, as 'informants will need training and perhaps follow-up visits to maintain motivation to keep the diaries' (ibid.: 72). All this seems to fly in the face of using diaries to reveal *private* forms of account, although in practical research terms what is suggested may seem perfectly reasonable for other purposes.

When considering time and time use in diary accounts more broadly, Adam (1993) usefully suggests that women's time 'cannot be placed in a meaningful way within perspectives that separate work from leisure, and public from private, subjective from objective and task from clock time' (Adam, 1993: 1972).

In my study I believe that I found evidence of, as Adam notes,

> time lived, time made and time generated. Often . . . mediated and derived time. It is rarely personal time but shared time, a relational time that is fundamentally enmeshed with that of significant others. This shared time can neither be forced into timetables, schedules and deadlines, nor be allocated a monetary value. Rather, it must take the time it needs to take. It needs to be open-ended. (Adam, 1993: 172)

Nevertheless I also found evidence in the locality where my research took place of women carefully counting time spent – for example, in their use of babysitting circles (Bell, 1995) – treating it as a resource, as 'currency'; in other words as 'clock time'. They were therefore (as Adam describes) fundamentally treating it as 'work time' for certain purposes. I found through examining both the actions and opinions of women in the research locality, that how they treated time as a resource (as clock time) or as 'time lived' would certainly vary, but it is important not to set up a false dichotomy here between public and private forms of time.[1] In my study, variations in approaches to time could be seen between individuals and between social contexts (Bell, 1994, chapter 6). Nevertheless in order to get at the idea of different sorts of time, I felt I needed to separate out the concept of time seen as a resource (see Wallman, 1984). This was so as to understand and be able to compare the experiences of my informants in relation to the time frames they experienced in common as mothers of young children. In separating out and examining time as a resource, which theoretically could not only be measured but also *exchanged*, I realized I was emphasizing the *instrumentality* of the activities I observed or was told about by informants. I felt, however, that this was necessary, if deeper meanings were to be uncovered and understood as grounded in women's own experiences. (See Tina Miller, this volume, on 'multi-layered voices'.) For example, when seen as a useful resource, time would clearly relate to a woman's length of residence in the area. However, what a woman *felt* about her experience of local residence does not just relate to the length of time involved, although her feelings on this issue might be reflected in the ways she used time as a resource in other contexts (e.g. in childcare arrangements).

Focusing specifically on 'activity' and 'time use' in diary accounts, I therefore attempted to consider mothers' potential for 'personal 'agency' and instrumentality through the everyday activities enmeshed within others' localized social networks. As noted above, the concurrence in many anthropological studies between three kinds of observation – finding out 'what people do', 'what people say' and 'what people say they do' – can be an attempt to give particular significance to the perspectives of interviewees themselves. But in my own research, the intention was to examine women's use and perceptions of time itself, on their own terms. How in practical terms could I then make use of this diary material, except by categorizing types of diary data and then making fairly rigid comparisons between informants?

I was aware that in analysing my data I did go on to reduce the personal accounts very much, to a series of categories and measured stretches of time. But in order to preserve the 'private nature' of accounts I also tried to examine the shape of each account as a whole; in doing this I had to draw not only upon diary data, but also on interviews and my own participant observation, so as to get at 'personal' meanings for what was being represented in the diaries.

Despite this, I found much of the diary data simply became lumped together and compared by virtue of some convenient external factor: for example, I decided to consider how much time each woman spent on paid employment, because the relevant information was available in the diaries I requested. My informant Rose, who had a very strong career orientation, turned out to spend the most time (i.e. measured in hours) on paid employment, compared with other informants – hardly a surprise. But of more interest to me was the way that the theme of her job as a teacher was 'woven' through her diary account, her interview and through the various occasions on which I spent time with her. Even a remark such as the following makes more sense when you understand how much Rose identified herself with her job:

[W]e don't go out that much and I haven't bothered to join a babysitting group . . . for the simple reason they hold a lot of coffee mornings and meetings during the day which *I haven't time to go to* . . . (Original emphasis)

I would therefore urge caution to anyone who is tempted to use diary material simply to produce categories of data for comparison. These categories can so easily show only a publicly recognized form, devoid of private, still less personal meanings (see also Jan Parr, this volume, on categorizing and analysing within a theoretical framework as a doctoral requirement). For me this became more of an issue as the research and writing up progressed, and as I realized it reflected a dilemma not only about methodological issues, but over how I personally was to represent my informants, their feelings and personal accounts of mothering to the world.

Connections between informant and researcher 'field' diaries

Shouldn't the researcher also be 'called to account' for his or her own experiences, in the same way as informants are asked to be? The field diary, written by the researcher her/himself, is surely the counterpart of the informant's account; a record of observation, activities and thoughts, which underlines further the link between diaries and observations as research instruments. (See also Melanie Mauthner, this volume, on the visibility of participant and researcher subjectivity.)

> How immensely difficult it is to formulate the endless variety of things in the current of a life. Keeping a diary as a problem of psychological analysis: to isolate the essential elements, to classify them (from what point of view?), then, in describing them to indicate more or less clearly what is their actual importance at the given moment, proportion; my subjective reaction etc. (Malinowski, 1967)

My own field diary was produced, I felt at the time, mainly in order to record events and activities which I observed through participant observation. As I commented in the thesis: 'This approach is intended to make visible many of the activities of mothers with young children locally, which might often seem to be a "closed book" to those not involved in them . . .' (Bell, 1994: 11). It therefore contains a careful record which

> describes my own involvement in local networks and activities, and records the opinions and perspectives of those whom I met over an extended period – the original informants plus many others – as well as showing in detail the mechanics and operation of individual local groups. (Bell, 1994: 11)

All this appears to be presented in such a straightforward and 'rational' way! It was clear, however, when looking through my own diary in preparation for this chapter that I was, as Stanley notes, presenting very firmly a diary account which contains a voice 'directed to an audience outside the text' (Stanley 1993: 48), relating personal to wider public meanings; this suggests my diary record is incomplete.

It may be that on some occasions I either failed to record conflict between myself and the women I was with; or much more likely, that I was extremely careful at the time, in my dealings with them, not to present any kind of 'dissent' from the expressed opinions I noted around me, and that this is what I therefore recorded in the diary. Although I was part of the crowd, my 'public' role as a researcher predominated: it was 'their opinions' I was listening for, not my own voice. Where there were differences of opinion between myself and some women, as in the example below, I played safe by siding with someone else's opinion and then only expressing mild dissent privately to my account. The way that I was undertaking the research seems to have meant that I maintained a 'public' voice (which I felt would be acceptable academically) even in my private diary:

[Coffee with Elizabeth and friends. Her husband is changing his job and will be home much earlier; also they are moving.] She is looking forward to seeing her husband earlier each day 'but I expect he won't know what's hit him, being with the kids such a lot'. She laughs but seems a little apprehensive. She says she thinks it will be 'great'. Kate happens to say that her husband is 'very good' with their son – he often gives him his breakfast. I say my husband does this for our son, too. Elizabeth and Kathleen both laugh, 'Where did we go wrong with our husbands?' Neither 'have ever done that'. Kathleen thinks her husband 'belongs to a different generation' (early 40s). *Note*: But all our husbands are all about the same age, late 30s/early 40s. (Field diary 30/3/85)

Did I fail to record my own private thoughts, problems and anxieties simply in order to remain 'objective' in my research? What were the events and themes which I left out? I had begun very clearly with the idea that I was not taking an objective or 'scientific' approach to research: I was listening for and then trying to represent women's own perspectives. Why then, through taking a public research role, did I allow my own perspective to be drowned out? Reviews of my work made by academic colleagues have in fact suggested that I must have 'suppressed' certain things in order to present the research account in the way that I did. I was rather shocked and dismayed by this appraisal, as it is so close to what happened; were my very private omissions so obvious to outsiders?

How, as Malinowski notes, do you cope with presenting what he glosses as 'my subjective reaction', when this includes anxieties and concerns which are thrown into particularly sharp relief by doing a piece of research on mothering: the attendant worries and feelings of guilt resulting from the birth of a premature child; the impact of my own mother's death during research; unemployment, depression, financial difficulties and inevitable marital strains. These were the things which I suppressed in my research diary, and did not want to dwell upon, or even to write about at all. Indeed my research project was the only space which I had to get away from all those difficulties, which crowded in on me during a very few years. I tacitly assumed that my informants too would suppress any significant but painful personal meanings of this sort in their private accounts. It was not simply a matter of trying to present a 'rosy picture' of motherhood from their accounts or mine; there were enough everyday difficulties to discuss in the research, particularly over our relationships with each other. And I justified my approach precisely by my research focus, which was on mothers' links with other mothers, and what I saw as the importance of publicly recognizing their significance. What price, then, should you be prepared to pay for setting full 'reflexivity' on the page? I am still not sure.

Some conclusions

Inevitably I feel that this chapter has probably raised more questions than it answers. In the light of it, how can I really decide whether to speak in favour or against the use of diaries as a data collection method? It is clear that a written, time-focused account of everyday experiences and activities can provide expression for observation, recording and comment by the writer/informant, and that this inevitably dovetails with unobtrusive observation by the researcher when the diary comes to be analysed.

I suggest we may tend to take for granted, as researchers, the idea that we should be expecting and encouraging women, in particular, to 'speak for themselves' in as personal a way as possible through using diary methods. But is it really possible (or desirable) for an informant producing a solicited diary to 'speak' on her own behalf in family/household-based research projects at all without significant intervention from the researcher? What about the researcher's own attempts to produce 'a diary' when, as in my own case, there seemed to be so many obstacles to producing a truly 'reflexive' account. How 'truthful' does that personal account have to be, or is the search for private truth a fruitless way to approach 'objectivity' by the back door? Which of the private and public voices which emerged through my research should I have listened to and written up? I eventually produced an account which satisfied the examiners of my PhD dissertation. Yet I am not satisfied. The hidden voices still keep me awake at night, although during the day I discuss the ones I did reveal with, it now seems, increasingly serious and detached 'academic' presentation.

Note

1 For some individuals (such as one of Adam's informants), time 'as a resource and a structural parameter [may be] acknowledged as integral to the complexity without being accorded greater importance than any other aspect of this meaning complex of time' (Adam, 1993: 173). See also Davies (1990).

References

Adam, Barbara (1993) 'Within and beyond the time economy of employment relations: conceptual issues pertinent to research on time and work', *Social Science Information*, 32 (2): 163–84.

Bell, Linda (1994) 'My child, your child; mothering in a Hertfordshire town in the 1980s'. Unpublished PhD dissertation, University of London (External), London.

Bell, Linda (1995) 'Just a token commitment? Women's involvement in a local babysitting circle', *Women's Studies International Forum*, 18 (3): 325–36.

Bell, Linda and Ribbens, Jane (1994) 'Isolated housewives and complex maternal worlds: the significance of social contacts between women with young children in industrial societies, *Sociological Review*, 42 (2): 227–62.

Berheide, Catherine White (1984) 'Women's work in the home: seems like old times', *Marriage and Family Review*, 7 (3/4): 37–55.

Boscolo, Luigi and Betrando, Paolo (1993) *The Times of Time: A New Perspective in Systemic Therapy and Consultation*. London: W.W. Norton.

Boulton, Mary G. (1983) *On Being a Mother: A Study of Women and Pre-school Children*. London: Tavistock.

Bryant, K. and Zick, C. (1996) 'An examination of parent–child shared time', *Journal of Marriage and the Family*, 58 (February): 227–37.

Burt, Christopher D.B. (1994) 'An analysis of a self-initiated coping behavior: diary-keeping', *Child Study Journal*, 24 (3): 171–89.

Charles, Nickie and Kerr, Marion (1986) 'Eating properly, the family and state benefit', *Sociology*, 20 (3): 412–29.

Cotterill, P. and Letherby, G. (1993) 'Weaving stories: personal auto/biographies in feminist research', *Sociology*, 27 (1): 67–79.

Coxon, T. (1988) 'Something sensational . . . the sexual diary as a tool for mapping detailed sexual behaviour', *Sociological Review*, 36 (2): 353–67.

Davies, Karen (1990) *Women, Time and the Weaving of the Strands of Everyday Life*. Aldershot: Gower.

Elchardus, Mark and Glorieux, Ignace (1994) 'The search for the invisible eight hours: the gendered use of time in a society with a high labour force participation of women', *Time and Society*, 3 (1): 5–27.

Evans, Mary (1993) 'Reading lives: how the personal might be social', *Sociology*, 21 (1): 5–13. (Special edition on autobiography and sociology.)

Gamarnikow, Eva, Morgan, David, Purvis, June and Taylorson, Daphne (eds) (1983) *The Public and the Private*. London: Heinemann.

Gates, Barbara Timm (ed.) (1991) *Journal of Emily Shore*. Charlottesville, VA: University Press of Virginia.

Gershuny, J.I. (1983) *Social Innovation and the Division of Labour*. Oxford: Oxford University Press.

Gershuny, J.I. and Robinson, John P. (1988) 'Historical changes in the household division of labour', *Demography*, 25 (4): 537–52.

Gibson, Vanessa (1995) 'An analysis of the use of diaries as a data collection method', *Nurse Researcher*, 3 (1): 66–73.

Harvey, Andrew S. (1990) 'Time use studies for leisure analysis', *Social Indicators Research*, 23 (4): 309–36.

Hill, Malcolm (1987) *Sharing Child Care in Early Parenthood*. London: Routledge and Kegan Paul.

Jackson-Beeck, Marilyn and Robinson, John P. (1981) 'Television nonviewers: an endangered species?', *Journal of Consumer Research*, 7 (4): 356–9.

Killien, Marcia and Brown, Marie Annette (1987) 'Work and family roles of women: sources of stress and coping strategies', *Health Care for Women International*, 8 (2/3): 169–84.

Lucca, Joseph A. (1991) 'Predicting maternal child care and personal care time inputs from maternal resources, maternal demands, and child demands in families with normal and handicapped children'. Dissertation Abstracts International.

Malinowski, Bronislaw (1967) 'A diary in the strict sense of the term', in R. Burgess (ed.) (1982), *Field Research: A Sourcebook and Field Manual*. London: Allen and Unwin.

Marini, Margaret Mooney and Shelton, Beth-Anne (1993) 'Measuring household work: recent experience in the United States', *Social Science Research*, 22 (4): 361–82.

Meiners, Jane E and Olson, Geraldine I. (1987) 'Household, paid, and unpaid work time of farm women', *Family Relations*, 36 (4): 407–11.

Nock, Steven L. and Kingston, Paul William (1988) 'Time with children: the impact of couples' work-time commitments', *Social Forces*, 67 (1): 59–85.

Nock, Steven L and Kingston, Paul William (1989) 'The division of leisure and work', *Social Science Quarterly*, 70 (1): 24–39.

Oakley, Ann (1986) *From Here to Maternity: Becoming a Mother* (2nd edition). London: Penguin.

O'Donnell, Lydia (1985) *The Unheralded Majority: Contemporary Women as Mothers*. New York: Lexington.

Plummer, Ken (1990) *Documents of Life: An Introduction to the Problems and Literature of a Humanistic Method* (2nd edition). London: Unwin Hyman.

Ribbens, Jane (1994) *Mothers and their Children: A Feminist Sociology of Childrearing*. London: Sage.

Robinson, Warren C. (1987) 'The time cost of children and other household production', *Population Studies*, 41 (2): 313–23.

Rosner, Tena Tarler, Namazi, Kevan H. and Wykle, May L. (1992) 'Health diaries and interviews: consistency in reporting by older adults', *Research on Ageing*, 14 (2): 248–66.

Sandelowski, Margarete, Harris, Betty G. and Holditch-Davis, Diane (1991) '"The clock has been ticking, the calendar pages turning, and we are still waiting": infertile couples' encounter with time in the adoption waiting period', *Qualitative Sociology*, 14 (2): 147–73

Shaw, Susan M. (1991) 'Research note: women's leisure time – using time budget data to examine current trends and future predictions', *Leisure Studies*, 10 (2): 171–81.

Smith, Jonathan A (1994) 'Reconstructing selves: an analysis of discrepancies between women's contemporaneous and retrospective accounts of the transition to motherhood', *British Journal of Psychology*, 85 (3): 371–92.

Stanley, Liz (ed.) (1984) *The Diaries of Hannah Cullwick*. New York: Rutgers University Press.

Stanley, Liz (1987) 'Some thoughts on editing Hannah Cullwick's diaries', *Studies in Sexual Politics*, 16: 88–99.

Stanley, Liz (1993) 'On auto/biographies in sociology', *Sociology*, 27 (1): 41–52.

Stanley, Liz (1995) 'Women have servants and men never eat: issues in reading gender, using the case study of Mass-Observation's 1937 day-diaries', *Women's History Review*, 4 (1): 85–102.

Stoller, Eleanor Palo (1995) 'Symptom reporting during physician consultation: results of a health diary study', *Journal of Ageing and Health*, 7 (2): 200–32.

Tietze, Wolfgang and Rossbach, Hans Gunther (1991) 'Care and education of preschool children' (Die Betreuung von Kindern im vorschulischen Alter), *Zeitschrift für Padagogik*, 37 (4): 555–79.

Tivers, Jacqueline (1985) *Women Attached: The Daily Lives of Women with Young Children*. London: Croom Helm.

Wallman, Sandra (1984) *Eight London Households*. London: Tavistock.

Werbner, Richard (1991) *Tears of the Dead: The Social Biography of an African Family*. Edinburgh University Press.

Zimmerman, D.H. and Wieder, D.L. (1977) 'The diary-diary interview method', *Urban Life*, 5 (4): 479–97.

6 Theoretical Voices and Women's Own Voices

The Stories of Mature Women Students

Janet Parr

Researchers approach the interviewing process both as academics and as individuals with a personal history. The application of theoretical perspectives can be experienced as either sharpening sensitivity to research participants' voices, or as shaping and silencing those voices. This chapter discusses the ways in which my academic and personal background informed my research topic and original methodology. It then moves on to chart the problems I had in shedding the positivist influence dominant in my undergraduate years and adopting a grounded theory approach. It discusses the changes in my thinking and the dilemmas created in being guided by research participants' stories and understandings whilst at the same time addressing a pre-existing body of theoretical academic knowledge as required by a PhD.

The research on which the discussion in this chapter is based was conducted for my doctoral thesis and examined the experiences of 49 mature women students who returned to learning after a number of years out of the education system and were attending college or university on a variety of courses in and around a northern city. The research began as an exploration of the barriers which mature women meet when they return to education – a topic in which I became interested around 20 years ago when I began my own career as a mature student with three children and a husband to care for as well as a home to run. My subsequent occupation as a lecturer in further and higher education brought close contact with mature students, many of whom talked to me about issues connected with their return to learning, including childcare, finance, travel, workload, timetabling as well as confidence and relationship issues. Interest in these issues encouraged research initially for a master's degree and a few years later for a doctorate.

The original theoretical structure

There was a gendered structure to many of the issues about which the students were talking and patriarchy seemed an appropriate theoretical construct within which to frame the experiences of mature women returners to education. However, I felt that a great deal of the writing on patriarchy tended to marginalize notions of agency. There seems little doubt that the major institutions in our society are male dominated – for example, at the time of writing, women still constitute only 120 Members of Parliament out of 658, and 2 per cent of the members of the Institute of Directors. There are also fewer women employed in the managerial, administrative and professional categories than men (Central Statistical Office, 1996). There was ample evidence from the earlier interviews I had conducted of patriarchal influences on women's experiences, but did this tell the whole story? The fact that women had made a conscious decision to return to learning appeared to be indicative of agency. Giddens' theory of structuration (1984) takes account of both structural influences and agency and the different levels and contexts in which power operates. Davis (1991) uses Giddens' theory of power in her study of the relationship between female patients and male GPs and concludes that however great the power imbalance appeared to be, the women did exhibit some control over their own lives. This led me to consider the characteristics of power and to reflect on the nature of ideology as an adjunct to the power relationship. I was particularly attracted to Lukes' three-dimensional view (1974) which suggests that the most effective exercise of power is when people are persuaded that a situation is right and proper. Although Lukes does not use the term 'ideology', this seemed to be an important concept to consider, particularly in relation to gender issues.

My initial theoretical framework then had a number of elements: patriarchy, power, ideology and the relationship between structure and agency. It was within this theoretical framework, influenced by pre-existing academic knowledge, that I developed the following research questions.

> *'Does patriarchy explain the erection and maintenance of the barriers which mature women experience when returning to further and higher education?'*
>
> *'If women surmount the barriers, does this call into question the explanatory reach of patriarchy as a theoretical structure?'*
>
> *'Is there a fit between the broad structure of patriarchy and women's everyday lives?'*

Implicit in these questions is the power of patriarchy, operating at a structural level, to erect and create barriers to women's return to education, but which may not reflect their lived experience. This tension between an existing body of academic theory and individual stories had implications for my research which are obvious to me now, though I did not recognize them at the time.

The original research design

The original research design to address these questions incorporated both quantitative and qualitative data collection. Initially, I decided that I would send out a questionnaire to mature students in colleges and universities in the local area. This was to be followed by in-depth interviews with a small group of students from both further and higher education institutions. As I saw it, the structure was clearly mapped out – research questions, albeit loosely formulated; clear data collecting methods; and a theoretical framework within which to analyse the data.

Positivist influence

My whole approach to the research was considerably influenced by positivist research methodology which had been dominant in sociology during my undergraduate years. Positivism has its roots in the approaches to research commonly adopted by the 'natural' sciences. Followers of this school of thought hold that social science can and should resemble the natural sciences both in the way research is conducted and in the way in which findings are presented. Simply, the starting point is a theory, or an attempt to put forward an explanation for some social phenomenon. From this general theory, a hypothesis is formulated and data collected to test it. Data have to be objectively observed and classified (which makes the assumption of course that there is a single, tangible 'reality' which everyone defines in the same way). Internal meanings, motives, feelings and emotions cannot be truly observed and so they cannot be measured in any objective way. There is considerable stress on the researcher's own values being kept out of the research arena and an emphasis on quantitative data collecting methods and statistical presentation.

Changing methodology

However, I grew increasingly dissatisfied with the idea of using quantitative data collecting methods for the primary research. The crucial factor was the growing awareness that I was looking more for explanations and processes rather than 'numbers of women who . . .' I realized over the months that if my real interest was in explanations and perceptions, then it was greater depth rather than breadth which was required in the research data. One of the ways of achieving this depth in terms of explanations and perceptions was by listening to, and hearing, what the women themselves had to say. During this period, I was also reading more of the literature on feminist methodology, where the emphasis is on understanding the social and cultural context of events as well as the events themselves. So I shed my original plan for a questionnaire and adopted a wholly qualitative approach to the data collecting.

In addition to this, I was increasingly influenced by the grounded theory approach developed by Glaser and Strauss, 1967 (see also Strauss and Corbin, 1990), and which has extensively informed qualitative research since then (Bryman and Burgess, 1994; Miles and Huberman, 1994). Taylor and Bogdan (1984) define this approach succinctly:

> The grounded theory approach – discovering theories, concepts, hypotheses, propositions directly from the data, rather than from a priori assumptions, other research or existing theoretical frameworks. (Taylor and Bogdan, 1984: 126)

In encompassing a grounded theory approach to analysing the data, I again struggled to shed the influence of positivism. I seemed constantly to have one foot in that camp as I adopted a much less secure approach to the analysis of the data. In addition, there is a considerable tension between putting a grounded theory approach into practice within the context of a PhD and the expectation that one should engage with pre-existing bodies of theory in the area of one's research topic. Fortunately, I had considerable support from my supervisor and from the Women's Workshop, whence this book has emerged. Nevertheless, putting this approach into practice was not easy as I discuss later.

The strengths of grounded theory are the emphasis on an open-mindedness and a willingness to listen, hear and act on the results at all stages of the research process, grounding the analysis in the research data rather than trying to fit the data into an a priori framework. This is consistent with a feminist framework which has rejected positivism, largely because of its emphasis on value-freedom and objectivity. Rather, what is emphasized is the importance of contextual factors regardless of whether qualitative or quantitative data collecting methods are used. Some feminists maintain that the positivist argument for distance, objectivity and the elimination of researcher bias is impossible to achieve in any research, regardless of methodology, not least because our perspective will determine what we study, what or whom we include in the research and how we present our data. As Mies argues:

> The postulate of value free research, of neutrality and indifference towards the research objects, has to be replaced by conscious partiality, which is achieved through partial identification with the research objects. For women who deliberately and actively integrate their double-consciousness into the research process, this partial identification will not be difficult. It is the opposite of the so-called 'Spectator-knowledge' (Maslow, 1966: 50) which is achieved by showing an indifferent, disinterested, alienated attitude towards the 'researcher objects'. (Mies, 1993: 68)

Mies' concept of 'conscious partiality' necessitates the researcher locating herself in the research process. My role as a former mature student clearly located me within the research process, but in addition, I felt that the reasons I had not pursued an academic career at the 'normal' age would also contribute to my understanding of the women's position and circumstances.

Locating myself in the research process

I was born and raised in a mining village, where the majority of men in my family and the neighbourhood worked at one of the local pits. There was a clear and rigid division of labour – the women did all the domestic chores and childcare, often helping one another out, especially in times of illness. The infant school was just down the road and was very much a neighbourhood school, attended by the majority of the local children. Because of the tied nature of the housing, there was at least one miner in each household in the village and all my friends' fathers 'worked at t' pit'. So the whole of my early socialization was very much influenced by traditional gendered divisions. There was also a very gendered attitude towards education, and although I attended grammar school and gained eight O-levels, education beyond compulsory schooling was never on the agenda, especially for girls. I left school at 16 to go into routine white-collar work where I stayed until I married and had children. A variety of part-time jobs ensued until I returned to learning at college and then university. My eventual profession as a lecturer in further and higher education brought close contact with mature students. This background gave me a range of experience to bring to the research arena and I felt that the students and I would have much in common.

Oakley (1981) argues that the richness of the material in her research on motherhood was due to the non-hierarchical nature of the relationship between herself and the women she spoke with and the investment of her personal identity in the relationship. This means of course responding both to personal questions and to questions about the research, which can be both problematic and advantageous as discussed further by both Tina Miller and Melanie Mauthner in this volume.

From the outset, the aim was to create an interactive situation in which the women could ask questions of me, but I did envisage a problem in answering any questions from the women as honestly as possible without driving the interview down a particular route. I felt that my background and experiences could be a double-edged sword, both enabling and limiting the women's voices. Considerable thought therefore needed to be given to my approach, particularly when I talked to the students in their course groups, since this first contact would clearly set the tone of the interviews. I needed to explain to the students what the research was, and why it was being done, but without leading them into responses they thought I was anticipating. Previous literature on the topic (ACACE, 1982; Charnley et al., 1985; Coats, 1989, 1994; Edwards, 1993; McGivney, 1993; Oglesby, 1989, 1991; Pascall and Cox, 1993; Schutze et al., 1987; Woodley et al., 1987) and my own experiences as a mature student and a lecturer showed that mature women who return to education are likely to face a number of barriers. However, I wanted to avoid presupposing the students' situations. My natural inclination was to be open and honest with students about my own position, but I wanted what they told me to be their story, not a reflection of my own.

My approach to the students then was very general, avoiding terms like 'barriers', 'difficulties' and 'problems', just talking in general terms about the areas I was interested in – such as childhood education, occupation, reasons for returning to learning, what domestic arrangements, if any, had to be made, how the course was financed and so on. Despite this, one of the women students asked whether I was only interested in students with difficulties. To my response of, 'Why do you ask?', she replied that she would quite like to talk to me but didn't have any difficulties this year because she had managed to organize childcare for the youngest and finished in time to get home before the other kids came in from school. She also managed to fit in the housework, shopping and cooking in the evenings and at the weekends. This student went on to say that going to university could be a problem because of the travel involved and timetabling structures. My response was immediate – that I was interested in all experiences, positive and negative, but her question was quite thought-provoking. It made me realize that women may not necessarily perceive some issues as barriers. This student accepted that childcare, domestic chores and cooking were her responsibility and she fitted everything in, so there was no problem.

Much of the existing literature uses the term 'barriers', and I had adopted this somewhat unquestioningly, even though I had not verbalized it to the students. This raised two issues – firstly, to what extent could a barrier be said to exist for a woman if she did not perceive it, and secondly, was there a danger of doing what I was trying to avoid, i.e. objectifying the women – putting my own, rather than their, categorization on their experiences? So, barriers *per se* may not be the issue, but the women's perception of them and the way they were dealt with.

Even though I was moving into a qualitative/interpretive mode, it seems that I was still working within a positivist framework. I was influenced by an existing body of knowledge on the topic and had developed research questions from this, looking for evidence to either support or refute them. The existing literature, which it was necessary to review for my doctorate, together with my own experience, led me into believing that I would find a mass of evidence indicating that women do meet obstacles when they return to education. Even though I wanted to listen to the women's stories, I was still looking for evidence that these obstacles existed. My reason for taking a very general approach was so that I did not unduly influence what the women said to me. However, I was still assuming that they would talk of barriers. On further reflection it is clear that I was also making the assumption that the women's experiences, however they perceived them, were framed by a patriarchal society.

One must also recognize that theory, in its loosest sense, does not just influence researchers. We all have prior frameworks into which we fit, examine, and make sense of new information. The question of whether I was just interested in women with problems could have been prompted by common perceptions of what research is about. Most of the research which is discussed in the public arena, particularly by television and the popular press, is concerned with issues which are regarded as problems for society. Coverage of topics such as crime, poverty, single parents and 'difficult' children has tended to take a wholly negative view, so there is little wonder that people will generally think that research is about problems rather than about positive experiences or ordinary lives. It could well be that it was perceptions of research which had influenced the student's question, 'Are you only interested in students with difficulties?', rather than anything I had said.

The interviews

From the start of the actual interviews, I aimed to create a relaxed and informal atmosphere, welcoming the student, thanking her for giving me her time
and asking whether she had any general questions. I explained how the material would be used, assuring anonymity, and told the women that at any time
they could refuse to answer a question, stop the interview or request at the
end that I did not use the material.

One of the early questions, asked almost as an icebreaker, was, 'Why did
you come back into education?' The students gave many reasons, such as
wanting to contribute to the family income, better qualifications and a more
stimulating job. By chance, I began one interview in a different way from the
others. I asked the question, 'Why have you come back into education?' later
rather than at the beginning of the interview and got another answer: 'I'm
doing it for myself really.' So was this a different response because it was a different person, or was it because the question had been asked at a different
point? I decided to ask the same question twice – first near the start and then
later in the interview and found that most women made links with employment initially, but then told me later that they were doing it for themselves.
They talked of much more personal issues such as confidence and status,
proof of ability, a public as well as a private identity and a more positive self-
image (see also Edwards, 1993).

Contradictory or complementary explanations?

So why would the students apparently alter the reasons they gave me for
returning to education? On the whole, I think there is no contradiction, rather
there is an expansion of reasons. Economic reasons and personal reasons are
not necessarily mutually exclusive since our status in this society is largely
influenced by the type of job we do. It seems to me that some women initially
advanced what they perceived as a socially acceptable reason for returning to
education. In our culture, women are constantly being told, both directly
and indirectly, to put others' needs before their own. Women are still seen as
the primary (and often unpaid) carers – of the young, their partners and the
elderly (see amongst many others, Brannen and Moss, 1988; Charles, 1993;
Nash, 1990; Warde and Hetherington, 1993), and this is reflected in most
institutions of our society. It can also clearly be seen in the types of jobs
women do, the patterns of their employment and their representation in the
media, particularly in advertising. Even though advertising has changed considerably, women are still represented as taking prime responsibility for family
care and domestic chores. This is of course a representation which both
reflects and creates a reality – that at least part of women's identity is located
in the domestic and caring role (see also Edwards, 1993).

It is perhaps not surprising then that for those women with domestic and
caring responsibilities, 'doing it for myself' was construed by the students as

a somewhat selfish reason and the economic reasons which were advanced were more socially acceptable reasons to give to a relative stranger. However, once the women felt more relaxed in the discussion and an element of trust had been created in the interview situation, they felt more able to give other, not necessarily mutually exclusive, reasons for their return to education. There is also of course the possibility that in thinking and talking to me about the many issues in their lives, the students became more aware of, and were able to verbalize more personal reasons for, their return (see also Tina Miller on this issue, this volume). Both Brannen and Oakley (Brannen et al., 1991) reported on the benefits of reflexivity for the women they interviewed and Robson (1993) maintains that listening, hearing and empathy create a situation in which people feel safe and comfortable, are able to be reflective and talk freely:

> People often derive considerable satisfaction from talking about what they are doing to a disinterested but sympathetic ear. Taking part in a study can often lead to respondents reflecting on their experience in a way they find helpful. (Robson, 1993: 297)

It also seems that within the relaxed and non-judgemental structure of the interview, women were willing to talk of issues which they may not have discussed in a more formal setting.

Emergent data and unexpected findings

Over half of the students interviewed spoke of painful life experiences which could be significantly linked with their education, both past and present. This is not what I anticipated would come out of the interviews and these stories were certainly unsolicited. Maybe the women had reached a point where they had a need and desire for their voice to be heard in relation to particular periods in their lives and were given the opportunity to do this as part of, and at different points in, their stories, within the relaxed format of the interviews. Sometimes the students made direct, clear and immediate connections between these experiences and their return to education, but in other instances, the associations were indirect and almost casual. This appears to be linked with the nature of the experiences, which ranged across the women's lives in terms of what and when they occurred. Some, such as child sex abuse, an alcoholic mother, and a manipulative and controlling father, were rooted in childhood and had major ongoing influences on women's lives. Other experiences were more recent and had had different but no less significant effects for the students. For example, women were telling me about things such as mental and physical abuse, the death of a child and other family members, teenage pregnancy and divorce.

I was surprised at the way these clearly painful experiences tumbled out with no prompting. I found these accounts very stressful and this was accompanied by a mixture of conflicting emotions: anger and distress at the women's experiences, but also excitement that they were actually telling me about them. The biggest problem here was keeping control over non-verbal communication – particularly facial expression – so that I was not appearing to be judgemental. At the same time though, my expression needed to be sufficiently open and receptive to encourage the women to keep talking to me.

Jane Ribbens suggests that one of the most important qualities for researchers is the ability to listen and hear what is being said – which may not always be what is being verbalized (Ribbens, 1989: 586). I would take this a step further and suggest that this not only means paying attention to verbal cues such as intonations, nuances, pauses and inflections, it is also necessary to pay attention to body language.

Watching body language, listening to hesitations and trying to get an overall impression of the student whilst at the same time appearing relaxed and receptive to their stories was quite demanding. I recorded some comments on body language afterwards, but my main aim was to pick up cues and respond accordingly. Although the interview schedule was loosely ordered, I tended to allow the women to move the interview along in their own direction and quite often points were mentioned in conjunction with other factors about which they were talking. I had to concentrate hard to remember whether particular issues had been covered or not, at the same time as listening to what they were saying now and picking up on any serendipity. It was also possible to locate myself clearly in much of what the women were saying and it was almost as though I was going through the whole experience of being a mature student at the start of my educational career again, only this time with knowledge and awareness which had not been there before. I had to work hard therefore to ensure that what I was getting was the women's story and not a reflection of my own.

Because the focus was on barriers, I did not at first see the importance of the painful experiences about which the women were talking, but I felt that if they had been prepared to give precious time in a busy schedule to talk to me, the least I could do was to listen to what they wanted to tell me. I noted these stories with interest though, and can remember commenting to my supervisor about the trauma in some of the women's backgrounds.

I used the word 'trauma' because of the powerful and painful nature of the stories which the women were telling me. These experiences had clearly had a major impact on the lives of the students, and the effects appeared to be ongoing. Interviewing more students, I began to be aware of the frequency of these stories which seemed to be as much the rule as the exception. I did consider though whether the impact of these stories was staying with me. Were these particular voices too loud, dominating and colouring my thinking? However, by the time the interviews had been completed, around half of the 49 women with whom I talked told me of painful life experiences which could be significantly linked with their return to learning as adults.

Della, for example, told me of considerable personal domestic violence prior to her divorce and her son's subsequent psychological problems because of his father's treatment. Her daughter persuaded her to return to education, and she went on to tell me of her growing confidence:

> I didn't want to but she bullied and bullied me until I actually came down and I ended up doing three GCSEs . . . She said I could do it, but I didn't think I could, for about the first six months I was packing it in every week . . . I got some confidence back then and I started the second year on access. It got to about February as we started in the September and I got all the credits done easy . . . I thought, 'God I've done it again!' I was so bloody proud of myself . . . (Interview data)

Dilys talked of her poor relationship with her mother who would not allow her to stay at school after the minimum leaving age. She went on to talk of her long-held desire to return to education: 'I've waited all these years to go back . . .'

Jenny had to leave her nursery nursing course when she became pregnant. She felt that she was and still remained, restricted and controlled by her subsequent early marriage. Education was her way of ameliorating this situation: 'It's not just job prospects . . . It's the way that I escape the unfairness I suppose.'

Gerry experienced sexual abuse as a child. Her return to education is helping to give her a more positive self-image:

> I sort of came to a point where I thought 'I can either carry on the way that I am going and make a total mess of my life or try and get something positive from the negative' – try to get to a position where I can actually carry on with my life . . . perhaps this was a way I could prove to myself, more to myself than anybody else that I wasn't a failure. Even if I didn't actually succeed it was something that I actually got the courage to go and try and to have a go at . . . (Interview data)

The links were not always this clear and direct, but education seemed to be a vehicle which the women were using to deal with some of the consequences of their experiences.

I was surprised and appalled at the frequency of these stories, overwhelmed by the implications for my research and faced with a sizeable dilemma. I had considerable data on the barriers, ranging from minor to major, which mature women have to negotiate when they return to education. The original intention had been to examine these hurdles and the students' perception of them. I felt that I could write up the thesis, using this data, the planned eclectic theoretical structure and a broad literature review, which was virtually done, completing the task without too much difficulty. The other option was to take as my central topic the trauma about which the women had spoken and the links they were explicitly or implicitly making with education. This was uncharted territory. I was very uncertain about what was going to emerge once I started to analyse the data in detail and could find no direct literature on this topic, although there was considerable anecdotal support for the women's stories from friends and colleagues in different walks of life. The task seemed to have formidable proportions; rather like being dropped into an unknown terrain with no map and no idea of what was in store or which way to go. My orientation though was towards focusing on the trauma despite my trepidation – I wanted the women's stories to be heard. After more thought and discussion I decided that this should be the focus of the thesis. However, because of the origins of the research, I felt that it was necessary to write at least a chapter on barriers. This is what had been the original plan and I felt that there should at least be some acknowledgement of that.

Nevertheless, I had great difficulty beginning to write the chapter on barriers and could not at first understand why. The evidence was there, backed up by my own experience and by others' research, so why was I having difficulty writing this up? After several false starts and considerable thinking about it, the light slowly dawned. My original ideas were still influencing my thinking. I was still trying to work within an 'a priori' positivist structure of validation and categorization, and subconsciously fitting the data into a neat theoretical framework of patriarchy and power. I was reluctant to let go of this convenient and safe way of working totally, but at the same time I was clearly not intellectually comfortable with it. I was still trying to impose my own view – a 'top-down' perspective – rather than listening to the women's own stories – a 'bottom-up' perspective grounded in the data. I was in a state of transition – adopting a methodology which recognized the value of the women's input much more and shedding (albeit slowly) a more structured methodology. The recognition of this dynamic process was both illuminating and frightening. Hard on the heels of recognizing the source of my 'barrier to writing' was the awareness that I had no clear-cut explanatory framework for the issues about which the women were talking.

Back to the drawing board

Going back to the transcripts of the interviews, I began to readdress the whole notion of barriers – a concept with which I had been working for many years. This necessitated shedding my own ideas and preconceptions and listening to the women's stories. The problems and issues were certainly evident in the data, but the women did not conceptualize what was going on in terms of barriers. Rather, they were perceived as difficulties to consider and deal with as part of their lives as mature students – accepted as part and parcel of their return to education. Importantly, and central to the discussion, is that whatever problems the women had to deal with, they did not constitute an insurmountable barrier to education for this particular group of students and were not verbalized as such. Recognizing this was part of the learning process of moving from positivism to an ethnographic grounded theory approach of hearing what the women were actually saying, rather than what I thought they were saying. The women with whom I talked had returned to education, and at all levels were interacting with their environment to get what they wanted within a positive personal framework. One must bear in mind of course that the women with whom I talked were a self-selected sample of successes in that they had returned to learning, and for many other women the story may be very different.

However, this does not mean that there are not constraints on what some students could do, and some women did tell me that their circumstances influenced and sometimes determined their choice of subjects, courses, and institutions. But even here, within the recognition of limitations on their lives, for the majority of women there was a positive note of, 'I can do this' rather than, 'I can't do that'.

Organizing the data and staying faithful to the women's stories

Initially, I used the word trauma to describe the women's painful experiences, since they appeared to have had a considerable negative effect on the women. However, I felt very uncomfortable with the word, since for me it implied almost a 'one-off' occurrence, which in some stories is true, but in others, women have and are coping with ongoing painful experiences. I spent more than a year trying to think of an alternative word or phrase to reflect what the women told me. I have been offered phrases such as 'post-traumatic syndrome' and 'significantly meaningful events', neither of which adequately portrays the women's stories.

Wrestling with this issue again, I thought about my original reasons for using 'trauma' to describe the women's experiences. My initial use of the word had been linked with the concept of barriers to education – that these experiences destroyed confidence which was a huge barrier for women to get over. I had moved away from this idea and had begun to think of these experiences as perhaps being a motivation for women's return to education, since clear links between the 'traumas' and education were emerging. However, I was still very much defining their experiences within a preconceived framework of barriers. I needed to understand how the women perceived their experiences and what links they were making with education. It seems that I had an almost constant struggle between trying to hold on to some security with the ideas I brought to the research arena and the excitement but uncertainty of negotiating uncharted territory within the grounded theory approach I was taking. My original concept of barriers gave me at least a working structure compared with the insecurity of putting these ideas on one side to broaden my framework. Again I refocused my thinking and concentrated on the content of the women's stories. The problem has been to find terminology to reflect adequately the range of ordeals about which the women were telling me. I considered again my use of the word trauma. A good dictionary suggests shock, ordeal or crisis as synonymous with trauma, and some recent reading in psychology defined trauma as the creation of psychological damage that can have lasting effects on lives and may engender a feeling of helplessness, creating an emotional wound. This much wider concept of the word does represent the broad range of the women's stories, so I now seemed to have come full circle back to the word 'trauma'.

During the initial analysis of the data, I found it very hard to get away from the impact of the stories. Each story was unique, had clearly been painful and had a major effect on the women's lives. I was pulled into the content of the stories, as a woman, as someone who had also been through some of what they were telling me and also as a past mature student whose return to education was for many reasons other than education itself. I was both angry and hurt for the women and it was difficult to see beyond this to any patterns or groupings in the data. Empathy, I discovered, definitely is a double-edged sword, both enabling and disabling. I wanted to present all the women's stories since they were unique and interesting, but the requirements of a doctorate meant that I had to categorize and analyse within a theoretical framework. I read and reread the stories and made summaries and notes until the anger and pain began to subside and I began to see some patterns emerging. I made many different attempts at grouping before finally settling on two broad groupings, the first of which was concerned with the impact of major life events or changes. These may have affected students either directly – for example divorce or serious injury – or indirectly – for example, the death of close family members. The second group was concerned with restrictive stultifying experiences – traumatic episodes with lasting and damaging psychological effects. These experiences generally took the form of interpersonal oppression and control, many of which have had severe, lasting and often ongoing effects on the life and identity of the student. So it is not just the trauma which is important, but the impact of the traumatic experiences too. Categorization in this manner is clearly not the only way of organizing the material and a reworking of the data may well produce different structures. What is important to remember though is that the structure used was drawn from what the women said; how they perceived and described their experiences and the links they made between these experiences and education. Their stories were presented very much in their own words, because I felt that the students were much better at telling their own stories than I was. Nevertheless, there was necessarily some selection, which meant that their voices were channelled through me which caused inevitable problems. (For further exposition of this, see Natasha Mauthner, Andrea Doucet and Kay Standing in Part III, this volume.)

I tried to avoid making a judgement on the intensity of the trauma according to my own criteria. The only basis I had for making this judgement was what the women said and the way they said it and this was open to varying interpretation. A short film used as part of an Open University Summer School (Course K668, *Mental Handicap: Changing Perspectives*) discusses the way people who have had harrowing personal experiences distance themselves emotionally when talking to others about them and present their ordeals in a very matter-of-fact way (see also Fisher et al., 1986). In addition to this, people do not have the same ability to verbalize their experiences. As Taylor and Bogdan maintain: 'People simply do not have equal ability to provide detailed accounts of what they have been through and what they feel about it' (Taylor and Bogdan, 1984: 84). If I was going to categorize in terms of trauma, then it had to be in terms of what the women told me, either directly or indirectly about how these painful experiences had affected their lives. This was a far cry from the positivist approach I had taken at the start of the research.

Changing the theoretical approach

The frequency of trauma in the women's stories, the ongoing effects and the links which the women were making with education was new, exciting and different from what I had expected would emerge from the interviews. This made me examine my original theoretical orientation. Grounding the theory in the data raised the question of the usefulness of an eclectic approach. However, working and reworking the data led me back to a single focus on patriarchy as a conceptual tool. What had emerged clearly from the women's stories was the extensive and pervasive nature of male dominance which affected all areas of the women's lives either directly or indirectly, and was linked with the trauma which the women presented. However, patriarchy did not seem to provide adequate explanations for many of the things about which the women had spoken, such as women's control over other women, the guilt feelings associated with sexual abuse, psychological violence and the extent of agency exhibited by the students. So rather than fitting the women's stories into a pre-existing theoretical framework, I decided to use the women's stories as a challenge to the theory. This was not without some trepidation as a doctoral student, since I appeared to be questioning a fairly weighty body of existing academic knowledge. (For greater discussion of this, see Parr, 1996.)

Conclusion

This chapter has discussed the dilemmas and difficulties of shifting from a positivist approach, fairly structured and organized, to an ethnographic feminist approach where the analysis is rooted in the data and the influence of all participants in the research process acknowledged. To what extent did this move sharpen my sensitivity to the women's voices?

Positivism argues for a structured approach to research, the distancing of the researcher from the 'researched' and for data to be objectively observed and classified, maintaining that researcher involvement will distort the data. Qualitative feminist methodology and a grounded theory approach on the other hand recognize the influence of all participants in the research process, arguing that it is there whether we acknowledge it or not. Had I continued down my planned route, an analysis of what I had defined as barriers in relation to women returners to education would have been the central focus of my thesis and this would clearly have been an inaccurate representation of the women's stories. Grounding the analysis in the data, though, raised my awareness of the women's perception of these issues, which was at variance with my own. Also revealed were interesting links in the data between trauma and education which were not at first obvious to me, but which became very apparent once I allowed the women's voices to be heard. I would argue that my sensitivity to the women's voices was clearly sharpened by the shift to a feminist grounded theory approach.

However, one cannot deny the power of the researcher in selecting, organizing and presenting the data, regardless of the approach taken. Whoever's voice is heard, it cannot be wholly the interviewees', but with an open and relatively unstructured approach, the filter is likely to be larger than with a more closely structured positivist framework.

References

ACACE (1982) *Continuing Education: From Policies to Practice*. Leicester: ACACE.

Brannen, J., Dodd, K. and Oakley, A. (1991) 'Getting involved: the effects of research on participants'. Paper given at BSA Conference, University of Manchester, Manchester, April.

Brannen, J. and Moss, P. (1988) *New Mothers at Work: Employment and Childcare*. London: Unwin Hyman.

Bryman, A. and Burgess, R. (1994) *Analyzing Qualitative Data*. London: Routledge.

Central Statistical Office (1996) *Social Trends*. London: HMSO.

Charles, N. (1993) *Gender Division and Social Change*. Hemel Hempstead: Harvester Wheatsheaf.

Charnley, A.H., McGivney, V. and Sims, D. (1985) *Education for the Adult Unemployed: Some Responses*. Leicester: NIACE.

Coats, M. (1989) 'Support for women learners: requirements and resources', *Adults Learning*, 1 (4): 104–5.

Coats, M. (1994) *Women's Education*. Buckingham: SRHE and Open University Press.

Davis, K. (1991) 'Critical sociology and gender relations', in K. Davis, M. Leijenaar and J. Oldersma (eds), *The Gender of Power*. London: Sage.

Edwards, R. (1993) *Mature Women Students*. London: Taylor and Francis.

Fisher, M., Marsh, P. and Phillips, D. (1986) *In and Out of Care: Final Report*. London: Batsford.

Giddens, A. (1984) *The Constitution of Society*. Cambridge: Polity Press.

Glaser, B. and Strauss, A. (1967) *The Discovery of Grounded Theory: Strategies for Qualitative Research*. Chicago: Aldine.

Lukes, S. (1974) *Power: A Radical View*. London: Macmillan.

McGivney, V. (1993) *Women, Education and Training: Barriers to Access, Informal Starting Points and Progression Routes*. Leicester: NIACE.

Mies, M. (1993) 'Towards a Methodology for Feminist Research', in M. Hammersley (ed.), *Social Research: Philosophy, Politics and Practice*. London: Sage.

Miles, M. and Huberman, M. (1994) *Qualitative Data Analysis*. London: Sage.

Nash, T. (1990) 'The Great No-Win Situation', *Director*, 43 (4): 46–50.

Oakley, A. (1981) 'Interviewing women: a contradiction in terms', in H. Roberts (eds), *Doing Feminist Research*. Routledge and Kegan Paul.

Oglesby, K.L. (1989) *Vocational Education for Women in Western Europe*. Report from European Bureau of Adult Education

Oglesby, K.L. (1991) 'Women and education and training in Europe: issues for the 90's', *Studies in the Education of Adults*, 23 (2): 133–44.

Parr, J. (1996) 'Education: what's in it for mature women?' PhD dissertation, University of Sheffield, Sheffield.

Pascall, G. and Cox, R. (1993) *Women Returning to Higher Education*. Milton Keynes: SHRE and Open University Press.

Ribbens, J. (1989) 'Interviewing: an "unnatural situation"?', *Women's Studies International Forum*, 12 (6): 579–92.

Robson, C. (1993) *Real World Research*. Oxford: Blackwell.

Schutze, H.G. (ed.), with Slowey, M., Wagner, A. and Paquet, P. (1987) *Adults in Higher Education: Policies and Practice in Gt. Britain and N. America*. Stockholm: Almqvist and Wiksell Int.

Strauss, A. and Corbin, J. (1990) *Basics of Qualitative Research: Grounded Theory Procedures and Techniques*. London: Sage.

Taylor, S. and Bogdan, R. (1984) *Introduction to Qualitative Research Methods.* Chichester: John Wiley.

Warde, A. and Hetherington, K. (1993) 'A changing domestic division of labour? Issues of measurement and interpretation', *Work, Employment and Society,* 7 (1): 23–45.

Woodley, A., Wagner, L., Slowey, M., Hamilton, M. and Fulton, O. (eds) (1987) *Choosing to Learn: Adults in Education.* Milton Keynes: SHRE and Open University Press.

PART III
HEARING AND REPRESENTING: REFLECTING THE PRIVATE IN PUBLIC

7 Hearing Competing Voices
Sibling Research

Miri Song

In this chapter, I discuss the dilemmas and insights I derived from comparing and interpreting two siblings' interviews, and issues around multiple perception in research more generally. The issue of competing siblings' perceptions and accounts constituted one part of my doctoral research, which examined the labour participation of 42 young people (mostly in their early twenties) and a few parents in 25 Chinese families running take-away businesses in Britain (Song, 1996).

Although 'family labour' has been noted as an important 'ethnic resource' in studies of so-called ethnic businesses, very little is known about children's work roles within them (Song, 1997b). Within this broader study I address the disjuncture between public knowledge and understandings of Chinese families running take-aways (and other ethnic groups running family-run businesses) and these families' lived experiences, at least as I understood them in this research. Chinese families' reliance upon the ethnic catering sector, and children's involvement in these family work strategies, had been depicted in a predominantly negative 'top-down' fashion by the few researchers who had explored this topic (for example, Baxter, 1988). However, the interviews with Chinese young people and their parents suggested much more complicated, ambivalent and even positive stories about the nature of the work and family relationships they experienced.

Therefore, one aim of the study was to privilege young people's own experiences and understandings of working with and for their families in Chinese family-run take-away businesses (see Pam Alldred's chapter, this volume, for a discussion of research dilemmas which arise in studies of younger children). I use the term 'children' throughout to refer to a family relationship, rather than to individuals of any particular age.

'Helping out' in these businesses was a widely shared expectation among Chinese families running take-aways in Britain. This belief in helping out was embodied in an implicit 'family work contract' upheld by these families (Song, 1997b). Children in most of these 25 families provided key forms of labour, for example, by working at the counter or in the kitchens of their take-away businesses, and by performing 'caring' labour, such as language mediation on behalf of their parents. In addition to the fact that helping out was crucial for family survival, it was expected on the basis of family obligations. Furthermore, helping out was regarded as an affirmation of Chinese cultural identity in Britain. This belief in helping out was widely held among the young people in this study, even though many of them felt ambivalent about contributing their labour.

I had not originally planned to obtain sibling interviews about 'helping out' in these families. However, in the initial interviews with Chinese young people, many of them talked about their work roles in relation to those of their siblings (Song, 1997a). In fact, many of the respondents referred to differences in labour commitments between themselves and their siblings, and it soon became clear that these differences could be the source of contentious issues in these families. Therefore, in spite of the widespread belief in helping out, in practice, individual siblings within families could differ in their commitments and feelings about working for their families.

Although I was excited about the prospect of interviewing siblings about their family and work experiences, I quickly realized that methodologically I had little idea of how I would 'take in' and digest two, rather than one, stories. Did interviewing two siblings, rather than one young person, entail a different way of listening or hearing in these interviews? How would I make sense of two accounts which seemed totally at odds with each other? As a sociologist, I had no prior expertise regarding siblings *per se*, or methodological approaches which dealt specifically with sibling interviews. Therefore, I searched out literature on the issue of multiple perception in various forms of family research.

Multiple perception in social research

In recent years there has been increased sensitivity and interest in the issue of multiple perception in social research, particularly in research on couples and on families. There is now a general recognition among researchers that the nature of the data collected is contingent upon the individual who was interviewed, and that, not surprisingly, individual interviewees may provide disparate perspectives and understandings of their situations and of social phenomena, depending upon their characteristics and backgrounds.

As a result, some analysts have critiqued the 'one-sided' nature of only interviewing, for instance, husbands (or wives), as opposed to both spouses, in research concerning married couples. Jessie Bernard's (1972) well-known assertion that there are 'his' and 'her' marriages pointed to the fact that men and women tended to experience and conceive of their marriages in quite distinct ways. From both a methodological and epistemological (and ideological!) point of view, this was an important point to make, because Bernard's research helped to legitimate the idea that individuals inhabited often different but equally valid terrains of 'reality' and existence.

Increasingly, feminist empirical research and writings on methodology and epistemology have challenged traditional notions of knowledge as presented and legitimated in the 'public' sphere. Such writings have addressed debates around which substantive topic areas are worthy of study, as well as debates on ways of knowing (see Ribbens and Edwards, 1995). Growing research on much social phenomena that occurs within the 'private' sphere, for instance intimate relationships between spouses or siblings, has pointed to the fact that research findings on many topic areas are based upon the complex and overlapping social realities of the individuals and groups studied.

However, the recognition of the complexity of investigating people's experiences and relationships has not necessarily meant that social research has successfully *combined* or interpreted multiple interviews or accounts from various family members. Most writings that have challenged the epistemological and ontological bases of much conventional social research have not addressed the issue of interpreting multiple accounts. The question of how to analyse and interpret competing interviews, whether by joint or separate interviews, has been little discussed – despite the fact that over the last few decades there has been a growing body of research on marriage and family life that has addressed aspects of spousal relationships (see, for example, Allan, 1980; Pahl, 1989; Safilios-Rothschild, 1976), such as marital satisfaction and divisions of labour, by relying upon the reports of both spouses.[1] Studies of marriage have tended to interpret wives' and husbands' points of view in ways that recognize the various differences in power between men and women and the different societal expectations of wives and husbands.

In comparison with studies including both spouses' accounts in marriage, there has been surprisingly little (at least, sociological) research investigating multiple perceptions in other family relationships, for instance, between siblings (see Jessop, 1981, and Smith and Self, 1980, for comparisons between parents and their children). However, there does generally seem to be a growing recognition of the need to include more than one perspective in recent research on family relationships. For example, Finch and Mason's study of how family responsibilities are negotiated illustrates the importance of relying upon interviews with various members of a kin group:

> We felt this [interviews with relatives] was important, given our focus on processes of negotiation between relatives: including a number of members of the same family would help us to understand negotiating processes from different perspectives and positions. (1993: 187)

Thus, for Finch and Mason, interviews with various relatives of the initial interviewee were important, not only because they provided another perspective, *per se*, but because additional interviews were crucial in understanding their object of interest – processes of negotiation in families. In such research it is imperative not only to report the existence of different perspectives, but also to piece together various accounts into a coherent story that the researcher must present. Their interviews with a host of kin provided Finch and Mason with a much fuller and more complex picture of how kin groups negotiated and understood various types of responsibilities.

The investigation of 'group properties', such as family divisions of labour, is greatly aided by drawing upon interviews with multiple family members. This was certainly the case in my research on children's labour commitments in Chinese families running take-away businesses; exploring sibling relationships within this broader study provided depth and insight which was, I believe, crucial to a fuller understanding of these families' relations of production and family relationships.

Although there has been considerable psychological research on sibling relationships (see Bank and Kahn, 1982; Hetherington et al., 1994; Lamb and Sutton-Smith, 1982), sibling relationships have received relatively little attention in sociological studies (as Melanie Mauthner, this volume, has pointed out). In comparison with marriage, or parent–child relationships, both of which are structured in terms of gendered and generational power differences, sibling relationships (particularly in Western societies) are usually characterized as being relatively equitable. Nevertheless, recent analysts such as Sulloway (1996) have argued that birth order is a very significant factor in shaping particular kinds of parent–child relationships for siblings.

Most of the existing literature on siblings has not centrally addressed the issue of interpreting and comparing siblings' accounts from a methodological or epistemological perspective. Undoubtedly, some of the broader findings about sibling dynamics and parent–child relationships do apply to the siblings in my study. However, the specific configurations of family, work and ethnicity that were central to Chinese families' lives in Britain (and thus their departure from broader studies of family and sibling relationships) meant that I approached these sibling interviews without a firm attachment to any particular way of hearing or analysis.

Siblings' labour commitments and family reputations

In order to explore how siblings understood their commitments to 'helping out', and the implications of these commitments for family relationships, I asked respondents to compare their work roles and commitments with those of their siblings. In asking this question, I wanted to gain a sense of how respondents made sense of their own and their siblings' commitments to helping out, rather than actually discern which sibling(s) had worked more than others. Therefore, like Finch and Mason (1993), I pursued these sibling interviews not only for the sake of obtaining different perspectives, but because sibling interviews ultimately provided important information and depth into how children's labour participation was elicited and negotiated.

Of the 42 young people in 25 families, I was able to interview two siblings in 17 families (nine sister pairs, five brother–sister pairs, and three brother pairs). Although siblings in four of the 17 families stressed *similarities* between their own and their siblings' labour commitments, most siblings reported *disparities* in work roles and commitments to helping out. These four sibling sets who stressed similarities seemed determined, in principle, *not* to compare themselves with their siblings (at least to me, an unknown researcher). This sense of loyalty (which Melanie Mauthner discusses in her chapter) was especially stressed by two sisters, Rita and Helen. When asked to compare herself with Rita, Helen replied, 'I don't like to compare. We don't count who does what. We help each other.' In a separate interview, Rita also said:

> I think she [Helen] did her bit and I did mine. It's difficult to say who's done more because I've done a lot in the earlier stage, then I was away studying for two years, and she was in the shop. Can't really compare the commitments.

Of course, such 'public' representations of their families – 'we don't count who does what' – could have belied underlying issues and tensions which neither sister was prepared to reveal to a researcher (Song and Parker, 1995).

Given the small numbers of sibling pairs I was able to interview, it was impossible to explore systematically any differences between same-sex and different-sex sibling pairs. As I illustrate later in this chapter, sister pairs in this study were not necessarily less inclined to compare themselves than brother pairs or brother–sister pairs.

Unlike the emphasis on *similarity* in labour commitments, reported *differences* in labour commitments between siblings clearly *mattered* in these families; if these respondents had any misgivings about 'talking about' their siblings, such doubts were overcome. Because the expectation that all children 'help out' was so widely held among these Chinese families, siblings who were less committed to helping out were regarded as contravening a valued Chinese norm in Britain. Respondents often spoke of the importance of equity in the sharing of labour between family members.

Therefore, perceived differences in labour commitments among siblings had ramifications for the status of individual children and for their relationships with family members. A key way in which respondents tended to explain differences in labour commitments among themselves and their siblings was in terms of their respective family reputations and cultural identities. Polarized reputations as 'good' or 'bad' children, in terms of their labour commitments, seemed to be widely shared in families where disparities in labour commitments were reported (Song, 1997a).

'Good' reputations were attributed to siblings who were seen to be very committed to helping out, and these siblings were regarded as possessing predominantly Chinese identities. In comparison, 'bad' reputations were attributed to siblings who were resistant to helping out; such 'selfish' and 'individualistic' siblings were thus seen to possess 'Western' or 'English' identities. No one act or record of commitment defined a 'good' or 'bad' reputation. Rather, these family reputations were formed in the context of long-term family relationships and dynamics.

Although I am unable to go into a detailed discussion of the ways in which such reputations were attributed in these families, there could be a heavy cost to a 'bad' reputation. In addition to the moral censure that 'bad' siblings had to endure, 'good' siblings could enjoy parental approval and a sense of 'the moral high ground' in relation to their 'bad' siblings.

'Gatekeeping' and access to siblings

In investigating siblings' labour commitments in these families, I conducted separate semi-structured interviews with both siblings, and transcribed all the interviews. Methodologically, I was limited by the fact that I was unable to be systematic about choosing siblings of any particular sex or age, in relation to the first respondent. While some siblings were too busy, or lived abroad, others simply did not want to participate. Based upon my first point of contact in these 25 families, the first respondent sometimes acted, either explicitly or implicitly, as a 'gatekeeper' to her/his sibling(s).

While no respondents actually told me that they did not want me to talk with a particular sibling, I sometimes had the impression that they steered me toward a sibling of their choice. In cases where respondents told me that a sibling was not willing to speak with me, I felt I had no choice but to accept such statements. In a few cases, respondents said that they were concerned not to impose *me* upon their sibling(s), and had to check with their siblings about my contacting them.

For instance, when I asked about interviewing one respondent's older sister, David told me that he would ask his sister about being interviewed. David had reported that he and his sister had had a somewhat conflictual relationship over the years, and that an important basis for their strained relationship had been the fact that his sister had reportedly been uninvolved in the family take-away. When David later told me that his sister was too busy to be interviewed, I couldn't help wondering if David had asked her at all, or dissuaded her from doing so in some way. Was it possible that David was concerned about her story contradicting his account? Was he concerned about his sister reporting unflattering things about him? One can obviously go too far with this kind of speculation; I am simply illustrating how the researcher may be subject to the gatekeeping prerogative of the interviewee in such situations.

So why might some respondents care so much about which sibling I interviewed? Given the sensitive nature of the interviews, in which I asked respondents to compare their labour commitments with those of their siblings, a whole array of issues and concerns could arise. As discussed before, perceived differences in labour commitments among siblings were understood in terms of various family reputations; as such, these differences affected the standing of individual children in these families. Not only was it important for individual children to have a 'good' reputation in their families, but respondents may also have wanted to assert a 'good' persona in a semi-public arena, through the interview. As Jordan et al. (1994) have observed, respondents are often anxious to provide accounts which demonstrate their 'moral adequacy' in interviews. Thus it is important to many interviewees, more generally, that they provide reasonable and credible accounts *and* that they appear to be 'good' people.

If respondents were concerned about preserving their credibility with me, or anxious to put forth a public account of their family which put them in a good light, they may have had an interest in my interviewing particular siblings over others. Through this gatekeeping process, I was made aware of the different kinds of motivations and interests that respondents had for providing particular accounts, and in some cases, steering me toward a certain sibling over others. Despite the fact that some young people exercised (or may have wanted to exercise) this gatekeeping prerogative, a number of respondents, as I discuss below, did not object to my interviewing a sibling who seemed likely to provide a different, even opposing point of view.

'Allied' and 'oppositional' sibling accounts

As I listened to these sibling accounts, I soon realized that respondents who stressed *differences* in labour commitments among siblings, and who explained these disparities in terms of polarized 'good' and 'bad' reputations, tended to do so in various ways throughout these interviews. In four sibling sets stressing similarities, the siblings who were interviewed seemed to be 'allied' together, for they both presented similar accounts of their families, *and* they also presented favourable accounts of other siblings' labour commitments (though they pointed to differences in labour commitments with other siblings who were *not* interviewed). Such 'allied' siblings reported that they had both been equally committed to helping out, and each of them gave congruent accounts which tended to focus upon other 'bad' siblings (see Segalen, 1984, for a discussion of 'alliances' among siblings).

In the other nine sibling sets, however, interviewed siblings, stressing differences, tended to provide 'oppositional' accounts about which siblings had been more committed than others, and for what reasons. Both 'allied' and 'oppositional' accounts, which relied upon discursive understandings of sibling reputations, were interactively created, in the context of sibling and family relationships, as well as in the context of participating in the interviews. After presenting examples of both 'allied' and 'oppositional' sibling interviews, I will discuss them in relation to the dilemmas I encountered in analysing and interpreting two sibling accounts.

Annie and Shirley: an 'allied' interview

Interviews with two sisters, Annie, aged 22, and Shirley, aged 26, exemplified a case in which they seemed to be 'allied' with each other – in terms of their close relationship with each other in their family and in terms of their match-ing accounts of why some siblings were more committed to helping out than others. Among the four children in their family, Annie and Shirley made no secret of the fact that they considered each other their best friend. I had first made contact with Annie, who then suggested that I interview her sister Shirley. Annie's brother lived in Hong Kong, and was not available, and while I was not explicitly discouraged from interviewing her other sister, Kelly, I had the strong impression that Annie did not want me to interview her. This was because Annie not only suggested that I contact Shirley, but because she demurred when I inquired about interviewing Kelly. Both Annie and Shirley considered themselves to be 'equally committed' to helping out, and were crit-ical of their other two siblings, who were seen to be selfish and uncaring. For instance, when I asked Annie why she thought Kelly was less committed to helping out, Annie responded,

> Because Shirley and I care about what happens. Kelly lets people know she hates it [the take-away]. She distances herself. It's her nature, same as my brother. Same as my father; they don't want to know. We [Annie and Shirley] used to get so angry with her [Kelly].

Annie's sister Shirley echoed this assessment of Kelly and their brother, Alan:

> *Shirley*: Alan left first, but not to move away. But he was studying, and so he didn't actually move away from the family, but he stopped work at the shop, and that caused big problems . . . My brother refused to come back to the shop, ever.
> *MS*: Why was that?
> *Shirley*: He hated it; he hated it more than all of us.
> *MS*: Did that cause a lot of tension between him and the parents?
> *Shirley*: No, it caused a lot of tension between us [siblings] and him. We thought he let the family down. He wasn't doing his part . . . He didn't have a lot of respon-sibility toward the family. I think he'd had enough . . . What we used to say, we've had this discussion before [she and Annie]. Me, Annie, and mum, we have simi-lar characteristics. We did it; we didn't like doing the work, but we did it because we're helping each other. We were very bonded, even now we're close . . .
> *MS*: So Kelly doesn't do much either?
> *Shirley*: Yeah. She and my brother were able not to attend work. They were able to do it without guilt. We hated it, but we felt we had to come back. She'd [mum] always count on us being there, whereas with my brother and Kelly, you don't know.

Lisa and June: an 'oppositional interview'

Unlike the 'allied' interviews, the majority of the sibling pairs (stressing dif-ferences in labour commitments) gave 'oppositional' accounts which compared their labour commitments with each other (as well as with non-interviewed siblings). In such interviews, the two respondents tended to disagree with each other about who or why some siblings were more com-mitted than others. While the 'allied' siblings were reportedly both committed to helping out, these 'oppositional' siblings seemed quite competitive about claiming the 'most committed' status in their families.

For instance, in one case the two interviewed siblings gave contrasting accounts about which of them had been more committed to helping out in their family take-away. I first interviewed June, aged 22, and then Lisa, aged 20. They were the two eldest of four children. June, whom I interviewed first, reported that she had been the most committed worker in her family:

> *MS*: What about your brother and sisters? Did they mind helping out?
> *June*: I think it's probably different from the way I see it. But I go home at holidays, and it's like, oh, great, she's back, we don't have to go [to the shop], we can stay at home.
> *MS*: Do you think their attitude toward working in the shop is similar to yours?
> *June*: No, different.
> *MS*: In what way is it different?
> *June*: They do it, but you sort of have to ask them. Whereas, if I'm home, I just go off and do it. And they sit around.

June reported that she had the strongest sense of filial piety and family obligation among her siblings: 'If I argue with my parents, then eventually, I will go around to their way of thinking, or I'll do it, whereas my sisters and brother don't.' Interestingly, June's sister, Lisa, was emphatic about having worked more than June:

> Even though June is older than me, I tended to tell her how to do things. I had more family responsibility than she did. On the shop front, I naturally had more responsibility because basically for her, her job involved just standing in the front, and maybe answering the phone, whereas I'm on the more difficult demanding side, actually cooking and doing what people think is a quite hard labour job.

Although both June and Lisa agreed that their other two siblings were less committed to helping out than either of them, each of them provided accounts which stressed the importance of their own work role and commitment to their family, albeit in different ways.

Analysing two siblings' accounts

Various dilemmas arose for me in relation to interpreting both 'allied' and 'oppositional' sibling interviews. Despite providing multiple perspectives, paradoxically, 'allied' interviews such as with Annie and Shirley could provide a limited and one-sided picture, because they excluded the viewpoints and stories of demonized 'bad' siblings. Because I did not interview Kelly or Alan, I had no way of knowing if their understandings of the situation were vastly different from those of Annie and Shirley. I initially experienced concerns about not giving voice to the 'bad' siblings in this family, especially because Annie had encouraged me to interview Shirley, rather than Kelly. This was because I wanted to provide as complete a picture of their family as possible.

I had to remind myself that I was not in a position to 'verify' Annie's and Shirley's accounts, since I did not have access to either Kelly or Alan. This is not to deny that actual divisions of labour between siblings mattered; they did, on various levels, for these respondents and for my data. However, what

I was in a position to investigate (and which was of primary interest to me) were Annie's and Shirley's motivations and interests in producing accounts in the ways they did. Without attributing Machiavellian designs to respondents, it is important to remember that it is highly unlikely that respondents are able to frame their accounts in a totally dispassionate and disinterested fashion.

The fact that Annie and Shirley provided congruent accounts did not, in and of itself, enhance the validity or 'truth' of their version; their close relationship seemed significant in shaping congruent beliefs and stories about their relative commitments to helping out. Annie and Shirley represented themselves in terms of a supportive 'alliance' of sorts, in relation to other siblings whom they deemed to be less committed to helping out. As such, 'allied' sibling accounts mirrored each other in a way which suggested that their versions of themselves and their families were co-produced and self-reinforcing. Through ongoing discussions and close relationships that had developed over many years, these siblings had woven together a story which explained who and why some siblings had been more committed to helping out in the business than others. Furthermore, there was no reason to believe that two 'oppositional' interviews, by virtue of presenting two different perspectives, were somehow more valid than the congruent stories presented in 'allied' interviews. In fact, they both tended to point to coalitions and contentiousness in these families about differential labour commitments among siblings.

Although I would argue that the researcher's access to certain lines of inquiry and knowledge may be limited in many interview situations, this does not mean that researchers cannot 'go with' their sense of scepticism, or query arguments and lines of thought which do not seem convincing or are blatantly contradictory. In the case of Lisa and June, it could be argued that, in theory, both siblings' accounts were equally valid to the extent that their accounts were sincere expressions of their beliefs and experiences, and reflected their own subjective realities; each seemed to believe that she had done more than the other.

However, these two sisters claimed the 'most committed' status through different means in their interviews. Regardless of whether or not Lisa had really worked more arduously than June, I felt that Lisa was absolutely determined to present herself (to me) as the most responsible person in her family; it was evidently of great personal importance to her that she was recognized as a committed child in her family. According to Lisa, her work in the kitchen was qualitatively more difficult and substantial than June's work at the counter.

Not only was I struck by the vehemence with which Lisa disparaged her sister's work role, but I was surprised by Lisa's characterization of counter work as 'just standing in the front'. Once again, although my main object was to understand how and why siblings explained differences in labour commitment (and not who had actually provided the most labour), Lisa's account immediately engendered scepticism on my part. First, I was doubtful of her claim that the work she had performed in the kitchen had been much more demanding than June's work at the counter. This was because I had heard much testimony from other young people about the stresses and difficulties of counter work, particularly because of racist abuse and condescension from their customers. I had also witnessed such incidents and the hard work involved in counter work through observation.

Despite the fact that she felt that she had done the most work, June acknowledged that her point of view differed from those of her siblings: 'I think it's probably different from the way I see it.' June recognized the partiality of her own account. In comparison, Lisa was much more bullish and definitive in the way she presented her story; I felt pushed to accept her account of her family. By comparison, June's account seemed much more balanced and less 'pushy'.

In general, more reflexive accounts from siblings who indicated an awareness that their reports were ultimately subjective (like June's) seemed more credible than those from siblings who were less reflexive. However, it is possible that some interviewees were affected by the social desirability of reflexive responses, and may have made a concerted effort to sound reasonable and balanced in their views. There seem to be links between issues of reflexivity and issues of credibility, both for us as researchers presenting our research to public audiences and for us as listeners within the semi-public (and yet very intimate) setting of the interview itself. Some accounts, such as June's, were more convincing to me if they were reflexively presented because we as researchers are expected, and often required to be, reflexive in the ways in which we engage in social research – at every stage of this process. Being reflexive for researchers includes a willingness to consider the subjective and often arbitrary positions from which we view and understand our feelings, experiences and social interactions with others.

Despite my recognition of the importance of reflexivity for the credibility of respondents' accounts, I found myself suppressing the notion that June's account was somehow more credible than Lisa's, as well as my rather negative feelings toward Lisa (see Jane Ribbens' chapter, this volume, about listening to her own voice on mothering). Various mantras about being 'fair', 'not taking sides' and not getting 'emotionally involved' circulated in my head. I found myself obsessed with the mantra that 'all accounts are equally valid' in a rather wooden way – without acknowledging that not all accounts may be *credible* in the same ways, or the possibility that I should trust my instincts and feelings about Lisa's non/credible account. My reluctance to view some siblings' accounts as more credible than others may have been related to an aversion to 'taking sides' as a researcher.

Researchers' own allegiances

In some interviews, I found myself aligned and much more sympathetic toward one sibling and that sibling's account, versus the other's. In June's and Lisa's case, I had been put off by what I considered to be Lisa's pushy insistence upon being the hardest working and most committed child in her family. I don't think that we, as researchers, can avoid some situations in which we may feel rather sympathetic or repelled by particular interviewees (and vice versa!). However, I do think it is important that researchers try to be aware of their sympathies and allegiances to a particular respondent in multiple interviews, particularly when sensitive issues are broached; some respondents may feel that they are being judged by the researcher if they detect that the researcher is more sympathetic with the other respondent.

In fact, I was aware that some respondents were un/consciously drawing me on to their 'side'. Particularly in 'oppositional' interviews such as these I was aware of interviewees' desires to elicit my support for their accounts. I believe that the respondents' knowledge of the fact that I would interview their sibling resulted in respondents giving accounts which positioned themselves in particular ways – *vis-à-vis* their siblings and their families, more generally.

For instance, in another case of 'oppositional' sibling interviews, Foon, aged 25, and Wong, aged 27, both reported that Foon had been more committed to helping out than Wong had been. While Wong had gone far away to university, and had distanced himself from his family and take-away business by doing so, Foon had attended university near his home, and had continued to help out in the evenings, combining his studies and his work in the take-away. Thus, according to Foon, he had a reputation for being 'good' and more Chinese than Wong, who was characterized as being relatively Western – that is, individualistic and selfish. Although both brothers agreed about who had been more committed to helping out (Foon), their interviews constituted oppositional accounts in that they disagreed about *how and why* Foon had become more committed than Wong. In this way, oppositional accounts could stem from a variety of contested claims and explanations about disparities in labour commitments.

When I interviewed Wong, following my interview with Foon, I had the sense that Wong had a prepared agenda, in which he would challenge Foon's account of Wong and their respective family reputation:

> I'd always had my mind on leaving [the take-away and home]. I'm not [pause] my view on all this isn't like Foon. I'm not a good boy that he is, like being responsible. It was something I've always felt – that I've got to get on with my life. I had to leave. Foon is someone who I think is living his life at the expense of the take-away . . .

Implicit in Wong's account was the sense that he wanted validation for his 'side of the story'. While undercutting Foon's reputation as the 'good' child, Wong stressed his own need to leave home as a positive act which required strength and courage.

Given the sensitivity of the issues discussed, and the siblings' knowledge that I had or would interview both of them, I had to be quite careful about the ways in which I probed them about their respective commitments to helping out (see Brannen, 1988). Other researchers have noted their roles in inadvertently 'stirring up trouble' in the interview process (see, for example, McKee and O'Brien's research on becoming a father (1983), in which they contacted fathers through their wives). Nevertheless, it seems to me that researchers still need to ask the hard questions – the (hopefully) pivotal

questions that may enable respondents to articulate often difficult and complex feelings and thoughts. I doubt that I could have obtained such rich
data if I had not explicitly asked respondents to compare their work roles
and commitments with those of their siblings.

Although 'oppositional' sibling interviews should not involve a researcher
openly 'taking sides' with either one of the respondents, in situations where
feelings of skewed sympathy and credibility arise, it is important for the
researcher to recognize such feelings and thoughts, and to be self-scrutinizing
about how her reactions may affect her interpretation of an account and the
broader situation (see also Andrea Doucet's discussion of analysing interviews with husbands and wives, Natasha Mauthner and Andrea Doucet, this
volume).

Conclusion

Interviewing two siblings, rather than an individual child, about their views
and experiences of helping out gave me crucial insight into the ways in which
children's labour participation was elicited and negotiated in Chinese families
running take-away businesses in Britain. Chinese children made sense of different labour commitments in their families in terms of individual children's
reputations and standings in their families. Although sibling relationships
have some distinctive qualities about them, in relation to other social relationships, they provided a good basis for exploring the dilemmas of analysing
and making sense of other kinds of multiple interviews.

Access to multiple accounts opens up the field of investigation for the
researcher, and may ultimately allow for a richer and more complete story.
The combination and interpretation of multiple accounts is not easily
achieved through any formulae or measurements. This was because while a
second respondent (in this case, a sibling) did provide a useful point of comparison with the first respondent, harnessing the interview material was far
from straightforward. That is, the result of combining and analysing two siblings' interviews was greater than the mere sum of the two interviews.

However, I learned that the simple addition of another perspective, *per se*,
did not automatically and necessarily provide depth and greater understanding of the object of study. Rather than assuming that multiple interviews
necessarily provide more information (which in many cases they can), it is
probably more accurate to say that multiple interviews help to reveal the
complexities, contradictions, and tensions in people's accounts and in their
daily lives. Such complexities and tensions were most evident in 'oppositional' interviews between siblings, where they tended to disagree about their
explanations of who or why some siblings had been more committed than
others. Although 'allied' interviews revealed a congruence in the two siblings' accounts, they too revealed tensions and dissensions in their families
about labour commitments and individual family reputations. Different
accounts from siblings did not mean that there was one 'true' story to be told,

and that I *had* to privilege one account over the other as the actual 'true' account. Each account was clearly valuable in and of itself, in revealing individuals' respective understandings of themselves and of their relationships with their siblings and their families more broadly.

Nevertheless, in spite of the fact that, in principle, many researchers such as myself qualify or even disdain the notion that there is one all-encompassing 'true' version of people's lives and relationships, it is important not to dismiss outright the notion of 'truth' or 'findings' in social research. Rather than speaking of 'true' accounts or 'truth' in the broadest terms, we need to ask ourselves what kind of knowledge we are after – 'truth' with regard to what? Who did what? What someone feels and understands? The sincerity of a respondent's story? In this sense, we often deal with various levels of 'truth' and knowledge which are differentially value-laden.

Not only do these various kinds of knowledge have different ontological statuses, but we, as researchers, have variable degrees of epistemological access to these various kinds of knowledge (see Pam Alldred's chapter, this volume, concerning strategic decisions about reflexivity and 'warrants' about knowledge claims). As Rosalind Edwards and Jane Ribbens point out in Chapter 1, 'We suggest that, rather than a relativistic despair, we need high standards of reflexivity and openness about the choices made throughout any empirical study . . .' (this volume, p. 4).

In fact, elaborating upon concerns around the relative credibility and 'truth' of siblings' accounts could actually be fruitful, rather than simply problematic, in the analysis and interpretation of these siblings' experiences. This is not to accept an unreflexive and antediluvian notion of 'truth'. Rather, issues of 'truth' (at various levels) which arise in the course of an interview can alert the researcher to the presence of contradictory reports which needed explanation, or the need to fill in gaps in information.

Therefore, scrutiny and scepticism on the part of the researcher should be equally exercised in relation to congruent as well as clashing accounts. The two categories of 'allied' and 'oppositional' can contain, of course, varying degrees of concurring or clashing accounts, and the researcher has to make sense of the intensity of dis/agreement. Just as two completely contradictory and polarized accounts may alert the researcher, two seamlessly congruent accounts may engender similar concerns and queries.

In providing an interpretation of both siblings' accounts it is necessary for the researcher to probe perceived inconsistencies, contradictions and/or unlikely depictions and scenarios. This may involve, for example, investigating a statement which seems to be at odds with one's understanding of a situation or person. To 'go with' feelings of scepticism in interviews (rather than suppressing them), or to be aware of sympathetic leanings toward one respondent over another, may ultimately be helpful rather than problematic for making sense of the interview material.

Rather than simply 'taking sides', in relation to one or the other sibling's account, the researcher must put forth her own interpretation and 'reading' of the interview material. As Natasha Mauthner and Andrea Doucet argue in their chapter, the processes involved in researchers transforming '. . . respondents' private lives into public theories are clearly critical to assessing the validity and status of these theories' (this volume, p. 119). All social researchers must grapple with the issue of not taking people's interviews only at 'face value', and this is perhaps heightened in a situation where respondents know that a person close to them is also being interviewed. It is therefore important to explore the dynamics and motivations behind people's accounts. Without a motivational context it would be very difficult to make sense of interviews, particularly multiple interviews, which may or may not cohere.

Lastly, in our efforts to present as complete a picture or understanding of various social phenomena as possible, we should not try to force a neat, coherent story if one is not forthcoming; this is especially the case in research that aims for a better understanding of social processes, which are subject to contingencies, change, and development. Because people's lived experiences and relationships with others are necessarily complex and 'messy' and not conducive to neat definitions, social researchers need to uphold a fairly wide latitude for what constitutes a coherent 'story' or 'finding'.

Note

I would like to thank Jane Ribbens and Rosalind Edwards for their hard editorial labour and their encouraging enthusiasm.

1   For instance, the *Journal of Marriage and the Family* has had a plethora of studies addressing aspects of marriage and family life.

References

Allan, G. (1980) 'A note on interviewing spouses together', *Journal of Marriage and the Family*, 42: 501–15.
Bank, S. and Kahn, M. (1982) *The Sibling Bond*. New York: Basic Books.
Baxter, Susan (1988) 'A political economy of the ethnic Chinese catering industry'. Unpublished PhD dissertation, University of Aston, Birmingham.
Bernard, J. (1972) *The Future of Marriage*. New York: World Publishing.
Brannen, J. (1988) 'The study of sensitive subjects', *Sociological Review*, 36 (1): 552–63.
Finch, J. and Mason, J. (1993) *Negotiating Family Responsibilities*. London: Routledge.
Hetherington, E., Reiss, D. and Plomin, R. (eds) (1994) *Separate Social Worlds of Siblings*. Hillsdale, NJ: Earlbaum.
Jessop, D. (1981) 'Family relationships as viewed by parents and adolescents: a specification', *Journal of Marriage and the Family*, 43: 95–107.
Jordan, B., Redley, M. and James, S. (1994) *Putting the Family First*. London: UCL Press.
Lamb, M. and Sutton-Smith, B. (1982) *Sibling Relationships*. Hillsdale, NJ: Earlbaum.
McKee, L. and O'Brien, M. (1983) 'Interviewing men: taking gender seriously', in E. Gamarnikow, D. Morgan, J. Purvis and D. Taylorson (eds), *The Public and the Private*. London: Heinemann.
Pahl, J. (1989) *Money and Marriage*. London: Macmillan.
Ribbens, J. and Edwards, R. (1995) 'Introducing qualitative research on women in families and households', *Women's Studies International Forum*, 18 (3): 247–58.

Safilios-Rothschild, C. (1976) 'A macro- and micro-examination of family power and love: an exchange model', *Journal of Marriage and the Family*, 38: 355–62.

Segalen, M. (1984) '*Avoir sa part*: sibling relations in partible inheritance in Brittany', in H. Medick and D.W. Sabean (eds), *Interest and Emotion*. Cambridge: Cambridge University Press.

Smith, M. and Self, B. (1980) 'The congruence between mothers' and daughters' sex-role attitudes', *Journal of Marriage and the Family*, 42: 105–9.

Song, M. (1996) 'Family, work and cultural identity: children's labour in Chinese take-away businesses in Britain'. Unpublished PhD dissertation, University of London, London.

Song, M. (1997a) '"You're becoming more and more English every day": investigating Chinese siblings' cultural identities', *New Community*, 23 (3): 343–62.

Song, M. (1997b) 'Children's labour in ethnic family businesses: the case of Chinese take-aways in Britain', *Ethnic and Racial Studies*, 20 (4): 690–716.

Song, M. and Parker, D. (1995) 'Commonality, difference, and the dynamics of disclosure', *Sociology*, 29 (2): 241–56.

Sulloway, F. (1996) *Born to Rebel*. London: Little, Brown.

8 Reflections on a Voice-centred Relational Method

Analysing Maternal and Domestic Voices

Natasha Mauthner and Andrea Doucet

In this chapter we discuss the issue of qualitative data analysis by drawing and reflecting upon our respective doctoral research projects: a study of women's experiences of motherhood and postnatal depression (Mauthner, 1994) and a study of heterosexual couples attempting to share housework and childcare (Doucet, 1995a). The question of data analysis has been of great interest to us because it is a relatively neglected area of the literature on qualitative research both in terms of general research texts and also within research accounts of specific studies. Yet the processes through which we transform respondents' private lives into public theories are clearly critical to assessing the validity and status of these theories. The particular issue which strikes us as central, yet overlooked, in qualitative data analysis processes and accounts is that of how to keep respondents' voices and perspectives alive, while at the same time recognizing the researcher's role in shaping the research process and product. In this chapter, we discuss our own attempts to tackle this issue and the questions and dilemmas we have faced in doing so. We detail the 'nitty-gritty' of how we analysed the interview transcripts gathered in the course of our doctoral work; and four years on, we also reflect back on our data analysis processes casting a more critical gaze on some of the beliefs and assumptions underlying the methods we used at that time. Thus, the chapter traces, but is also part of, an ongoing research journey as we continue to reflect on the ways in which we conduct qualitative research. We are writing this chapter together because we worked closely at the time of our doctoral studies, and have continued to do so despite now being separated by the Atlantic Ocean.

Transforming private stories into public theories: thinking about qualitative data analysis

Qualitative data analysis: a neglected issue?

While the question of qualitative data analysis has received increasing attention over recent years (see, for example, Coffey and Atkinson, 1996; Delamont, 1992; Denzin and Lincoln, 1994; Dey, 1993; Hammersley, 1992; Miles and Huberman, 1994; Patton, 1990; Riessman, 1987, 1993; Silverman, 1993; Strauss and Corbin, 1990; Wolcott, 1994), we would nevertheless maintain that, compared to other stages of the research process, such as entering the field or data collection methods, data analysis is still largely neglected. Of particular concern is the relative paucity of guidance in the literature, the lack of training on data analysis, the difficulties of finding appropriate support, mentoring and supervision from other researchers, and the increasing move to equate computer 'coding' with qualitative data 'analysis'. These neglects are particularly surprising given that the robustness and validity of our research claims largely lie in the precise methods through which we transform people's private lives and stories into public categories, theories and texts. Miles and Huberman similarly note that ' . . . the strengths of qualitative data rest very centrally on the competence with which their analysis is carried out' (1994: 10; see also Bryman and Burgess, 1994; Glucksmann, 1994).

We first became aware of this neglected area in 1992 when we faced the task of having to make sense of the enormous amounts of data we gathered for our PhDs. We searched the literature for guidance on data analysis and while we found several important texts (Glaser and Strauss, 1967; Hammersley and Atkinson, 1983; Miles and Huberman, 1984; Strauss and Corbin, 1990), it was unclear to us how to translate these ideas into practice without the advice and guidance of a researcher familiar with one of these particular methods. We also searched for discussions of data analysis in the context of specific research studies but found few detailed presentations of the step-by-step processes of how transcripts are analysed. Indeed restrictions on length of publications, particularly in journals, often preclude lengthy discussions of such methods. As we now reflect back to this period, we also realize that the social context, and the constraints and resources available at the academic institution within which we were conducting our research, had an impact on this stage of our projects. We were working within a faculty where quantitative, positivistic approaches dominated. In addition, there was pressure to get our theses completed and submitted within a three-year period, so that any inclinations to spend a great deal of time in data analysis tended to be discouraged. There was tremendous enthusiasm over computer software packages for analysing data. The debates about qualitative analysis in our department revolved very much around which software package to employ, and issues of 'coding' the data. Broader and more holistic questions about how to do 'analysis', and the links between data analysis and the research project as a whole, were not addressed.

In reading the literature on qualitative research we also paid particular attention to that written by feminist scholars, an impressive body of work which has influenced and helped us over the years (for example, DeVault, 1990; Harding, 1987; Roberts, 1981; Smith, 1987). However, two aspects of this literature have puzzled us. Firstly, the issue of listening to women, and understanding their lives 'in and on their own terms', has been a long-standing and pivotal concern amongst feminist researchers (Finch, 1984; Gilligan, 1982; Graham, 1983; Oakley, 1981), yet there are very few examples of how this general methodological principle can be practically operationalized within the actual research process and, in particular, in terms of data analysis.

A second theme which lies at the heart of feminist research is that of reflexivity. Reflexivity means reflecting upon and understanding our own personal, political and intellectual autobiographies as researchers and making explicit where we are located in relation to our research respondents. Reflexivity also means acknowledging the critical role we play in creating, interpreting and theorizing research data (Du Bois, 1983; Harding, 1992; Maynard, 1994; Stanley and Wise, 1983, 1993). Feminist discussions of reflexivity have largely addressed two aspects of the research process. First, the nature of the research relationship, and the extent to which similarities or differences between researcher and researched in characteristics such as gender, race, class, age, sexuality, or able-bodiedness influence this relationship (Olesen, 1994). Second, reflexivity has been widely debated in relation to issues of theory construction and epistemology (Braidotti et al., 1994; Harding, 1987, 1992). Feminist scholars point out that the production of theory is a social activity which is culturally, socially and historically embedded, thus resulting in 'situated knowledges' (Haraway, 1988). Nevertheless, while much has been written by feminists about reflexivity in methodology and epistemology, it remains surprising to us how little attention has been given to issues of reflexivity and power, voice and authority specifically in the data analysis stage of the research.

As it happened, we spent an intensive period of about 17 months analysing our data. Clearly, we had the time and access to financial resources to allow us to do this. More importantly, perhaps, we had the opportunity to learn a particular method of data analysis with the help of a committed and enthusiastic facilitator and the support of a research group. These resources enabled us to give data analysis the time, energy, and detailed and thorough attention it deserves. This experience, which we relate in this chapter, has focused our minds on the difficulties, dilemmas, importance, but also relative neglect, of data analysis.

The difficulties of articulating what we do when we analyse qualitative data

Over the years, and more recently in the context of struggling to write this chapter, we have pondered why writing about data analysis, in both theoretical and practical terms, is such an elusive task. The latter stages of data analysis, which tend to be structured, methodical, rigorous and systematic, are often easily described. For example, once a critical set of issues has been identified, the data are systematically scanned for examples of particular themes. However, the initial stages of actually getting to know the data and identifying what *are* the key issues feel more intuitive than anything else. As Bryman and Burgess have noted: '. . . much of the work in which investigators engage in this phase of the research process is as much implicit as explicit' (1994: 12). Thus, as qualitative researchers, we engage in a somewhat unsystematic process of following up certain leads and seeing where they take us. In deciding which ideas to follow up we are undoubtedly influenced, whether consciously or not, by our own personal, political and theoretical biographies. But the reasons why we choose some ideas rather than others are not always immediately obvious to us; nor are there necessarily logical reasons for our choices and decisions. The early phases of data analysis can therefore feel messy, confusing and uncertain because we are at a stage where we simply do not know what to think yet. Indeed, this is the whole point of data analysis – to learn from and about the data; to learn something new about a question by listening to other people. But while this sense of not knowing and of openness is exciting, it is also deeply uncomfortable. These kinds of processes are very difficult to articulate, especially in the logical, sequential, linear fashion that tends to be required in a research text.

Perhaps data analysis is also difficult to articulate because in doing so we are directly confronted with the subjective, interpretive nature of what we do – having to interpret respondents' words in some way, while realizing that these words could be interpreted in a multitude of ways. It is now well recognized in many feminist critiques,[1] as well as within work associated with postmodernism and with the longer-standing hermeneutic (Dilthey, 1976; Gadamer, 1975; Ricoeur, 1979) or interpretive traditions (Blumer, 1969; Mead, 1934), that all research contains biases and values, and that knowledge and understanding are contextually and historically grounded, as well as linguistically constituted. These critiques, while distinct in many ways, share a common emphasis on deconstructing Enlightenment and modernist ideals of objectivity, scientific thought, dualisms and rationality (see Du Bois, 1983; Harding, 1992; Hekman, 1990; Mies, 1983; Stanley and Wise, 1983, 1993). Feminists, for example, have argued for over two decades that understanding and knowledge come from being involved in a relationship with our subject matter and respondents, and not through adopting a detached and objective stance; indeed the production of knowledge must contain a systematic examination and explication of our beliefs, biases and social location (Harding, 1992). This reflexivity ensures that the politics underlying the methods, topics, and governing assumptions of our scholarship are analysed directly and self-consciously, rather than remaining unacknowledged (Crawford and Marecek, 1989). While these are laudable intentions, these biases and beliefs may be extremely difficult to uncover or even to notice: we may not have the practical means to do so in the busy process of analysing interview transcripts; it may be quite uncomfortable to do so; a profound level of self-awareness is required to begin to capture the perspectives through which we view the world; and it is not easy to grasp the 'unconscious' filters through which we experience the world.

In other words, in analysing data we are confronted with ourselves, and with our own central role in shaping the outcome. Indeed, perhaps this is part of the reason why computer programs have been so popular: the use of technology confers an air of scientific objectivity onto what remains a fundamentally subjective, interpretative process. This is not to deny the obvious practical benefits to be gained from computer programs (Coffey and Atkinson, 1996; Miles and Huberman, 1994; Weitzman and Miles, 1995). Indeed, one of us used such a program as part of the analysis process. The point we wish to make is that we need to think critically about how and why we use these programs.

A further reason why we might be tempted to gloss over the question of how we analyse our data stems from our anxiety about whether we have analysed the data in 'the right way'. Even when researchers draw on specific methods of data analysis they use and interpret these methods in their own individual ways. Indeed, researchers who jointly develop a particular method can actually use the same method differently. The case of Glaser and Strauss (1967), and the difference of opinion or 'head on clash' (Melia, 1996: 368) that developed between them as to what exactly 'grounded theory' is, provides a particularly good example of this (see Glaser, 1992; Melia, 1996). We might follow the general principles of a method but not go through all the steps that are specified. Or we might go through all the steps for a select number of cases, and analyse the remainder of the data set in a more speedy fashion particularly when resources of time, energy and money are running out. This can engender a sense of anxiety that we have not proceeded correctly; and rather than be open about exactly what we did and did not do, we might be tempted simply to gloss over the details of data analysis. But this issue has raised a number of unanswered questions for us. Are research texts on data analysis intended to be literally followed step by step? How many researchers who describe using particular methods actually follow all the steps as specified within the original texts? To what extent is it necessary to go through all the steps with each one of the transcripts? Do the researchers writing these texts actually go through all these steps themselves? Is there one right way to use a particular method? And to what extent do methods evolve as different researchers use and adapt them (see also Strauss and Corbin, 1990)?

Data analysis is our most vulnerable spot. It is the area of our research where we are most open to criticism. Writing about data analysis is exposing ourselves for scrutiny. Perhaps it is for these reasons that data analysis fails to receive the attention and detail it deserves.

Analysing maternal and domestic voices: how we did it

In this section we discuss the detailed processes of how we analysed verbatim transcripts of depth interviews gathered in the course of our doctoral research projects. Throughout the discussion we draw on examples from our research which employed individual, joint, and repeat, semi-structured, open-ended interviewing. Natasha Mauthner's research explored women's experiences of motherhood and postnatal depression through interviews with 40 mothers (and 25 of their male partners) of young children living in England, 18 of whom experienced postnatal depression (see Mauthner, 1993, 1994, 1995, 1998a, 1998b). Andrea Doucet's research investigated the experiences of 23 British dual earner couples with dependent children who identified themselves as 'consciously attempting to share the work and responsibility for housework and child care' (see Doucet 1995a, 1995b, 1996).

In focusing specifically on the *analysis of interview transcripts* in this chapter we are inevitably obscuring other aspects of data analysis and presenting a somewhat static and simplified picture of what is in fact a complex, dynamic process. Two particular issues are worth highlighting here, issues which are critical to how we analyse our data but which we do not discuss due to lack of space.

First, we recognize that 'data analysis' is not a discrete phase of the research process confined to the moments when we analyse interview transcripts. Rather, it is an ongoing process which takes place throughout, and often extends beyond, the life of a research project. For example, our interpretive work started when we first accessed the sample of people we wished to include in our studies. During the interviews, we were *actively* listening to participants' stories, asking questions and leading respondents down certain paths and not others, making decisions about which issues to follow up, and which to ignore, and choosing where to probe. We were guided by our initial research agenda and questions, what each respondent said to us, and our interpretations and understandings of their words. The interview content was therefore a joint production (see Mishler, 1986) and part of what we were doing in shaping the interview was following our own analytical thinking. Moreover, with each interview, and with the analytical work we did during and after each interview, we formulated new ideas or approaches, and modified our interview questions so as to 'check these out'. The process of analysis continued in a more explicit way as we transcribed the interviews and began to immerse ourselves in the data through full transcript readings. We began to interpret the meaning of each respondent's story, and noted areas of difference and overlap with other participants' accounts. Finally, data analysis overlapped with and was ongoing during the writing up of the research.

Second, in discussing the analysis of narrative accounts told within an interview we are paying less attention to more informal types of information such as field notes; information gleaned during the setting up of interviews; incidental meetings or conversations with respondents; observational data during the interview; and non-linguistic 'data' such as bodily and facial expressions, and non-verbal interactions between the couple in the case of joint interviews.

While we recognize the critical importance of these various processes, for the purposes of this chapter we wish to place the spotlight specifically on data analysis as a discrete stage, and on the interview transcript as the source of data, because these aspects of the research process have been particularly neglected.

We were able to devote a full 17 months specifically to analysing interview transcripts and our chapter focuses on the analytical procedures which we conducted during this concentrated period. We describe these in two distinct phases of data analysis: (1) a 'voice-centred relational method' of data analysis involving four readings, case studies and group work; and (2) summaries and thematic 'breaking down' of the data. The first stage took about 15 months and the second one about two months.

Stage 1– a voice-centred relational method of data analysis: four readings, case studies and group work

In the autumn of 1992 we had the opportunity to join a small graduate research group set up by Carol Gilligan on her arrival as visiting professor at the University of Cambridge.[2] The aim of the group was specifically to learn how to use a particular method of data analysis, the voice-centred relational method, as well as to explore the theoretical and methodological ideas which underpin it. This method of data analysis was developed over several years by Lyn Brown, Carol Gilligan and their colleagues at the Harvard Project on Women's Psychology and Girls' Development at the Harvard Graduate School of Education (see Brown and Gilligan, 1992, 1993; Brown et al., 1988; Gilligan et al., 1990).[3] The method has its roots in clinical and literary approaches (Brown and Gilligan, 1992), interpretive and hermeneutic traditions (Brown et al., 1989, 1991; Gilligan et al., 1990), and relational theory (Belenky et al., 1986; Brown and Gilligan, 1992; Gilligan, 1982, 1988; Gilligan et al., 1990; Miller, 1986).

While using the method under the guidance of Carol Gilligan, we were also simultaneously developing our own version of it. Thus we drew on the excellent work which had begun at Harvard University, but we adapted it so as to reflect our interdisciplinary backgrounds and our specific research interests. In particular, we were both interested in emphasizing and refining its application for projects that include a sociological focus. While the method holds at its core the idea of a *relational ontology* that arose out of the extensive research on girls and women conducted within the fields of developmental psychology and education, it is important to highlight that this relational ontology has been uncovered and theorized in other disciplines, particularly in political theory, feminist philosophy, and feminist legal theory (see Baier, 1993; Benhabib, 1987, 1992; Gilligan, 1988; Held, 1984, 1995; Minow and Shanley, 1996; Ruddick, 1989; Tronto, 1989, 1993, 1995). The ontological image which has predominated in liberal political thought and the Western philosophical tradition is that of a separate, self-sufficient, independent, rational 'self' or 'individual'. In contrast, the 'relational' ontology posits the notion of 'selves-in-relation' (Ruddick, 1989: 211), or 'relational being' (Jordan, 1993: 141), a view of human beings as embedded in a complex web of intimate and larger social relations (Gilligan, 1982), and a 'different understanding of human nature and human interaction so that people are viewed as interdependent rather than independent' (Tronto, 1995: 142).

A relational ontology is not dissimilar to the sociological emphases on understanding individuals within their social contexts and on exploring the 'duality' of social structures and human agency (see Giddens, 1984). Furthermore, we would argue that a relational ontology is consistent with many of the assumptions espoused by the interpretive or symbolic interactionism tradition within sociology (Blumer, 1969; Mead, 1934). What we are emphasizing here is that, in contrast to the focus on individualism, autonomy and independence which figure in much of the feminist sociological work on gender and household life, we wish to bring to the centre of our analysis of domestic life the interrelated ontological and theoretical issues of interdependence, dependence and independence (see Ahlander and Bahr, 1995; Finch and Mason, 1993; Morrow, 1996; Thorne, 1987).

The voice-centred relational method, and our version of it presented here, represents an attempt to translate this relational ontology into methodology and into concrete methods of data analysis by exploring individuals' narrative accounts in terms of their relationships to the people around them and their relationships to the broader social, structural and cultural contexts within which they live. Our version of the method is also deeply rooted within the broader tradition of feminist research practice and the increasingly rich and wide field of qualitative research.

Having read the work of other researchers who have also used this method at Harvard University (Geismar, 1996; Macuika, 1992; Rogers, 1994; Tolman, 1992; Way, 1994), we realize that, as we pointed out above, individual researchers use and adapt particular methods in their own individual ways. Researchers' individuality, their particular topics, their samples, the theoretical and academic environments and social and cultural contexts in which they work all influence the ways in which these methods are used. Although we both used this method, we picked up on and emphasized variable elements of it. The method worked differently for us because of our distinct topics but also because of differences in our own biographies. In discussing how we used a voice-centred relational method we are therefore not discussing *the* method but rather our own individual interpretations, understandings and versions of it.

The method revolves around a set of three or more readings of the interview text, and the original tapes can be listened to as these readings are carried out. We actually conducted four readings of selected interview transcripts.

Reading 1: reading for the plot and for our responses to the narrative   The first reading comprises two elements. First, the text is read for the overall plot and story that is being told by the respondent – what are the main events, the protagonists and the subplots. We listened for recurrent images, words, metaphors and contradictions in the narrative. This element is one which is common to many methods of qualitative data analysis (see Riessman, 1993; Strauss and Corbin, 1990).

In the second 'reader-response' element of this first reading, the researcher reads for herself in the text in the sense that she places herself, with her own particular background, history and experiences, in relation to the person she has interviewed. The researcher reads the narrative on her own terms – how she is responding emotionally and intellectually to this person. Lyn Mikel Brown describes this process:

> ... the first listening or reading requires the listener/interpreter to consider her rela-
> tionship to the speaker or text and to document, as best she can, her interests, biases
> and limitations that arise from such critical dimensions of social location as race,
> class, gender and sexual orientation, as well as to track her own feelings in response
> to what she hears – particularly those feelings that do not resonate with the
> speaker's experience. (1994: 392)

This allows the researcher to examine how and where some of her own
assumptions and views – whether personal, political or theoretical – might
affect her interpretation of the respondent's words, or how she later writes
about the person:

> Writing out our responses to what we are hearing, we then consider how our
> thoughts and feelings may affect our understanding, our interpretation, and the
> way we write about that person. (Brown and Gilligan, 1992: 27)

Brown (1994) and Brown and Gilligan (1992) therefore highlight the issue of
reflexivity in terms of the researcher's social location and emotional responses
to the respondent. What we would wish to give greater emphasis to and make
more explicit is the role of the researcher's theoretical location and ideas in
this process and how these influence the interpretations and conclusions
which are made. Thus being reflexive about our data analysis processes
involves for us: (1) locating ourselves socially in relation to our respondent;
(2) attending to our emotional responses to this person (see also Miri Song,
this volume); but also (3) examining how we make theoretical interpretations
of the respondent's narrative; and (4) documenting these processes for ourselves and others.

An example from Andrea's research

I became aware that in analysing a joint interview and two individual
interviews from one of my couples, Mandy and Christian, I had
listened more closely to Mandy than to Christian and I therefore had
to examine my own beliefs and prejudices on men's roles in
household life. The research group pointed out that I was more critical
of Christian and more sympathetic to Mandy and this reflected, in
part, the fact that I had been immersed in a literature which clearly
sees women as disadvantaged within household life. In addition, my
own emotions were brought into play as I realized that I had difficulty
hearing Christian's anger, and when I heard it, I shut it off.

The first reading of the interview text thus represents an attempt to come to
know our response to the respondent and her or his story. The underlying
assumption here is that by trying to name how we are socially, emotionally
and intellectually located in relation to our respondents we can retain some
grasp over the blurred boundary between their narratives and our interpretations of those narratives. If we fail to name these emotions and responses,

they will express themselves in other ways such as in our tone of voice or the way in which we write about that person. The aim of this reading is also to lay down the evidence of our responses for others to see. A further assumption underlying this 'reader response' reading is that our intellectual and emotional reactions to other people constitute sources of knowledge; it is through these processes that we come to know other people (see also Hammersley and Atkinson, 1983; Miles and Huberman, 1994).

Reading 2: reading for the voice of the 'I'   The second reading we conducted was similar to that described by Brown and Gilligan (1992) and focused on how the respondent experiences, feels and speaks about herself. In an attempt to get some sense of this through the empirical data, we followed the method of using a coloured pencil to physically trace and underline certain of the respondent's statements in the interview transcript – namely where the respondent uses personal pronouns such as 'I', 'we' or 'you' in talking about themselves. This process centres our attention on the active 'I' which is telling the story; amplifies the terms in which the respondent sees and presents herself; highlights where the respondent might be emotionally or intellectually struggling to say something; and identifies those places where the respondent shifts between 'I', 'we' and 'you', signalling changes in how the respondent perceives and experiences herself. Spending this time carefully listening to the respondent creates a space between her way of speaking and seeing and our own, so we can discover ' . . . how she speaks of herself before we speak of her' (Brown and Gilligan, 1992: 27–8).

An example from Natasha's research

Reading for the 'I' was particularly valuable in pulling out what became a central issue in my understanding of postnatal depression, namely that the women seemed caught between two 'voices' which articulated opposing positions, different viewpoints or ways of assessing their situation. One voice, or set of voices, reflected the mothers' expectations of themselves, and their interpretations of cultural norms and values surrounding motherhood. These expectations and interpretations were in turn related to the personal, social, and structural contexts in which mothering occurred, in that certain conditions (e.g. degree of social support; mother's and father's employment situation; employment policies) impeded or facilitated certain options. The other perspective, voice, or set of voices, seemed to be informed by the women's actual, concrete and day-to-day experiences of mothering their particular child, in the particular circumstances in which they found themselves. During the depression, the mothers explained that the latter voice was drowned out by the former. The mothers found it difficult to accept their feelings and experiences; they tried to change parts of themselves, and suppress certain of their needs and feelings, in order to live up to their ideals of 'the good mother'. Sonya's account tells of how she attempted to fit herself into a mould which violated her needs and desires:

> ... sometimes I think if I hadn't been ill, would I have gone to work quicker possibly and maybe felt happier? Because it's more my natural personality to have part work, part Suzie [her daughter] but I kept thinking, 'No, if I'm going to do this mother thing properly, I'm going to be at home, I'm going to watch *Neighbours*, I'm going to make jam and I'm going to go to the local play-groups.' What I did was almost again sort of sweep the business woman under the carpet and say, 'Ah, but I'm this now' but by denying the skills there, right, I was harming myself ... I think I damage myself by trying to shut that off ... I was intent on, 'This is my big sacrifice, this is me changing my life style for the good of Suzie' and pushing my own needs completely down to the bottom of the bag ... which is a stupid thing to do but that's what I did because I thought ... 'I will be the best mother of all time', you know, like people do and then they start putting pressure on themselves because of unrealistic expectations.

An example from Andrea's research

Sean began his individual interview with the words, 'I dropped out'. He said it three more times, followed by a long chain of recurring words like, 'I left', 'I fell into that', 'I gave up', 'I was bored', 'I didn't like', 'I hated', and 'I quit'. He told the story of a 41-year-old man who had moved from job to job all his life, never settling into 'a straight career path'. He reiterated at least seven times the fact that 'I've never been career minded', and that 'a career path never existed for me'. Tracing the 'I' in his interview transcript, how he spoke about himself and the matrices of his life, brought me to an interpretation of Sean's account which I feel I would have missed had I not paid close attention to the way he spoke about himself and the constant contradictions that emerged around this 'I'. For example, I soon noticed a recurring discrepancy between the 'I' who emphatically states that he has never been 'a career minded person' and a looming sense of regret and subtle admission that indeed, a career is actually tremendously important to him. This is evident in Sean's back-to-back contradiction where he stated one feeling and then immediately stated another which was at odds with the first: 'I wouldn't have wanted a sort of straight career pattern. I mean it would have been quite useful to have some sort of career behind me.' These mixed sentiments became important to me in attempting to sort out whether Sean's decision to stay at home as a full-time carer was a 'choice' or a 'forced' option; a decision which, in turn, related to his experience of caring for his children which he actually found quite difficult because he found it socially isolating as a lone man within large networks of mothers. At times, he felt: 'embarrassed'; 'smug'; 'patronized'; like 'a bit of a lemon'; and that he was in a 'female agenda' where 'some people don't want to talk to me – I'm not always sure what I should be saying to them'.

This second reading represents, in a sense, the first step of a phased process of listening to respondents as they speak about themselves, the lives they live and the worlds they inhabit. From the point of view of psychology which is interested in the 'psyche', and in how individuals experience themselves and the broader social contexts within which they live, this attention to the 'I' is a welcome and valuable empirical technique. From the point of view of sociology, this second reading represents an attempt to hear the person, agent or actor voice her or his sense of agency, while also recognizing the social location of this person who is speaking. This stage of the data analysis represents an attempt to stay, as far as it is possible, with the respondents' multi-layered voices, views and perspectives rather than simply and quickly slotting their words into either our own ways of understanding the world or into the categories of the literature in our area. In our view, this detailed and focused attention on the voice(s) of the 'I' increases the possibility of creating more or less space within which to hear our respondents' voices; and to take more or less time doing so.

This reading for the personal pronoun statements strikes us as being one of the key features which distinguishes a voice-centred relational method of data analysis from grounded theory, a method which is used widely by sociologists conducting qualitative data analysis. According to Strauss and Corbin, grounded theory is less interested in 'persons *per se*' and more interested in action/interaction:

> The aim of theoretical sampling is to sample events, incidents, and so forth, that are indicative of categories, their properties and dimensions, . . . we sample incidents and not persons *per se*! Our interest is in gathering data about what persons do or don't do in terms of action/interaction; the range of conditions that give rise to that action/interaction and its variations; how conditions change or stay the same over time and with what impact; also the consequences of either actual or failed action/interaction or of strategies never acted on. (1990: 177)

Thus grounded theory seems more concerned with action and interaction and less so with the processes of reflection and decision making which are key concerns of a voice-centred relational method of data analysis. Thus, it may be that in researching areas of 'private' life where process-oriented values and ways of being are emphasized rather than the more 'public' goal-oriented values and ways of being (Rosalind Edwards and Jane Ribbens, this volume), the voice-centred relational method was quite instrumental in helping to shed light on the meanings, processes, relationships and contradictions which are central to domestic life.

The first two readings are the 'staples' of the method in that researchers using this method of data analysis would always undertake these. Generally speaking, researchers have conducted two further readings of their own choice depending on their research topic. The third and fourth readings we carried out are a version of the third and fourth readings conducted by Brown and Gilligan (1992).

Reading 3: reading for relationships In the third reading we listened for how the respondents spoke about their interpersonal relationships, with their partners, their relatives, their children, and the broader social networks within which they lived, parented, and worked. Again using a pencil, this time of a different colour, we physically traced their words as they spoke about these relationships. Consciously reading for relationships was particularly valuable in revealing the theoretical framework which quietly and pervasively underlines the bulk of research carried out on gender divisions of household labour, as well as on mothers' experiences of post-natal depression.

An example from Andrea's research

I charted how women and men described their relationships and the differences which occurred across gender, class, and the children's ages. Looking at how other studies did or did not concentrate on issues of relationships revealed that the informing framework of much of the literature on gender divisions of household labour is that of an 'equality' or 'equal rights' framework (see Doucet, 1995a, 1995b) rooted, in turn, in larger sets of ontological assumptions which have predominated in liberal political thought and the Western philosophical tradition of a separate, self-sufficient, independent, rational 'self' or 'individual'. Reading for relationships enabled me to achieve a sense of balance between justice and care concerns, rights and responsibilities, independence and interdependence, and issues of autonomy and connection for women, men and children within household life.

An example from Natasha's research

Drawing on Andrea's work, I found that an equal-rights perspective has similarly prevailed in feminist research on post-natal depression where the latter is explained in terms of the *transition* to motherhood and the 'public world' losses this incurs for women, including loss of identity, autonomy, independence and paid employment (Mauthner, 1998b). Influenced by the work of relational psychologists (Jack, 1991) and clinicians (Miller, 1986; Stiver and Miller, 1992) which indicates that women's psychological and emotional difficulties are linked to impasses within their relationships, I highlighted the relational difficulties the mothers in my study were experiencing by reading for relationships which the women regarded as positive ones in their lives (for example, relationships in which they felt able and willing to confide their thoughts and feelings, and felt listened to, heard and supported) and tracing the relationships which the women described as difficult and constraining (for example, relationships in which they felt silenced or rejected).

Reading 4: placing people within cultural contexts and social structures In the fourth reading, we placed our respondents' accounts and experiences within broader social, political, cultural and structural contexts.

An example from Andrea's research

I emphasized the wide array of social structures and social institutions that form the social worlds my respondents lived within and experienced. I was interested in whether and how my respondents recognized or alluded to these social factors and thus began to link the person into their social context in a more significant way. I listened for how they described the structural and ideological forces as constraining and/or enabling. Did they recognize them as such or accept them as 'personal' and 'private' troubles rather than as more 'public' and socially located ills? For example, Eve spoke about what she saw as a personal 'battle' at work where, in spite of her efforts to demonstrate that '. . . everything's carrying on really smoothly and that the children haven't affected the way I feel about work or the way I carry out my job', she nevertheless conceded that '. . . I know that the way my colleagues look on me has changed'. Eve's analysis of this 'battle' keeps coming back to how she is the 'only woman consultant' in her firm of tax consultants and she feels that she was 'prejudged' with regard to the ability to combine parenting with full-time employment. However, I could also root what Eve perceives as a personal 'battle' into a larger social issue relating to how the social institution of work is still very much a 'male' institution within which many women, and an increasing number of men, feel that they cannot bring family-related issues. This final reading or listening to the interview transcript thus focuses on how individuals experience the particular social context from within which they are speaking.

An example from Natasha's research

In this fourth reading, I paid particular attention to the ideological context of motherhood as well as structural and political issues. I looked for the ways in which the women's accounts voiced and/or reflected dominant and normative conceptions of motherhood. For example, the use of moral terms such as 'should', 'ought', 'right', 'wrong', 'good' and 'bad' indicated places in their narratives where the women were speaking in terms of, or through, the cultural norms and values of society. These 'moral voices' often conflicted with, and constrained, the mothers' concrete day-to-day mothering experiences.

For example, Sandra's difficulties stemmed from the pressure she felt to work full time *and* look after her children as full-time mothers do: 'I've found that the hardest, having to assume *as well* as working that I should do everything else that mums at home do, you know, I should bake and clean and whatever.' Another part of Sandra, or another 'voice', expressed a different viewpoint, grounded in her actual experiences of mothering. On this basis, Sandra felt that '. . . to a degree, *it's impossible* practically to do that', 'I'd set myself these goals which were *impossible*' because 'I couldn't work out how you were supposed to deal with the baby and do everything else as well, *which you can't.*' She explained:

> It tends to be mothers who are at home that seem to go everywhere with the kids, go swimming, go to ballet classes, do this, do that . . . and that's what I feel I should be doing. I should be sewing and baking and cooking and going swimming with her and I mean . . . that's cloud cuckoo land. I'm not very good at sewing anyway. I don't particularly like baking.

While Sandra and the other mothers in the study clearly questioned these 'moral voices' and the values embodied within them, during the depression it seemed that the moral voices were 'louder' and 'drowned out' their questioning voice.

Case studies and group work   The work in our research group involved us writing up our ongoing thoughts and analyses about a particular respondent in the form of case studies. This detailed and time-consuming work was valuable for understanding the depth and complexity of individuals' experiences, as well as the very significant differences between our respondents' narratives. Working within the context of a group was useful because, having read extracts from our transcripts, others were able to point out where we might have missed or glossed over what they regarded as key aspects of the interview narrative. This made us acutely aware of our own role and power in choosing the particular issues we emphasize and pick up on, and which we ignore or minimize. Working with other colleagues highlighted the fact '. . . that people have more than one way to tell a story and see a situation through different lenses and in different lights' (Gilligan et al., 1990: 95).

One of the drawbacks of how we used a voice-centred method is that ideally it requires a great deal of time. As a result we found it impossible systematically to conduct all four readings with each and every one of our respondents; we were only able to focus such detailed attention on a select number of cases.[4] Nevertheless, the energy and time we put into these few cases served the function of 'tuning our ear'. We read the remaining narratives listening for the issues or voices we had by then identified as both critical in terms of understanding the experiences of our respondents, and also 'new' or challenging within our particular disciplinary areas. What is clear to us, however, is that in moving from the slow and careful work with individual cases to the more speedy process of reading through the other transcripts, we begin to focus in selectively on certain issues while shutting out others. This seems inevitable to us. In part, we reach a 'saturation point' where we have enough and even too many 'new' issues we wish to write about and contribute to our areas of work. But shortages of time and resources are obviously a further constraint on the extent to which we analyse the data. It is important to recognize and acknowledge that these processes are taking place.

Overall the four readings of the interview transcripts emphasize the multi-layered nature of narratives and trace voices across and within a particular transcript. This approach is fundamentally different to the thematic organization characteristic of most methods of data analysis, including those assisted by computer programs. It delays the reductionistic stage of data analysis when transcripts are cut up into themes and aggregated. This process shifts data analysis away from traditional 'coding', which implies fitting a person into a pre-existing set of categories, whether those of the researcher or those of established theoretical frameworks. Furthermore, tracing voices through individual interview transcripts, as opposed to linking themes across interviews, helps maintain differences between the respondents.

An example from Natasha's research

I found this approach particularly valuable because it highlighted underlying processes of the depression – such as the discrepancy between women's expectations and experiences of motherhood, and their sense of individual failure in the face of this conflict – which all the women experienced despite the numerous and important differences between them in terms of their age, class, parity, quality of the marital relationship, social support, birth experience, method of feeding the baby, employment situation and so on. This dual emphasis on similarities and differences between the women might have eluded me had I adopted a more thematic approach focusing on 'factors' or 'variables' such as 'the marital relationship', 'social support', or the birth experience.

The detailed and lengthy focus on individual interviews embodies respect for individual respondents within the research context. If we do not take the time and trouble to listen to our respondents, data analysis risks simply confirming what we already know. If this is the case, in no way has the respondent changed our view or understanding, thus defeating the point of doing the study in the first place. At the same time, this approach respects the role of the researcher and indeed the necessity of the researcher having her own voice and perspective in this process. By providing a way of reading and listening to an interview text '. . . that takes into account both our stance as researchers and the stance of the person speaking within the text' (Gilligan et al., 1990: 96), this approach respects and to some extent exposes the *relationship* between researcher and researched. As Gilligan notes, 'the relationship has to be maintained throughout the writing, and you don't write over, or voice over, other people's voices . . . It's an attempt to try to work as a writer would work, by giving people their voice, by giving ourselves a voice in our work, and then thinking very consciously about the orchestration of the pieces we write' (Kitzinger with Gilligan, 1994: 411). It is in bringing the listener into responsive relationship with the person speaking that this approach or method is characterized as a relational one.

Stage 2– summaries and thematic 'breaking down' of the data

In addition to the detailed case studies, which we did for 10 individuals (or five couples), we wrote up summaries for the remaining individuals which represented short portraits of each respondent of one to two pages. We also both felt it was necessary and important to try to move from the holistic understandings of individual respondents described above to tackling the data set as a whole. This decision to 'cut up' the transcripts was a difficult moment in our research. Having spent so many months on a relatively small number of respondents, we felt anxious to make the huge volume of data more manageable. At the same time, we were frustrated not to be able to devote the same amount of time and energy to each one of our respondents. We felt we were short-changing many of them; we missed the process of getting to know and understand another story; and above all we feared that in 'cutting up' the data we would lose much of its complexity. Despite this apprehension, we proceeded to break up each transcript into a number of overlapping themes and sub-themes. Natasha did this manually on the computer (through cut and paste) while Andrea conducted a two-staged process of working manually and then using a computer-based program (text-base alpha). Many of these themes, and sub-themes in particular, emerged as a direct result of the intensive case study work and provided a way of linking the details of individual respondents with the stories told by the datasets as wholes.

The analysis of the data therefore involved organizing the data in different ways (tapes, verbatim transcripts, four readings, case studies, summaries, themes) in order to tap into different dimensions of the data sets. It also involved a dialectical process of moving between different ways of organizing or representing the data, and between the details and particularity of each one of the individual respondent's experiences, and the overall picture of the samples as wholes.

Reflecting on our data analysis processes

Reflecting on 'stories', 'voices' and 'self'

This method of data analysis was enormously valuable to us but more recently it has presented us with a number of difficult questions. There are now a number of discussions around this method (Beiser, 1993; Charmaz, 1993; Gold, 1993; Wilkinson, 1994) which we cannot fully address here due to lack of space. However, the issue of 'self' or 'voice' is probably the most contentious one within this method of reading or listening, particularly in the midst of postmodern discussions of discursively constructed or fragmented selves (Butler, 1990, 1994; Davies, 1989a, 1989b; Weedon, 1987). One of the difficulties is that terms such as 'self' and 'voice' are used without adequately defining them. Clearly, for many researchers, 'voice' has become a shorthand way of referring to the person speaking or even to the account or story spoken. We struggled around these terms while we were in the processes of analysing our data and writing up our theses, and we have since come to believe that when we analyse interview transcripts we hear stories/accounts/narratives spoken by a person in a voice/voices. With regard to the story, it occurs within a social context and we hear and read the story from within a/nother social context and in a particular research relationship (see Mishler, 1986; Riessman, 1993).[5] Rather than wrestling with these age-old theoretically contentious issues such as 'self' and 'voice', we wish to highlight, as Ken Plummer so eloquently does, that we 'coax' stories and listen with an open mind and an open heart to this person and her or his story, both of which are ever-changing and continually constituted in relationships. As Plummer points out:

> I have slowly come to believe that no stories are true for all time and space: we invent our stories with a passion, they are momentarily true, we may cling to them, they may become our lives, and then we may move on. Clinging to the story, changing the story, reworking it, denying it. But somewhere behind all this story telling there are real active, embodied, impassioned lives. Is this a process of peeling back stories to reveal better and better ones? And if so, when do we know a story is better? Or is it a process of constant readjustment of stories to be aligned with the time and the place of their telling? I am suggesting here that multiple stories engulf us, and we need tools for distinguishing between layers of stories or even layers of truth. (1995: 170)

While emphasizing the dynamic and fluid quality of these stories, we believe there is a person within and telling this story, who – in those minutes and hours that we came to speak with them – makes choices about what to emphasize and what to hold back from us. We pay attention to what we think this person is trying to tell us within the context of this relationship, this research setting, and a particular location in the social world, rather than making grand statements about just who this person or 'voice' is. We are drawn to the words of Lorraine Code who writes against the idea of the totally fragmented 'self' and for the importance of being able to refer to 'this person' with whom we have had a fleeting research relationship and from whom we hear many stories which 'engulf us':

> The contention that people are *knowable* may sit uneasily with psychoanalytic decenterings of conscious subjectivity and postmodern critiques of the unified subject of Enlightenment humanism. But I think this is a tension that has to be acknowledged and maintained. In practice, people often know one another well enough to make good decisions about who can be counted on and who cannot, who makes a good ally and who does not. Yet precisely because of the fluctuations and contradictions of subjectivity, this process is ongoing, communicative and interpretive. It is never fixed or complete; any fixity claimed for 'the self' will be a fixity in flux. Nonetheless, I argue that something must be fixed to 'contain' the flux even enough to permit references to and ongoing relationships with 'this person'. Knowing people always occur within the terms of this tension. (1993: 34; original emphasis)

Reflexivity in data analysis

It is only recently that we have come to appreciate fully the meaning of reflexivity in the context of our own research. We have come to understand the extent to which our own theoretical stances have influenced the theoretical accounts we have given concerning our respondents' lives. For example, in analysing our data, we were to some extent reacting against the work which had come before us and which we regarded as telling only one story about our respondents' lives. In contrast to the feminist 'equal rights' framework which had prevailed in our respective research areas where the focus was on issues of identity, autonomy, independence and paid employment, we found ourselves drawing on different feminist theories, including discussions around justice and care, relational theory and feminist ethics as well as methodological and theoretical works on symbolic interactionism, feminist methodologies, phenomenology and hermeneutics. Feminist qualitative researchers have highlighted the difficulties involved in hearing and theorizing the 'muted voices' of women's lives in 'private' domains when the facilities for hearing are predominantly male-stream public language, concepts, and theories (DeVault, 1990; Edwards and Ribbens, 1991; Gilligan, 1982; Graham, 1983; Smith, 1987; Stacey, 1981; Westkott, 1990). However, it can also be difficult to hear stories which might contradict dominant feminist understandings such as those within an equal rights framework; and it is here that locating ourselves within a different relational, but still feminist, vantage point was particularly valuable.

At the end of the day, whether consciously/explicitly or not, we are in effect choosing a particular theoretical and ontological framework within which to locate ourselves, and through which to hear and analyse our respondents' lives. The difficulty is not so much the choice of paradigm, but rather having to accept that this is the case and that as a result we will focus our attention on certain issues and perhaps ignore others (see also Anderson and Jack, 1991: 12; Riessman, 1993; Strauss and Corbin, 1990: 75). The best we can do then is to trace and document our data analysis processes, and the choices and decisions we make, so that other researchers and interested parties can see for themselves some of what has been lost and some of what has been gained (see also Pam Alldred, this volume). We need to document these reflexive processes, not just in general terms such as our class, gender and ethnic background; but in a more concrete and nitty-gritty way in terms of where, how and why particular decisions are made at particular stages. Holland and Ramazanoglu make a similar point when they note that:

> Feminists have had to accept that there is no technique of analysis or methodolog-
> ical logic that can neutralize the social nature of interpretation . . . Feminist
> researchers can only try to explain the grounds on which selective interpretations
> have been made by making explicit the process of decision-making which produces
> the interpretation, and the logic of method on which these decisions are made.
> (1994: 133)

We wish to highlight data analysis as a particularly critical site for issues of reflexivity because, in our view, this is a point where the voices and perspectives of the research respondents are especially vulnerable. They might be lost and subsumed to the views of the researcher, or to the theoretical frameworks and categories that she brings to the research. Furthermore, we believe that if researchers are to implement their theoretical and methodological commitments to being reflexive about the research process, both in the data analysis stage and throughout the entire research endeavour, a practical method of doing this is vital.

The power of the researcher and the vulnerability of the researched

Acknowledging the central role of the researcher in shaping the research process and product means recognizing the power relations between researcher and researched. In particular, the data analysis stage can be viewed as a deeply disempowering one in which our respondents have little or no control. Far removed from our respondents, we make choices and decisions about their lives: which particular issues to focus on in the analysis; how to interpret their words; and which extracts to select for quotation. We dissect, cut up, distil and reduce their accounts, thereby losing much of the complexity, subtleties and depth of their narratives (see also Kay Standing and Maxine Birch, this volume). We categorize their words into overarching themes, and as we do so, the discrete, separate and different individuals we interviewed are gradually lost. Unlike in the interview, we can simply stop reading (or listening) whenever we choose, and thus cut off the conversation at any point without concern that we will offend the respondent. We replace respondents' names and identities with pseudonyms and disguise their distinguishing features for the purposes of anonymity. We extract and quote their words, often out of context of the overall story they have told us. Though we might adopt a bottom-up approach in that the starting point for our research is the perspectives and words of the individuals we study, we are nonetheless the ones who will be speaking for them. We are in the privileged position of naming and representing other people's realities. Thus, in turning private issues into public concerns, and in giving our respondents a voice in public arenas, we have to ask ourselves whether we are in fact appropriating their voices and experiences, and further disempowering them by taking away their voice, agency and ownership.

Despite the attempts we might make to ensure that the voices of our respondents are heard and represented, and in the process trace our research journeys and make our own thinking and reasoning explicit, we must also recognize the impossibility of creating a research process in which the contradictions in power and consciousness are eliminated (see also Acker et al., 1991; Holland and Ramazanoglu, 1994). We have to accept that the entire research process is most often one of unequals and that, as researchers, we retain power and control over conceiving, designing, administering, and reporting the research. Researcher and researched have a '. . . different and unequal relation to knowledge' (Glucksmann, 1994: 150), and within most research projects, 'the final shift of power between the researcher and the respondent is balanced in favor of the researcher, for it is she who eventually walks away' (Cotterill, 1992: 604).

This power differential between researcher and researched is likely to be particularly pronounced when doing research both *on* and *in* the private, rather than the public, sphere. For example, powerful professionals, public bodies and institutions are in a (better) position to 'police' research output.[6] Furthermore, participatory research, action research or experiential research projects might not face the same kinds of difficulties with power imbalances we are describing here (see Birch, this volume; Hall, 1992; Olesen, 1994; Reason and Rowan, 1981; Reinharz, 1983, 1992). Feminist scholars have suggested that one strategy for keeping participants' voices alive is to involve participants in the data analysis, either during the interview or with the transcript of the interview, so that the analysis is more collaborative and meaning is negotiated (Crawford and Marecek, 1989; Lather, 1991; Reinharz, 1992). Such research is not without its difficulties and dilemmas. For example, participants might not all wish to become involved in such a way; the goals and aims and time-frame of the research project may not accommodate such an interactive phase of data analysis; and there is a risk that the researcher and the respondent might disagree in their interpretation (Acker et al., 1991; Borland, 1991; Thompson 1992), thus raising the issue of whose, if any, perspectives will take precedence.

Conclusions

We believe that data analysis is a critical stage in the research process for it carries the potential to decrease or amplify the volume of our respondents' voices. As the site where their stories and 'voices' become 'transformed' into theory, what goes on during data analysis strikes us as being central to the fundamental concern of feminists: 'the intertwined problem of realizing as fully as possible women's voices in data gathering and preparing an account that transmits those voices' (Olesen, 1994: 167). We cannot emphasize enough how these processes between 'data gathering' and transmitting 'those voices' has received only sparse attention in feminist research and in the more general field of qualitative research. Indeed in place of a move towards greater links between empirical research practice and epistemological discussions, we would concur with Maynard (1994: 22) who has noted that '. . . arguments about what constitutes knowledge and discussions about methods of research are moving in opposite directions'. Our purpose in writing this chapter is to join those authors who are concerned about this increasing gap between abstract philosophical discussions about epistemology and research revealing the daily lives of women and men in domestic and private settings.

As we have gradually come to appreciate our omnipresence throughout all the stages of the research, we now feel that the feminist aim of listening to women 'in and on their own terms' is to some extent impossible. We are thus critical of the tendency by some feminist researchers to simplify the complex processes of representing the 'voices' of research respondents as though these voices speak on their own (see, for example, Reinharz, 1992: 267), rather than through the researcher who has already made choices about how to interpret them and which quotes and interpretations to present as evidence. There is therefore a contradiction, as we see it, between two of the principles that are fundamental to feminist research: the commitment to listen to women on their own terms and the recognition that it is the researcher who ultimately shapes the entire research process and product. Instead, we have found it helpful to think of the research process as involving a balancing act between three different and sometimes conflicting standpoints: (1) the multiple and varying voices and stories of each of the individuals we interview; (2) the voice(s) of the researcher(s); and (3) the voices and perspectives represented within existing theories or frameworks in our research areas and which researchers bring to their studies. We view research both in terms of process (how we do research) and product (the production/social construction of knowledge) as a journey in which these three 'voices' or perspectives must be listened to, maintained and respected, and the processes whereby we make critical shifts between these three 'voices' be charted for other researchers to build on or to critique (see also Rosalind Edwards and Jane Ribbens, this volume).

We also find it useful to think of the research process and product in terms of degrees rather than absolutes. There can be no 'pure', 'real' or 'authentic' experiences or voices of respondents because of the complex set of relationships between the respondents' experiences, voices and narratives, and the researcher's interpretation and representation of these experiences/voices/narratives. However, there are ways in which we can attempt to hear *more* of their voices, and understand *more* of their perspective through the ways in which we conduct our data analysis. Our chapter has highlighted one of the key dilemmas we face as researchers: on the one hand, we play a critical role in transforming private lives and concerns into public theories and debates and in voicing what might otherwise remain invisible and/or devalued issues pertaining to domestic life. On the other hand, in the process of transformation, the private account is changed by and infused with our identity – and thereby becomes a different story to that originally told by the respondent(s). We cannot be sure we have faithfully reported our respondents' concerns. At the same time, as academic researchers, our role involves more than this for we are also required to theorize our respondents' accounts and lives, and locate them within wider academic and theoretical debates. We have to accept the losses and gains involved in this process, and hope that a version of our respondents' concerns is made public, even if it is not their exact version nor necessarily all of the issues they regard as paramount. Moreover, whatever the losses and gains involved in moving from talk, to text, to theory, we must document the paths, detours, and shortcuts we have chosen at each stage of the research journey.

Notes

We thank the mothers and fathers who agreed to participate in our studies and share their experiences with us. We are extremely grateful to Jane Ribbens and Rosalind Edwards for their comments and advice on earlier drafts of this chapter, and for pushing us in our thinking. Several other colleagues gave extensive and invaluable comments for which we are grateful: Claudia Downing, Kathryn Geismar, Lorna McKee, Kathryn Milburn, Steve Pavis, Stephen Platt and Danny Wight. We thank Joy Emmanuel for her excellent research assistance supported by a Saint Mary's University Senate Research Grant. We also thank Carol Gilligan for giving generously of her time, insights and support in our work. This chapter draws on our doctoral research which was funded by the British Medical Research Council, in Natasha Mauthner's case, and by the Commonwealth Association of Canada and the Social Sciences and Humanities Research Council of Canada (SSHRC), in Andrea Doucet's case. The chapter is also based on research and teaching Natasha Mauthner carried out at the Harvard University Graduate School of Education in 1994–5, made possible by an International Fellowship from the American Association of University Women, a Wingate Scholarship, and a Fulbright Scholarship.

1 Feminist critiques are not uniform but vary, for example, in approaches to the links between methodology and epistemology. Here we can refer to Harding's (1987) now classic distinction between three kinds of approaches: feminist empiricist, feminist standpoint and feminist postmodernist.

2 Our research group met for three hours, every two to three weeks, over a period of 17 months and evolved over this time in terms of its membership from an initial group of seven PhD students and one post-doctoral researcher to a core of three graduate students (ourselves and Jane Ireland, 1994). We alternately brought transcripts, ongoing analyses and/or written up case studies to the group for comments, suggestions, criticisms and support.

3 The method is detailed in Brown and Gilligan (1992, chapter 2).

4 We selected these case studies in different ways: interview(ee)s which we found exciting or moving; interview(ee)s which we found difficult, challenging or perplexing; interview(ee)s which seemed particularly illuminating in terms of our research questions; and interview(ee)s which provided a different, contrasting or conflicting story to a previously analysed interview(ee).

5 The ability to 'coax' stories (Plummer, 1995), however, is critically linked with the aims and goals of the particular research project as well as the format and structure that the interview

relationship takes. In the words of Elliott Mishler, 'We are more likely to find stories reported in studies using relatively unstructured interviews where respondents are invited to speak in their own voices, allowed to control the introduction and flow of topics, and encouraged to extend their responses' (1986: 69).

6 We are grateful to Lorna McKee for clarifying this point for us.

References

Acker, J., Barry, K. and Esseveld, J. (1991) 'Objectivity and truth: problems in doing feminist research', in M.M. Fonow and J.A. Cook (eds), *Beyond Methodology: Feminist Scholarship as Lived Research*. Bloomington, IN: Indiana University Press.

Ahlander, N.R. and Bahr, K.S. (1995) 'Beyond discourse, power and equity: toward an expanded discourse on the moral dimensions of housework in families', *Journal of Marriage and the Family*, 57 (1): 54–68.

Anderson, K. and Jack, D. (1991) 'Learning to listen: interview techniques and analysis', in S. Gluck and D. Patai (eds), *Women's Words: The Feminist Practice of Oral History*. London: Routledge.

Baier, A.C. (1993) 'What do women want in moral theory?', in M.J. Larrabee (ed.), *An Ethic of Care: Feminist and Interdisciplinary Perspectives*. London: Routledge.

Beiser, H.R. (1993) 'Meeting at the crossroads: women's psychology and girls' development', *Journal of the American Medical Association,* 11 (4): 1446–7.

Belenky, M.F., Clinchy, B.M., Goldberger, N.R. and Tarule, J.M. (1986) *Women's Ways of Knowing: The Development of Self, Voice, and Mind*. New York: Basic Books.

Benhabib, S. (1987) 'The generalized and the concrete other: the Kohlberg–Gilligan controversy and feminist theory', in E. Kittay and D. Meyers (eds), *Women and Moral Theory*. Totowa, NJ: Rowman and Littlefield.

Benhabib, S. (1992) *Situating the Self*. Cambridge: Polity Press.

Blumer, H. (1969) *Symbolic Interactionism: Perspective and Method*. Berkeley, CA: University of California Press.

Borland, K. (1991) '"That's not what I said": interpretive conflict in oral narrative research', in S. Gluck and D. Patai (eds), *Women's Words: The Feminist Practice of Oral History*. London: Routledge.

Braidotti, R., Charkiewicz, E., Hausler, S. and Wieringa, S. (1994) *Women, the Environment and Sustainable Development: Towards a Theoretical Synthesis*. London: Zed Books in association with INSTRAW.

Brown, L.M. (1994) 'Standing in the crossfire: a response to Tavris, Gremmen, Lykes, Davis and Contratto', *Feminism and Psychology,* 4 (3): 382–98.

Brown, L.M. and Gilligan, C. (1992) *Meeting at the Crossroads: Women's Psychology and Girls' Development*. Cambridge, MA: Harvard University Press.

Brown, L.M. and Gilligan, C. (1993) 'Meeting at the crossroads: women's psychology and girls' development', *Feminism and Psychology,* 3 (1): 11–35.

Brown, L.M., Debold, E., Tappan, M. and Gilligan, C. (1991) 'Reading narratives of conflict and choice for self and moral voices: A relational method', in M. William and J.L. Gewirtz (eds), *Moral Behaviour and Development, Volume 2: Research*. Hilldale, NJ: Lawrence Erlbaum.

Brown, L.M., Tappan, M.B., Gilligan, C., Miller, B.A. and Argyris, D.E. (1989) 'Reading for self and moral voice: A method for interpreting narratives of real-life moral conflict and choice', in M.J. Packer and R.B. Addison (eds), *Entering the Circle: Hermeneutic Investigation in Psychology*. Albany, NY: State University of New York Press.

Brown, L.M., Argyris, D., Attanucci, J., Bardige, B., Gilligan, C., Johnston, K., Miller, B., Osborne, R., Tappan, M., Ward, Janie, Wiggins, G. and Wilcox, D. (1988) *A Guide to Reading Narratives of Conflict and Choice for Self and Relational Voice*. Cambridge, MA: Harvard Graduate School of Education.

Bryman, A. and Burgess, R. (1994) *Analyzing Qualitative Data*. London: Routledge.

Butler, J. (1990) *Gender Trouble: Feminism and the Subversion of Identity*. London: Routledge.

Butler, J. (1994) 'For a careful reading', in S. Benhabib, J. Butler, D. Cornell and N. Fraser (eds), *Feminist Contentions: A Philosophical Exchange*. London: Routledge.

Charmaz, K. (1993) 'Meeting at the crossroads: women's psychology and girls' development', *Gender and Society*, 7 (4): 614–16.

Code, L. (1993) 'Taking subjectivity into account', in L. Alcoff and E. Potter (eds), *Feminist Epistemologies*. New York and London: Routledge.

Coffey, A. and Atkinson, P. (1996) *Making Sense of Qualitative Data: Complementary Research Strategies*. London: Sage.

Cotterill, P. (1992) 'Interviewing women: issues of friendship, vulnerability, and power', *Women's Studies International Forum*, 15 (5/6): 593–606.

Crawford, M. and Marecek, J. (1989) 'Psychology constructs the female 1968–1988', *Psychology of Women Quarterly*, 13 (1): 147–65.

Davies, B. (1989a) 'The discursive production of male/female dualism', *Oxford Review of Education*, 15 (3): 229–41.

Davies, B. (1989b) *Frogs and Snails and Feminist Tales*. Sydney: Allen and Unwin.

Delamont, S. (1992) *Fieldwork in Educational Settings: Methods, Pitfalls and Perspectives*. London: Falmer Press.

Denzin, N.K. and Lincoln, Y.S. (1994) *Handbook of Qualitative Research*. London: Sage.

DeVault, M. (1990) 'Talking and listening from women's standpoint: feminist strategies for interviewing and analysis', *Social Problems*, 37 (1): 96–116.

Dey, I. (1993) *Qualitative Data Analysis: A User-friendly Guide for Social Scientists*. London: Routledge.

Dilthey, W. (1976) 'The development of hermeneutics', in W. Dilthey, *Selected Writings* (edited and translated by H. Rickman). Cambridge: Cambridge University Press. (First published 1900.)

Doucet, A. (1995a) 'Gender equality, gender differences and care: towards understanding gendered labour in British dual earner households'. Unpublished PhD dissertation, University of Cambridge, Cambridge.

Doucet, A. (1995b) 'Gender equality and gender differences in household work and parenting', *Women's Studies International Forum*, 18 (3): 271–84.

Doucet, A. (1996) 'Encouraging voices: towards more creative methods for collecting data on gender and household labour', in L. Morris and S. Lyon (eds), *Gender Relations in the Public and the Private*. London: Macmillan.

Du Bois, B. (1983) 'Passionate scholarship: notes on values, knowing and method in feminist social science', in G. Bowles and R.D. Klein (eds), *Theories of Women's Studies*. London: Routledge and Kegan Paul.

Edwards, R. and Ribbens, J. (1991) 'Meanderings around "strategy": a research note on strategic discourse in the lives of women', *Sociology*, 25 (3): 477–89.

Finch, J. (1984) '"It's great to have someone to talk to": the ethics and politics of interviewing women', in C. Bell and H. Roberts (eds), *Social Researching: Politics, Problems, Practice*. London: Routledge and Kegan Paul.

Finch, J. and Mason, J. (1993) *Negotiating Family Responsibilities*. London: Routledge.

Gadamer, H. (1975) *Truth and Method*. New York: Seabury Press.

Geismar, K. (1996) 'Bodies of knowledge: transfiguring the pain of childhood trauma'. Unpublished PhD dissertation, Harvard University Graduate School of Education, Cambridge, MA.

Giddens, A. (1984) *The Constitution of Society*. Cambridge: Polity Press.

Gilligan, C. (1982) *In a Different Voice: Psychological Theory and Women's Development*. Cambridge, MA: Harvard University Press.

Gilligan, C. (1988) 'Remapping the moral domain: new images of self in relationship', in C. Gilligan, J.V. Ward, J.M. Taylor, with Betty Bardige (eds), *Mapping the Moral Domain: A Contribution of Women's Thinking to Psychological Theory and Education*. Cambridge, MA: Harvard University Press.

Gilligan, C., Brown, L.M. and Rogers, A. (1990) 'Psyche embedded: a place for body, relationships and culture in personality theory', in A.I. Rabin, R. Zucker, R. Emmons and S. Frank (eds), *Studying Persons and Lives*. New York: Springer.

Glaser, B.G. (1992) *Emergence vs Forcing Basics of Grounded Theory Analysis*. Mill Valley, CA: Sociological Press.

Glaser, B.G. and Strauss, A.L. (1967) *The Discovery of Grounded Theory*. Chicago: Aldine.

Glucksmann, M. (1994) 'The work of knowledge and the knowledge of women's work', in M. Maynard and J. Purvis (eds), *Researching Women's Lives from a Feminist Perspective*. London: Taylor and Francis.

Gold, J.H. (1993) 'Meeting at the crossroads: women's psychology and girls' development', *American Journal of Psychiatry*, 151 (1): 281.

Graham, H. (1983) 'Caring: a labour of love', in J. Finch and D. Groves (eds), *A Labour of Love: Women, Work and Caring*. London: Routledge and Kegan Paul.

Hall, B.L. (1992) 'From margins to center: the development and purpose of participatory research', *American Sociologist*, 23 (4): 15–28.

Hammersley, M. (1992) *What's Wrong with Ethnography?* London: Routledge.

Hammersley, M. and Atkinson, P. (1983) *Ethnography: Principles in Practice*. London: Tavistock.

Haraway, D. (1988) 'Situated knowledges: the science question in feminism and the privilege of partial perspective', *Feminist Studies*, 14 (3): 575–99.

Harding, S. (1987) 'Is there a feminist method?', in S. Harding (ed.), *Feminism and Methodology*. Bloomington, IN: Indiana University Press.

Harding, S. (1992) *Whose Science? Whose Knowledge?* Milton Keynes: Open University Press.

Hekman, S.J. (1990) *Gender and Knowledge: Elements of a Postmodern Feminism*. Boston: Northeastern University Press.

Held, V. (1984) 'The obligations of mothers and fathers', in J. Trebilcott (ed.), *Mothering: Essays in Feminist Theory*. Totowa, NJ: Rowman and Allenheld.

Held, V. (1995) 'The meshing of care and justice', *Hypatia*, 10 (2): 168–74. (Symposium on care and justice.)

Holland, J. and Ramazanoglu, C. (1994) 'Coming to conclusions: power and interpretation in researching young women's sexuality', in M. Maynard and J. Purvis (eds), *Researching Women's Lives from a Feminist Perspective*. London: Taylor and Francis.

Ireland, J. (1994) 'Gender, work and identity in the lives of women and men in nursing and engineering trades in the south of England'. Unpublished PhD dissertation, University of Cambridge, Cambridge.

Jack, D. (1991) *Silencing the Self: Depression and Women*. Cambridge, MA: Harvard University Press.

Jordan, J. (1993) 'The relational self: a model of women's development', in J. van Mens-Verhulst, K. Schreurs and L. Woertman (eds), *Daughtering and Mothering: Female Subjectivity Reanalysed*. London: Routledge.

Kitzinger, C. with Gilligan, C. (1994) 'The spoken word: listening to a different voice', *Feminism and Psychology*, 4 (3): 399–403.

Lather, P.A. (1991) *Getting Smart: Feminist Research and Pedagogy with/in the Postmodern*. New York: Routledge.

Macuika, L. (1992) '"When their world has been rocked": profound learning and psychological change in adults'. Unpublished PhD dissertation, Harvard University, Cambridge, MA.

Mauthner, N.S. (1993) 'Towards a feminist understanding of "postnatal depression"', *Feminism and Psychology*, 3 (3): 350–5.

Mauthner, N. S. (1994) 'Postnatal depression: a relational perspective'. Unpublished PhD dissertation, University of Cambridge, Cambridge.

Mauthner, N.S. (1995) 'Postnatal depression: the significance of social contacts between mothers', *Women's Studies International Forum*, 18 (3): 11–23.

Mauthner, N.S. (1998a) 'Re-assessing the importance and role of the marital relationship in postnatal depression: methodological and theoretical implications', *Journal of Reproductive and Infant Psychology* (forthcoming).

Mauthner, N.S. (1998b) '"It's a woman's cry for help": a relational perspective on postnatal depression.' *Feminism & Psychology* (forthcoming).

Maynard, M. (1994) 'Methods, practice and epistemology', in M. Maynard and J. Purvis (eds),

Researching Women's Lives from a Feminist Perspective. London: Taylor and Francis.

Mead, G.H. (1934) *Mind, Self and Society.* Chicago: University of Chicago Press.

Melia, K.M. (1996) 'Rediscovering Glaser', *Qualitative Health Research,* 6 (3): 368–78.

Mies, M. (1983) 'Towards a methodology for feminist research', in G. Bowles and R.D. Klein (eds), *Theories of Women's Studies.* London: Routledge and Kegan Paul.

Miles, M.B. and Huberman, A.M. (1984) *Qualitative Data Analysis: A Sourcebook of New Methods.* Beverly Hills, CA: Sage.

Miles, M.B. and Huberman, A.M. (1994) *Qualitative Data Analysis: An Expanded Sourcebook.* London: Sage.

Miller, J. B. (1986) *Towards a New Psychology of Women.* London: Penguin Books. (First published 1976.)

Minow, M. and Shanley, M.L. (1996) 'Relational rights and responsibilities: revisioning the family in liberal political theory and law', *Hypatia,* 11 (1): 4–29.

Mishler, E.G. (1986) *Research Interviewing: Context and Narrative.* Cambridge, MA: Harvard University Press.

Morrow, V. (1996) 'Rethinking childhood dependency: children's contributions to the domestic economy', *Sociological Review,* 44 (1): 59–76.

Oakley, A. (1981) 'Interviewing women: a contradiction in terms', in H. Roberts (ed.), *Doing Feminist Research.* London: Routledge and Kegan Paul.

Olesen, V. (1994) 'Feminisms and models of qualitative research', in N.K. Denzin and Y.S. Lincoln (eds), *Handbook of Qualitative Research.* London: Sage.

Patton, M.Q. (1990) *Qualitative Evaluation and Research Methods.* London: Sage.

Plummer, K. (1995) *Telling Sexual Stories: Power, Change and Social Worlds.* London: Routledge.

Reason, P. and Rowan, J. (1981) *Human Inquiry: a Sourcebook of New Paradigm Research.* Chichester: John Wiley.

Reinharz, S. (1983) 'Experiential analysis: a contribution to feminist research', in G. Bowles and R. D. Klein (eds), *Theories of Women's Studies.* London: Routledge and Kegan Paul.

Reinharz, S. (1992) *Feminist Methods in Social Research.* Oxford: Oxford University Press.

Ricoeur, P. (1979) 'The model of a text: meaningful action considered as a text', in P. Rabinow and W. Sullivan (eds), *Interpretive Social Science: a Reader.* Berkeley, CA: University of California Press.

Riessman, C.K. (1987) 'When gender is not enough: women interviewing women', *Gender and Society,* 1(2): 172–207.

Riessman, C.K. (1993) *Narrative Analysis.* Newbury Park, CA: Sage.

Roberts, H. (1981) *Doing Feminist Research.* London: Routledge and Kegan Paul.

Rogers, A. (1994) *Exiled Voices: Dissociation and Repression in Women's Narratives of Trauma.* Wellesley, MA: Stone Center Working Paper Series.

Ruddick, S. (1989) *Maternal Thinking: Towards a Politics of Peace.* Boston, MA: Beacon.

Silverman, D. (1993) *Interpreting Qualitative Data: Methods for Analysing Talk, Text and Interaction.* London: Sage.

Smith, D. (1987) *The Everyday World as Problematic: A Feminist Sociology.* Milton Keynes: Open University Press.

Stacey, M. (1981) 'The division of labour revisited, or overcoming the two Adams', in P. Abrams, R. Deem, J. Finch and P. Rock (eds), *Practice and Progress: British Sociology 1950–1980.* London: George Allen and Unwin.

Stanley, L. and Wise, S. (1983) *Breaking Out: Feminist Consciousness and Feminist Research.* London: Routledge and Kegan Paul.

Stanley, L. and Wise, S. (1993) *Breaking Out Again: Feminist Ontology and Epistemology.* London: Routledge and Kegan Paul.

Stiver, I.P. and Miller, J.B. (1992) *From Depression to Sadness in Women's Psychotherapy.* Wellesley, MA: Stone Center Working Paper Series.

Strauss, A.L. and Corbin, J. (1990) *Basics of Qualitative Research: Grounded Theory Procedures and Techniques.* London: Sage.

Thompson, L. (1992) 'Feminist methodology for family studies', *Journal of Marriage and the Family,* 54 (February): 3–18.

Thorne, B. (1987) 'Revisioning women and social change: where are the children?', *Gender and Society*, 1 (1): 85–109.

Tolman, D. (1992) 'Voicing the body: a psychological study of adolescent girls' sexual desire'. Unpublished PhD dissertation, Harvard University, Cambridge, MA.

Tronto, J. (1989) 'Women and caring: what can feminists learn about morality from caring?', in A.M. Jaggar and S.R. Bordo (eds), *Gender/Body/Knowledge: Feminist Reconstructions of Being and Knowing*. New Brunswick, NJ: Rutgers University Press.

Tronto, J. (1993) *Moral Boundaries: A Political Argument for an Ethic of Care*. New York and London: Routledge.

Tronto, J. (1995) 'Care as a basis for radical political judgements', *Hypatia,* 10 (2): 141–9. (Symposium on care and justice.)

Way, N. (1994) 'In their own words: listening to inner-city adolescents speak their worlds'. Unpublished PhD dissertation, Harvard University, Cambridge, MA.

Weedon, C. (1987) *Feminist Practice and Poststructuralist Theory*. Oxford: Basil Blackwell.

Weitzman, E.A. and Miles, M.B. (1995) *Computer Programs for Qualitative Data Analysis: A Software Sourcebook*. London: Sage.

Westkott, M. (1990) 'Feminist criticism of the social sciences', in J.M. Nielsen (ed.), *Feminist Research Methods: Exemplary Readings in the Social Sciences*. Boulder, CO: Westview Press.

Wilkinson, S. (1994) 'Editor's introduction', *Feminism and Psychology,* 4 (3): 343–4.

Wolcott, H.F. (1994) *Transforming Qualitative Data: Description, Analysis and Interpretation*. Newbury Park, CA: Sage.

9 Ethnography and Discourse Analysis

Dilemmas in Representing the Voices of Children

Pam Alldred

Particular ethical and political dilemmas arise in representing the lives of people who are marginalized within, and by, the domain of public knowledge. In order to remain critically self-aware about the decisions we take as researchers we need to be able to make explicit both the nature of the dilemmas we face, and the losses, as well as gains, that result from our decisions. This chapter discusses some of the representational dilemmas of research work with children, that is, issues arising in our production of research accounts for dissemination in the public sphere. What claims to represent children's voices can adult researchers legitimately make? And what meanings may we unwittingly reinforce as we make such public re/presentations?

Different research methodologies provide different claims for the status of the knowledge produced. Whilst both ethnographic and discourse analytic approaches can enable a response to the political call to 'hear the voices of children', and provide a means of re/presenting their opinions in 'the public sphere', they often entail radically different ideas about language. As a consequence they make different kinds of representational claims about the status of their accounts. What are the implications of these different claims and warrants for knowledge in terms of the strategies they provide for feminist or critical researchers?

In order to make a particular intervention in public debate, I want to be able to claim that the research account I produce represents participants, yet I have political and theoretical doubts about the representational claims that have conventionally warranted research, and about the particular notion of 'the subject' which metaphors of voice serve. The dilemmas arise from my recognition, or suspicion, that, despite these doubts, the discourse of voice and the claims of objectivism and realism to guarantee my 'findings' do still provide the most powerful warrant for my research account. What are the pitfalls or limitations of responding to the 'voices of children' discourse within the terms of existing debates? Might a 'hybrid' approach of discourse–ethnography offer a way forward?

To what extent are these representational issues common to research with any marginalized group, or specific to research work with children? I believe that the issues themselves apply to research with any less powerful social group which has little access to the practices of public knowledge production.

However, the dilemmas we face must involve the consideration of the specific meanings attributed to particular social groups since, for instance, in the case of children, certain ideas about their psychological development can allow them to be more easily disqualified as participants of research. Exploring the dilemmas in relation to children therefore engages both specific discussion within contemporary childhood research (Alanen, 1990; James and Prout, 1990; Kitzinger, 1990; Mayall, 1994; Waksler, 1991), and more general debates in feminist theory about the status of knowledge after the 'crisis of representation'.

For three years I was the researcher on the Children's Representations of Family Life project with Dr Margaret O'Brien in the Department of Sociology at the University of East London. I conducted individual interviews and group discussions with children at a primary school and also piloted some graphic approaches. Whilst this chapter doesn't draw specifically from material gathered for this study (but see O'Brien, Alldred and Jones, 1996), my consideration of the issues raised was stimulated by this fieldwork and came to be articulated more theoretically during my subsequent PhD research.

Hearing children's voices: the political discourse of voice

In the West, there are now established popular discourses of the moral imperative to 'hear the voices' of women, of black and Asian peoples, of lesbians and gay men, of postcolonial subjects, of people with disabilities, and now, tentatively, of people with learning difficulties, PWAs (people living with AIDS) and 'mental health'/system and abuse survivors. The struggles that these reflect have been about striving to be recognized fully as 'subjects'. These, along with inter-ethnic conflicts, are struggles over identities and the status granted them, rather than over material resources and economics. Political philosophers such as Nancy Fraser identify these as forms of the 'recognition' rather than 'redistribution' struggles which have come to characterize contemporary politics (Fraser, 1995). The 'recognition' granted these hitherto marginal subjects has begun a process of decentring 'the (Western) subject', and has shaken the unthinking confidence with which the dominant masculinist, Eurocentric perspective has been assumed to be *the* perspective.

Children are another socially silenced group: their opinions are not heard in the public sphere and they wield little power as a social group. Adults are generally more powerful relative to, and specifically over, children. As Brannen and O'Brien note, there is increasing consciousness of the fact that '. . . children's worlds have typically become known through adult accounts' (1996: 1). The demand to 'hear the voices of children' relies upon these earlier struggles as 'conditions of possibility' and employs the same discourses of empowerment and metaphors of voice and perspective. The cultural spaces for children's voices which have opened up over the past decade in the UK are illustrated by the increasing concern in the legal sphere to take children's

'. . . wishes and feelings and self-defined preferences into account whenever possible' (Roche, 1996: 27) (expressed, for instance, in the Children Act 1989, the Scottish Law Commission, 1992 and supported, at least in principle, by the UK government's ratification of the UN Convention on the Rights of the Child in 1991), as well as by the emergence of organizations and advice centres which are predicated on children's participation and articulation (children's magazines such as *Children Express*, and organizations such as Who Cares?, which aims to give children in residential care more of a public voice). The process of recognizing children as subjects is similar in rhetorical character to these earlier struggles, but has lagged somewhat behind.

Children's voices (or my re-presentation of their voices) are notably absent from this chapter. Instead, I focus on the claims of adult researchers, and how we may warrant our accounts of what children say. Of course, some of the arguments I make about the difficulties surrounding researchers' claims to represent children apply to my representation of the work of other researchers. However, there are also significant differences: firstly, I am representing *adult* researchers, not *child* participants (although I will consider whether this alters or simply intensifies the issues); and secondly, material I re-present is from published research that researchers have already placed in the public sphere (so I am not serving up privately elicited accounts for public consumption, as is the case for much research). Following Spivak's (1988) distinction between representation meaning *proxy*, or meaning *portrayal*, I am representing other researchers in the sense of portrayal (the 'photographic' meaning of representation), but not in the sense of advocacy. However, in our research roles, these two may not be clearly distinguished, or indeed, we may wish to 'represent children' in both senses. Interrogating the doctrine of empiricism raises problems with both these meanings of 'representing children'.

James and Prout (1990) note the elision of a temporal (re-presenting) and a significatory meaning of 'representation'. Whilst the temporal meaning of repeating raises the possibility of seeing representation as an active process, and therefore one which is conducted from a particular perspective, the word re-presentation does not insist on this. Indeed, both of these meanings may assume that an object exists and is then truthfully reflected in (portrayed by) its representation. I think this ambivalence about what the word means epistemologically is what Hall (1992) identifies when he notes that the term is used currently not only as an unproblematic notion of 'image of' (portrayal or signification), but also to indicate a radical displacement of that notion. I prefer to use the terms 're-presentation' and re/presentation to indicate that my research account is actively produced by me and embodies my perspective, using the former when emphasizing process and the latter when emphasizing its significance for cultural politics. However, neither seems to allow me to distinguish the epistemological positions which this chapter discusses. By making reference to the word 'representational' (even when doing so critically) they each suggest to me both an empirical meaning of portrayal, and the significance for cultural politics of either images of a social group or their advocacy. I like the way in which 're/presentation' admits this ambivalence.

My use in this chapter of the 'discourse of voice' must be distinguished from the specific approach of Carol Gilligan and co-workers (however, see Andrea Doucet and Natasha Mauthner, this volume). I am referring to the particular, but loose, set of metaphors of voice which circulate in popular political discourse and link (political) perspective closely with 'who the speaker is'.

Childhood research: giving voice to children?

The empirical study of children in the West has, for the last 150 years, been regarded as the domain of psychology. Within this discipline children have been treated as the (passive) objects of study; scrutinized, tested and measured (Burman, 1994; Rose, 1985). The focus has been on what happens to them (and processes they undergo), rather than what they do or say. The psychological construction of the individual which underpins this is hegemonic and has provided the foundation for sociological thinking too. However, for children, it is confounded with developmentalism: the construction of a linear, sequential and normalized process by which children become adults. As Qvortrup (1987) notes, this constructs children as more like 'human becomings', than human beings. Developmental discourses, therefore, exacerbate children's objectification within research. It is not unless children are seen as people in their own right that they can be thought of as participants of research (Speier, 1973, cited by Corsaro, 1981).

As the children's rights movement has been developing in the UK, ethnographic research has 'given voice' to children, enabling them to begin to play a more direct part in the production of sociological knowledge than the adult/researcher-determined categories of survey or experimental methods (James and Prout, 1990). Hence discourses of 'giving voice' offer a way of constructing children as active subjects, not objects, and of recognizing that they may have distinct perspectives on the world. The recognition that meaning embodies perspective is at least an implicit challenge to objectivism and the arrogant assumption that a perspective is universal, an account definitive. Ethnography has the most established place in the social sciences and humanities as an approach which attempts to place subjects' own perspectives centrally. Its ethical promise rests on its (compatibility with) voice metaphors; its political force, on the salience attributed to identity in contemporary political discourses; and its immense appeal, on its 'promise to delve into the "concrete" (in the hope of finding "real" people living "real" lives)' (Probyn, 1993: 72). Because it matters 'that some speak and that others are merely spoken' (Probyn, ibid.), it offers to meet feminist concerns to 'give voice' to those whose opinions are rarely heard.

Research is, therefore, seen as one of the ways of providing spaces in which hitherto silenced people can 'be heard' and be recognized as subjects. It is hoped that interview-based research and the dissemination of 'findings' in the public sphere can provide a platform for, or can amplify, these voices. Like most researchers, I imagine, my personal investment in the hope that research has a progressive impact means that there are personal, as well as institutional, risks involved in explicating the politics of research relations and the effectivity of research as an intervention in particular public debates or broader cultural politics.

Ethnographers often use the discourse of voice empirically to mean something akin to perspective, and perhaps some use it in a less literal, illustrative way. Whilst discourse analysis is an approach which can be employed to analyse the things children say, it rejects some of the theoretical underpinnings of the voice-as-perspective discourse. However, both approaches can recognize that interviews are a particular form of social interaction in which the discursive exchange is constructed jointly by researcher and participant; see meanings as grounded in their contexts; and base analysis and interpretation on a theory of discourse and meaning (Mishler, 1986).

What Oakley (1981) called the 'hygienic', traditional approach to interviewing obscures the relations of power that characterize the research relationship. However, a discursive approach requires us to consider reflexively the institutional power carried by researchers, and to avoid creating the illusion of 'democratized' research through the fantasy of empowerment (Marks, 1993). Whilst ethnography can lodge a powerful critique of the conventional research practices Oakley described, it can also be employed within an otherwise conventional approach. The following three sections describe key tensions that can arise within the ethnographic study of children, which are, I believe, general representational dilemmas for researchers. They challenge the assumption that adults' benevolent attempts to represent children (as proxy or advocate) are necessarily always in their interests, and the simplicity with which it is assumed that what children say can be represented (portrayed) through research.

Ethnography of 'children's culture'

In order to gain access to children's perspectives, William Corsaro employed the ethnographic technique of participant observation through which he became '. . . a participant in children's culture' (Corsaro, 1981: 118), '. . . joining in the children's activities whilst not affecting the nature or flow of peer episodes' (ibid.: 133). Notions such as '. . . entering *the child's world*' (Mandell, 1986; 1991) and interacting 'with children *in their perspective*' (Mandell, 1991: 59; emphasis added) imply that adults and children occupy separate social spheres. It constructs children as little aliens to the dominant culture, the exotic objects of some other culture. 'Other', that is, to the presumed norm or centrality of adult culture (which is itself thus imputed with homogeneity and consensuality). The centrality of the researcher and the pseudo-colonialist relation of rendering the strange in terms familiar to the observer culture – which is sometimes reinforced by metaphors of travel

(Pratt, 1986a, cited in Hammersley and Atkinson, 1995) – is, of course, not particular to work with children. For contemporary childhood research there is surely a tension between studying children simply as people, and giving them research (or political) attention because they are currently marginalized, which then risks reinforcing the idea of them as a 'special case'. So fundamental is our 'knowledge' of adult–child difference that it's difficult to imagine research in which participants happen to include adults and children, yet no between-groups comparison is made. Although, for the present, a strong case can be made for the benefits of 'special case' attention.

When considering his power as researcher, Corsaro notes that '. . . adults are much bigger than children and are perceived as being socially more powerful' (Corsaro, 1981: 118). Physical size may well have been significant (although he did not attempt the 'least-adult' role that Mandell (1986, 1991) developed), but it is only one of the features that may have affected the interaction between the children and himself. He might also have considered the ways in which the interaction was informed by dominant cultural meanings assigned to his age and gender, such as ideas about paternal playfulness or pedagogic authority. However, in later debates amongst researchers about the extent to which adults can enter children's worlds, Corsaro (1985, cited by Mandell, 1991) insists that age and authority continue to separate adults and children and so qualifies his participation as partial, whereas others argue that all aspects of adult superiority except physical differences can be cast aside and that adults can participate fully in children's culture (Goode, 1986 and Waksler, 1986, both cited by Mandell, 1991).

Beyond the interaction, in later stages of the research process, there is also an unequal power relationship. Not only are adult researchers '. . . perceived as being socially more powerful', they *are* more powerful by virtue of their role as researchers, through which they are in a position to interpret, as well as to represent (Burman, 1992). The reflexive consideration of researchers' power and status is limited by a focus on the dynamics of the interaction 'in the field', with little consideration of the broader power relations within which this is constituted. This is a criticism that Probyn (1993) makes of even some recent ethnography: that reflexivity extends only to the immediate context of meaning production (here, the classroom), and not adequately to the production of meaning in the account (processes occurring back in the academy).

Corsaro does identify the problem of adult assumptions and interpretations of children's behaviour and abilities, so recognizes that *how* children are heard is an issue. He believes that an adult perspective is the result of removing the interaction from its full social context. However, although '. . . adult interpretations and assumptions about children's behavior are themselves topics for inquiry (Schwartzman, 1978)' (Corsaro, 1981: 118), such a study is viewed as separate:

> One of the central aims of ethnographies of childhood culture is the suspension of such interpretations. The researcher must attempt to free himself [sic] from adult conceptions of children's activities and enter the child's world as both *observer* and *participant*. (Ibid.: 119; original emphasis)

The idea that it is possible to suspend, or step outside of, the cultural meanings assigned to childhood must be viewed with scepticism. From where might the researcher's conceptual framework – indeed, the words to speak – then come from? A more realistic aim might be to attempt to examine the 'adult conceptions' closely alongside, and in relation to, the observations that one makes. In this way one could begin to reflect upon the concepts and processes of the analysis as an '. . . interrogation of the methods . . . simultaneously with, and as an integral part of, the investigation of the object (Woolgar, 1982)' (Woolgar and Ashmore, 1988: 8).

The approach adopted by both Corsaro and Mandell is realist and implicitly objectivist: children's culture is seen as existing prior to, and independently of, the researcher's gaze, so that they may enter that culture, observe it without altering it, then objectively report without distortion what they have 'merely observed'. Therefore, the ethnographer's perception is the key warrant for the knowledge produced. Corsaro's 'escape from' an adult perspective into the 'real' children's culture demonstrates his reliance on conventional notions of language as reflective or representational (rather than constitutive) and consequently he presents his work as a straightforward representation or portrayal of children's culture. Claiming this representational status is so conventionalized in Western scientific discourse that the warrant need not be made explicit. Ethnographic techniques can embody a realist epistemology even where they have rejected (unitary) objectivism. So that whilst a researcher explicitly recognizes the existence of different perspectives (hence studying the participants'), it is simply assumed that readers of the research will rest their faith in the researcher's own perspective as the basis for knowledge.

Otherness and the centre

Ethnography is '. . . a writing practice in which the other is inscribed within, and explained by, the power of the ethnographer's language' (Grossberg, 1989: 23) with '. . . the onus on the other to fit her experiences into an understandable order' (Probyn, 1993: 63). As in the classical anthropological monographs documenting the West's cultural Others, the crucial relation is of the observed culture to the researcher's culture. Can a description by an outsider remain faithful to the framework of the subjects, as it is inevitably rendered in the observer's terms? Is the representation to a dominant group or culture of 'other' perspectives necessarily imperialist, serving to bolster their own sense of centrality and extend cultural power through 'knowledge of'? But how else can that centrality be challenged?

Adult-(ethno)centrism can be seen to operate at both an individual level, whereby adults tend to interpret the actions and utterances of children as immature versions of their own speech and behaviour (Bruner et al., 1976), and also at a cultural level. A researcher employing a discourse analytic approach might share the concern with adult-centrism without expecting to be able to avoid it. Since representation is through language, and the language and hegemonic concepts are those of the dominant culture, marginalized groups have described how the dominant conceptual framework which is not 'their own' may be imbued with negativities for them (for instance, Spender, 1985, on the androcentricism of the English language). For adult-dominated culture, language is, 'by definition', reflective and productive of adult power, status and authority. Since the whole frame of reference is adult-centred, it is difficult to see to what extent children could, as ethnographic subjects, present 'their own' account of their worlds. Furthermore, it can be argued that children are having to render themselves meaningful in adult-centred terms, and explain themselves convincingly to those in power over them (this parallels the discussion by Rosalind Edwards and Jane Ribbens, this volume). Seen in this light, children's interviews, because they entail the requirement to make sense for adults, might not necessarily be empowering occasions for children. The idea that any ethnographic subjects are free to present their own meanings in any radical sense neglects the ways in which the dominant culture provides hegemonic meanings.

   Post-structuralist approaches to language disallow the fantasy of speaking from outside of the language system, which is why feminist writers influenced by post-structuralism (Butler, 1990; Diamond and Quinby, 1988; Weedon, 1987) emphasize the recognition of resistance to powerful discourses. Recognizing the fact that in providing a research voice for a particular group we may simultaneously reinforce their construction as Other, and concurrently our own perspective or the dominant cultural perspective as central, prevents us from naively assuming that our work is bound to be liberatory. Patai (1991) believes that ethical research is simply not possible in an unjust world, since researchers replicate structures of privilege through the institution of knowledge. Taking up a position as one who knows, in relation to those who are oppressed, is fraught with ethical problems which are not assuaged by good intentions. At the very least, this requires that we focus on the potential losses as well as gains of particular approaches to research. In relation to placing children's voices in the public sphere, we need to examine the broader context of meanings that will be brought into play. Through what cultural understandings of children are the words of any child heard?

How we hear what children say

Corsaro (1981) notes that adults often describe as 'silly' or unimportant what they do not understand in children's speech or behaviour. Berry Mayall describes how discussions of 'methodological issues' in childhood research sometimes construct children '. . . as cognitive incompetents, . . . routinely wrong and misunderstand[ing]; likely to confuse fact with fiction; and . . . give the answers they think adults want rather than reply accurately' (1996: 13). She reminds us that adults also vary in their knowledge and experience, and that '. . . we [all] interweave fact and fiction both consciously and unconsciously and tell interviewers what we think they want to know' (ibid). This illustrates how the specific cultural positioning of children within developmental discourses of incompleteness, and as 'not yet there', can further extend the doubts that some have about the validity of 'subjective' research in general. Where objectivism prevails, the subjectivity that is understood as a problem for research is seen as exaggerated in the case of children. There also exist particular ideas about children's communication skills, knowledge and self-reflection. Therefore, it is not just a case of hearing children's voices, but of *how* we hear their voices. In terms of feminist intervention, it might be that providing a public platform for children's perspectives is not enough. We need to attend to the meanings that will be made of the accounts.

Both possible meanings of the title of this section are in operation. By emphasizing the *how* of 'How we hear what children say', I am arguing that, as researchers, we face decisions about *how to go about* trying to hear what children say. Different methods are underpinned by alternative epistemological perspectives which provide different ways of thinking about the relation between participants' voices and the knowledge that is produced about them. Alternatively, when *hear* is emphasized, attention is drawn to the way in which children's voices are actually heard. This problematizes the passivity which 'to hear' usually conveys and highlights issues of interpretation. How do both specific context and broader cultural discourses affect the ways in which what children say is understood? Although not conceptually distinct, we can consider this at the level of how researchers hear children, and then how research reports are heard in the public sphere.

Children's voices are heard through cultural constructions of childhood. It is simultaneous attention to child*hood*, as opposed to a sole focus on (particular) children, that distinguishes writers influenced by social constructionism, such as Burman (1992), James and Prout (1990), Marks (1996) and Mayall (1996) from more conventional ethnographers such as Corsaro (1981, 1986) and Mandell (1986, 1991). Some discourse analytic approaches, such as Parker's (1992), can take into account the social construction of childhood, by insisting that we bring in knowledge of discourses from 'outside' the research, including those that our politics identify as broader power relations, in order to analyse discourse.

The status of 'voice' in discourse analytic research

In post-structuralist informed discourse analytic research, representations of interviewees' accounts are made without a realist, objectivist warrant. Research is recognized to be a practice of re-presentation, and 'findings' a re/presentation through a particular lens. This invites reflexivity about the production of the account. The participant's 'voice' is seen as produced from what was culturally available to her/him, rather than from a private reserve of meaning. The fantasy of the authentic subject, one whose subjectivity is imagined to be independent of, or prior to, culture is rejected. Deborah Marks interviewed young people about exclusion from school. She writes:

researching into people's experience is fraught with epistemological and ontologi-cal dilemmas. Social constructionist theory has warned that giving our 'subject' a 'voice' involves the fantasy that it is possible to have unmediated direct knowledge of experience (James and Prout, 1990). Derrida has challenged the phonocentricism implicit in the notion of speech as a direct and immediate form of expression. Giving primacy to interviewees' talk about their experience of exclusion suggests that their speech may refer to themselves as a unified authentic subject. This Cartesian subject, whose self-consciousness acts as guarantor of meaning, is chal-lenged both by versions of psychoanalysis (Althusser, 1971; Frosh, 1987) and discourse analysis (Parker, 1992), which see the subject as being fragmented and constituted within language. (Marks, 1996: 115)

Marks does not treat the accounts obtained as final and fixed, rather they are '. . . often ambivalent, contradictory and changing' (ibid.: 115). She notes that 'the relationship between an original exclusion and the way pupils talk about it in their interview or discussion group is highly complex', and therefore she doesn't ask about their experiences in order to try to establish 'what really hap-pened'. She does not position herself as able to 'penetrate the manifest content in order to reveal its hidden kernel' and so she is not central in her warrant for the research knowledge: 'I cannot say how participants *really* experienced the exclusion. However, asking about the experience of exclusion brings forth a number of productive ways of seeing the event' (ibid.: 116; original emphasis).

For some pupils, the tone of the interview was confessional as they took responsibility for bad behaviour. Other accounts took the form of factual reports and had a disengaged tone, and in a third type, pupils protested their innocence. The complexity of thoughts and feelings about their exclusions meant that they might be positioned in a variety of conflicted ways. Whilst identifying how these may have functioned psychologically and emotionally for the individuals, and indeed for herself – since she too experienced exclu-sion by the children during a group discussion – she deliberately avoids '. . . establishing an opposition between emotional, conflicted and hence "authentic" accounts and generalised, jargon-laden "inauthentic" accounts' (Marks, 1996: 129). The imperative that discourse analysts attend the broader social meanings within which research occurs leads Marks to consider these interviews in relation to powerful psychological discourses of self-regulating individuals who, on reflection, repent their misdemeanours. The possibility that the interviews functioned to regulate some participants further by pro-viding a space in which they drew themselves under disciplinary gaze to produce themselves as good children and self-governing individuals prevented Marks from assuming the interviews to be necessarily (or only) liberating.

Warranting discourse analytic work

Many feminist theorists use post-structuralist approaches to show how knowledge claims entail plays of power. Without an appeal to objectivity and without asserting the centrality of one's own perspective, with what authority can one present discourse analytic research? Is there an alternative rhetoric of research? Most importantly, could an alternative support effective feminist or critical intervention? This issue is key in debates about feminism and postmodernism, as well as having exercised researchers who have taken the reflexive 'turn to language'. Burman et al. (1996) argue that rejecting conventional ideas of authorship and of knowing through personal identities need not mean losing the relevance of individual experience, nor the possibility of political critique. Losing faith in objectivity need not mean completely undermining our own warrants for speaking critically (Burman, 1990). Fraser and Nicholson (1990) argue that feminists might present local empirical accounts, without the grand narratives which universalize and ahistoricize. Empiricism without objectivist foundations, they argue, requires us to extend self-reflexivity to recognize that our analyses, as well as their objects, are culturally specific.

Erica Burman (1992) interviewed primary school-aged children, but neither warrants her analyses by appeal to objectivism, nor grounds her interpretation solely in her ontology. Her own psychological processes form part of her reflections on her interpretation, but are not the warrant for it. She argues that reflexivity must include the broader context; relations not just within, but also beyond, the interview:

> One of the places where feminist and post-structuralist concerns meet is in affirming reflexivity, both as structured within research relationships (no longer colluding in the sanitization of subjectivity, identification and emotion from research encounters) and within the theory–method relation (e.g. Hollway, 1989; Walkerdine, 1986). (Ibid.: 47)

Through an analysis of interview excerpts, Burman demonstrates how the structural relations of power and discursive positioning (of interviewee and interviewer), as well as broader social relations of power and knowledge, can inform the micro-analysis of statements from an interview. She argues that drawing on the broader context in this way prevents her refusal to claim objectivity from collapsing into a complete relativization of her analysis. This theoretical position treads a careful path between naive realism and an idealism which could fall prey to relativism and immaterialism.

In the research, Burman set up an agreed exchange of interviewer and interviewee roles with the children, which allowed moments in which the children occupied powerful positions in relation to her. The concept of researcher and researched occupying particular 'subject positions' (rather than being thought of as subjects whose position is unitary and fixed) facilitates recognition of the complexity of the play of power in these exchanges. A particular statement from a boy is open to various interpretations, including that of a threat to steal Burman's bicycle. Her interpretation of it recognizes cultural adult–child relations, the specific context of the co-operative switch of 'roles', and her actual retention of certain authority despite this. She comes to understand it as a request that the topic of conversation shifts. Its implicit nature prevented the shift from being abrupt or from challenging her (supposedly relinquished) conversational control. Thus, such an analysis can conceptualize power as operating through both the manipulated (in the 'role exchange'), and the underlying, positions of researcher and researched (and show the children's understanding of this distinction), without simplifying to a model of power as summative. Burman goes 'beyond simply affirming different accounts' and warrants her own interpretation by arguing that it is produced and fixed by the power relationships (though it is not the only one warranted by them): 'The point here is not to arrive at a unique and unambiguous interpretation, but to demonstrate that an analysis of power relations privileges some interpretations over others' (ibid.: 54).

Indeed, this indeterminacy, she argues, is itself only a function of the text being taken out of its linguistic and wider discursive context. Thus, discourse analytic work which is informed by post-structuralist understandings of power can demonstrate how power enters into the interpretation, as well as the production, of discourse (ibid.). This includes how power inheres in the processes of analysis 'back in the academy' as well as in the research encounter. However, this type of micro-analysis still, inevitably, abstracts the interaction from its context to some degree, and places it in another context for viewing from other perspectives. We can be critical of a researcher's (political) judgement, and hopefully, such critical scrutiny is invited by a reflexive style that acknowledges that the analysis is an artefact, produced in a particular moment by a person occupying particular subject positions, and within the particular power relations described.

A 'new ethnography'?

Some discursive approaches employ qualified empiricism, as the above illustrates, and some ethnographic approaches recognize that representation is an active, not merely reflective, practice. So, moving beyond my oppositional account, there are now, in fact, researchers who occupy a range of epistemological positions 'within' each approach.

Ethnography has not remained untouched by the 'turn to language'. In addition to radical critiques across the disciplines of cultural studies, critical anthropology and sociology (Clough, 1992; Nencel and Pels, 1991; Probyn, 1993), there are also ethnographers who are developing a 'more textual' ethnography within sociology (Hammersley and Atkinson, 1995: 239), for instance, Plummer's (1995) sociology of sexual stories. In a chapter about the rhetorics or poetics of ethnographic writing – perhaps tellingly at the end of the book – Hammersley and Atkinson argue that an ethnography '. . . is produced as much by how we write as by the processes of data collection and analysis' (ibid.: 239). Therefore, unlike in Corsaro's much earlier work, their reflexivity does include textual production within its remit. However, they maintain a broadly objective–realist perspective, illustrated by their remark that it is 'knowledge of', rather than politics, which motivates them.

Similarly, Berry Mayall's (1996) research with children is strongly influenced by ethnography, yet – as with many others in contemporary UK childhood studies – is also informed by social constructionism. She writes of how children's lives are framed within adult understandings of what children are like, and problematizes the conceptualization of children as Other. She partially relativizes her account by recognizing that '. . . no doubt another approach would lead to another story of where and how children's lives are lived' (ibid.: 19), but retains an empiricist warrant and employs the 'up the mountain' discourse of new scientific knowledge improving on the old (Kitzinger, 1987; Rorty, 1980). Her position is neither that of radical social constructionist nor 'naive' objective–realist, but the empiricist epistemology locates her closer to realist ethnography than post-structuralism.

Mayall presents statements from children's accounts 'contextualized' within comments from interviews with adults. Inevitably it is Mayall's own conceptual frame that allows her to articulate the comments from children with those of adults. She recognizes the power imbalance between herself and the child interviewees and is modest about the extent to which it can be rectified. She even wonders: '. . . [i]f one is not a child, can one and should one attempt to understand and convey what children's experiences are?' (ibid.: 1). She describes child-friendly measures she took during the interaction (sitting on low chairs, letting children choose their companions), and she briefly reflects upon her position as author of 'children's accounts', acknowledging that it is her own argument and mentioning her hope that in future research she will co-write with participants. She therefore engages both of Probyn's (1993) two levels of reflexivity: that is, within the interaction, and in the interpretation and production of the research account. However, on the issue of textual authority, whilst she is explicit about the authority of her account *vis-à-vis* the child participants, she does not open up issues of the text's authority as one claiming an empirical warrant. This might have been explored through reflexivity about the processes by which she produced her analysis (for instance, meshing together adult and child accounts) and the rhetorical style in which it is presented.

This raises several points. First, we are reminded that how researchers present their work, including their epistemological warrants, relates to considerations of forum, format, and funding. Working within a research unit that is grant-dependent (as does Mayall) does not lend itself to radical critique of the research enterprise. Secondly, it illustrates the complexity of positions we may take up as researchers: recognizing the productivity of language, yet incorporating such insight into empiricist ethnographic methodology. The radical challenges the concept of discourse may present can be neutralized by an appropriating gesture (Burman, 1990), and the 'findings' of discourse analytic research (about interaction between researcher and 'subject') can even be taken up to 'improve' mainstream experimental work (Potter and Wetherell, 1987). Thirdly, the issue of research strategies provides an alternative way of seeing this second point: retaining an objective–realist research warrant provided Mayall with a more powerful position and may have made the particular intervention she desired more effective. However, as readers of the study we cannot actually distinguish between an unreflexive conventional style, and an account which for strategic purposes employs conventional rhetoric and '. . . deliberately conceal[s] any ostensive signs of reflexivity' (Woolgar and Ashmore, 1988: 6). Thus, Mayall's approach may either be straightforwardly realist, or her account may reflect a decision to take up the authoritative 'voice' of the researcher.

Some possibilities and pitfalls of hybrid approaches

The warrant we claim for our research knowledge, whether stated explicitly or implied by rhetorical style, is the basis of its authority. Feminists have identified the danger of 'kicking the platform from under our own feet' (Burman, 1990) by deconstructing the warrant for our preferred account, but some (Burman et al., 1996; Weedon, 1987) see feminist possibilities in the selective use of post-structuralist arguments such as those employed here. The privilege accorded empirical knowledge makes research powerful, and because the discourse of 'hearing the voices of children' is highly persuasive in contemporary UK cultural politics, ethnographic realism probably provides the most effective warrant for intervention, say, in debates about health or education services for children. So, might I adopt the discourse of voice and employ qualified empirical warrants? The sections above illustrated how empirical claims are sometimes made alongside differing degrees of reflexivity, or recognition of ethical issues surrounding a researcher's power to interpret and to produce an account and the significance of the broader cultural meanings assigned to childhood. If one refuses to employ arrogant, 'self-centred' assertions of objectivity, yet can see current political value in them, could a self-reflexive, re-presentation of others' 'voices' enable partial uptake of research authority? This would not resolve the dilemma once and for all, but neither is that desirable. Burman et al. (1996) argue that we might consider our research as a series of strategic decisions, rather than wed ourselves to any particular approach. Such commitment to an approach would be to imagine that any approach could contain, and therefore guarantee (our), politics, and would pay inadequate attention to the context which informs how our research is heard. As a temporary strategy it allows movement beyond the impasse, but is tentative and resists closure – thereby requiring its context-specific reinvention.

A strong case can be made for presenting research as 'hearing the voices of children', and children as deserving and capable of articulating their perspectives, whilst there are still important political gains for children in being granted full subject status. However, we must consider the potential risks of employing the voice rhetoric in each particular case: generalized assertions cannot be made about how it may operate. So, for each research account, we must assess whether the particular research issue or the general affirmation of children as subjects outweighs the pitfalls described above: the reification of 'the centre' at the expense of the Other; the reassertion of objective–realism; and the obscuring of the researcher's role and denial of perspective in the discourse of representation as portrayal.

Might a 'hybrid' position be possible in which the discourse of voice is employed, but subjects are not attributed authenticity outside (dominant) culture? Instead, we can present them as finding 'their voices' within and through the networks of meanings made available to them, including where they resist the dominant meanings ascribed them (as does Marks, 1996). Employing the discourse of voice risks reinforcing ideas about the psychological subject, but perhaps there are some ways of limiting this, such as by surrounding the term voice with quotation marks to indicate its metaphorical status. Referring to 'subject positions' allows for an individual to be multiply or shiftingly positioned and hence avoids complicity with the fantasy of unitary, logical beings whose experiences are stable, fixed by identity and internally coherent (Butler, 1990). We might retain the distinction in this chapter between *children's voices* themselves and the discourse of *'the voices of children'* and it may be appropriate to make this distinction explicit. The discourse may still be heard in the singular ('the voice of the child') but for this piece I did not feel the compromise of reinforcing homogeneity amongst children was necessary. The argument for the recognition of differences amongst children might appear, in the abstract, to be robust and incontestable, but there may be times when we decide this oversimplification is worthwhile. James and Prout (1990) suggest that we use the past tense in empirical narratives, because the present tense fixes children in a timeless place devoid of context thereby contributing to their objectification. These suggestions sketch an approach which could still link perspectives to social location, but would aim to avoid relying on the concept of identity in such a way as to fix and oversimplify the connection. In these ways, local empirical narratives employing the voice metaphor in a qualified way – what we might call discourse–ethnography – could provide ways of doing politics and research without grounding positions in reified identities.

However, some cautionary notes are needed: methods rest upon methodologies, which themselves embody particular epistemological positions. Given that the most crucial aspect of the context of the public research account to be considered relates to the authority necessary to intervene, the risk of a hybrid method is that it makes neither epistemological claim authoritatively. For instance, it would be problematic to present a realist warrant (such as for ethnography) within an account that has set up a non-realist framework. 'Triangulation' – using more than one method to study an object – could not employ a discursive approach alongside a non-discursive one, because triangulation assumes realism for its object. Such separation of methods from their epistemological perspectives is not only an issue of theoretical coherence: in order to take up 'the voice' of knowledge authoritatively one usually has to state one or other type of claim. If we assume that such epistemological inconsistencies may go unnoticed in a given forum, questions arise about how explicit we ought to be about our epistemological commitments.

Reflexivity

If reflexivity involves being explicit about the operation of power within the actual processes of researching and representing people (Burman, 1992; Ribbens, 1989), we become suspicious of the techniques (as well as epistemological claims) through which accounts are rendered authoritative. Researchers' power can be conceptualized as operating through multiple levels: through the hegemonic cultural perspective contained within the language we (must) use; through the subject positions we take up and are positioned within (including our deliberate claims to researcher positions); and through our particular individual relationships with participants and to our field of inquiry. In relation to research with children, the first was illustrated earlier through the adult-centrism of language and the second was explored through Burman's study, where the particularity of research with children is the conflation of adult/child with researcher/researched. The third level raises very interesting questions in relation to research with children: how do we account for our own unconscious projections and fantasies concerning children, which include those stemming from our own experiences, above and beyond culture-wide ones?

Ethnographic research raises questions about how much to listen and how much to interpret (Ribbens, 1989), but discourse analytic approaches highlight how the two cannot ultimately be separated out. If we necessarily hear others through culturally dominant meanings, an unacknowledged perspective is most likely the hegemonic one. The task of reflexivity, according to Mishler (1986), is to make explicit the theoretical basis of interpretation. Deconstructing the photographic meaning of representation, as a critique of objectivism begs, means taking greater caution over our representational claims and avoiding obscuring the perspectival nature of knowledge. This issue emerges in considering how close to keep to participants' actual words (see Kay Standing, this volume). Whilst their language and concepts will be of central interest if we wish to (and believe it is possible to) re-present (portray), we might wish, or be drawn, to employ more politically relevant terms and analytic frameworks when we want to make representation for/about children either as advocacy, or when we take it upon ourselves to intervene in what Stuart Hall (1992) calls 'the relations of representation'. The options can be understood as being about the representative role we adopt. Finch (1993) described the conflict she faced between using women's own terms, and providing the structural analysis she felt their position called for, and Ribbens (1989) argued that if we do not agree with what our participants say, we will have to decide in the context whether and how we try to respect their opinions. In research with children, this conflict is between promoting particular re/presentations of children as a social group, and re-presenting the accounts of the particular children who participated. We must be clear about when our priority is to make an admittedly flawed (say, qualified empirical) re/presentation of children's voices, and when it is for the presentation of *our* analyses, reflecting an adult, and perhaps personal, agenda within cultural politics.

The dilemma can then be located within the realm of research strategy if, from the start of a given piece of research, we are clear about whether we are engaging in representational politics, and in which case will present aspects of the research in particular ways to intervene on particular issues, or we are attempting to hear and re-present particular children's voices. I would want to be decisive about this from the outset in order to be explicit with my participants about which type of representative role I was taking, and clear, though not necessarily explicit within it, about my priorities for any particular representative act. It appears that, in either case, we might employ literal ('naive'), or reflexive, or covertly reflexive representational warrants (as discussed earlier).

Of course, the two horns of the dilemma are an ideal separation because even if we adopt an empirical warrant for placing the 'voices of children' in the public sphere, we surely retain responsibility for not re-presenting uncritically, say, a racist discourse. Hammersley and Atkinson (1995) and Parker and Burman (1993) agree that the researcher's responsibility extends to consideration of the default meanings of the context of research publication. What we consider to be progressive re/presentations could be subverted and carry undesirable meanings in another context. We cannot completely control the meanings that can be made of our research (Foucault, 1983). Not only might our careful wordings, qualifiers and warrants be lost, but another context might produce meanings that we could not have predicted. We cannot ensure our preferred readings, but we must attempt to ward off ones we believe to be oppressive. These, as well as decisions about how to frame, how to write, how and where to publish, are more than mere 'editorial control' over the accounts, and our politics are clearly highly significant, yet because of the taboo on speaking of politics in academic work (a legacy of objectivism), I have found few spaces – although the Women's Workshop has been one – for discussing these concerns. Without recognition and discussion of these dilemmas we risk relying on unexamined assumptions. Reflexive discussion amongst researchers and activists can thus inform our strategies, but is sometimes blocked by the presumption of realism. Hopefully, being reflexive enables us not simply to reproduce the cultural positions, but to ask new questions about the existence of these positions.

Reflexivity can be extended to make explicit the warrants we employ for the status of our accounts, to attempt to disassemble them where we feel it is appropriate, but perhaps taking up some positions of authority and presenting our research as knowledge where we feel it is politically expedient to do so. To demonstrate our recognition that we actively provide narratives for our material, and construct the authority of knowledge, we may use active verbs such as 'producing' (also avoiding the realist implication of pre-existing data), and might undo the specular metaphors of research which obscure the processes, deny the particularity of perspective and the differential investments in particular kinds of knowledge. However, it might sometimes be useful to *exclude* discussion of our methodological dilemmas in our finished reports. This goes against the grain of recent feminist research debates about making explicit both our practices and dilemmas, but there might be good grounds for considering which 'public' we are open with about issues; an audience of feminist and critical researchers (such as I assume here), or a broader audience (when we aim to disseminate our reports widely). Could we choose a strategy of omitting the discussion of decision-making processes or the political nature of knowledge production, that is, maintaining these conventional silences? For instance, might we deliberately employ the specular metaphors of research despite their implicit objective–realist warrants? The description earlier of different epistemological warrants within either discourse of representation suggests moments at which this might be useful. However, is it ever acceptable to present a piece of research with a contradiction between its re/presentational claims and our actual confidence in these claims? This is one of the ethical/political questions politically motivated researchers might begin to discuss more broadly. One of the contributions of a book such as this is the opportunity to voice questions and discuss the dilemmas we work with, without the same pressure to find 'answers' that writing for a broader public usually requires.

How our accounts might be heard

Being critical of the presuppositions of the voice discourse would not necessarily prevent me from insisting that 'children be heard' in a particular forum. However, when employing it, I would be concerned that my research might satisfy the demand that 'the voices of children' be heard, without actually altering *how* they are heard, or challenging the limited impact that what children say usually has.

Discursive approaches, by rejecting the possibility of escape from the cultural web of meanings, direct our attention to the consideration of what ideas we unwittingly reinforce. Given that the cultural construction of childhood is dominated by discourses of developmental psychology, there is a danger of reifying these particular ideas about children through our research. Even our strategic use of 'voice' metaphors may endorse the hegemonic notion of the rational, integrated, psychological subject (of which post-structuralist positions and some non-post-structuralist feminist positions are critical), but furthermore, these may have particular implications for children.

Children, in particular, can be closely associated with the emotions, through ideas which link them to nature, and through discourses of their development towards rationality (Walkerdine, 1988). Where rationality is privileged, 'emotionality' can disqualify them as research participants. Similarly, failure to meet the expectations of conventional interview research (of consistency, and of 'independence' from the researcher), can be interpreted as failings of children to be successful interviewees, rather than problems with the mythical notion of the 'individual' which underpins the approach. This too can function to undermine the idea that children can, or should, be 'given voice'. The concept of attitude (or opinion) involves a single, stable or consistent perspective (Potter and Wetherell, 1987). However, interviewing anyone about 'family', for instance, will elicit a range of contradictory ideas, so a contribution of discourse analytic work is to demonstrate that multiplicity, complexity and contradiction are features of our linguistic repertoire, rather than the incompetent expression, or limited cognitive sophistication, of a particular child. In conventional accounts, the ambiguity of children's talk would either not be recognized, or, if acknowledged, would be interpreted as evidence of immature logical reasoning or loss of narrative control because of its abstraction from social relationships (Burman, 1992).

For the above reasons, we may be critical of children being 'given voice' only if they can present themselves as subjects or individuals in this (Cartesian) sense, and ambivalent about some of the policy changes which require such bases for recognition. For instance, my support for the 1989 Children Act's requirement that children's wishes be heard on decisions that affect them is tempered by the knowledge that popular psychological notions about children (about fantasy, 'impressionability', reliability as witnesses) form the inescapable context within which statements will be heard. The complexity of issues that we face is illustrated by the fact that these same psychological discourses of the subject which allow some children to be heard will disallow other children, including those who present contradictory or illogical accounts and don't manage to make themselves understood by (particular) adults, in 'adults' terms'. Attaining subject status in current hegemonic discourse is fraught with risks as well as benefits for those currently on its margins.

Even after we have adopted a strategy either of engaging in representational politics or of claiming to re/present particular children, further issues may arise which repeat this question. Within either approach, particular discourses may have apparently contradictory implications. For instance, the discourse of child protection can reinforce the idea that children are weak, vulnerable and in need of (adult) protection (Kitzinger, 1990), even as they simultaneously provide help for particular children. Alternatively, there may be times when this kind of emphasis benefits children as a social group, say in securing funding for services, but is unhelpful for an individual child.

Even though 'the voices of children' discourse is deliberately plural (as mentioned above), there is the danger that invoking the category, despite taking care to speak of particular children, risks reifying children as an homogeneous social group whose 'nature' is different from that of adults. As for the category 'women', there may be times when the benefits of naming the social group outweigh the costs. Throughout this chapter I have retained 'children' as an unproblematized category in order to focus on questions of representation. I have presumed the constituency of childhood when, perhaps, the dilemmas in representing children depend crucially on *which* children.

Kay Standing (this volume) also explores the risk that our research reinforces assumptions about the research participants. There is the danger that our critiques reify what we would rather dispel if we concentrate too much on dominant meanings, with too little attention to times and places in which they are contested (Alcoff, 1988). Parker and Burman remind discourse analysts of the importance of theorizing the '. . . fluctuations and transformations in discursive relations to ward off a reading of them as unchanging' (1993: 164). This dilemma can be aligned crudely with the tension between 'gritty realism' ('showing it like it is') and 'positive images' (presenting a preferred version). It restates the alternative between re-presentation (understood as empirical, realist) or re/presentation (as an intervention in cultural politics). I have argued that, although this is a false opposition (as Walkerdine, 1990, and others have shown) and risks reasserting a truth/ideology distinction (see, for example, Barrett, 1991), it can be useful for thinking strategically about our research.

Representations in the public sphere: choosing a strategy

To summarize, our strategic decisions might include not only which approach to adopt and what representational claims to make, but also precisely how reflexive to be about these in a given forum. One could be aware of the rhetorical ploys and epistemological imperialisms by which one's textual authority is supported, but choose not to deconstruct it at a given point, in which case the strategic use of conventional research rhetoric might be indistinguishable from its unreflexive use (Woolgar and Ashmore, 1988). However, in doing so, hitherto taken-for-granted notions may have been displaced. For example, James and Prout (1996) call for children to be studied within family contexts once again because they are an '. . . important social context in which children discover [*sic*] their identities (James, 1994)' (James and Prout, 1996: 42), rather than, unthinkingly, because the family has been naturalized as the place where children exist. Another illustration might be using the discourse of 'public sphere' in order to emphasize the broader political consequences of our research, even though we might reject theoretically the idea that there can be a separate sphere of (private) meanings which are not cultural which it sometimes implies. Perhaps another illustration is my use of the notion of strategy despite its implication of rational, goal-oriented subjects (and its militaristic resonances) (Edwards and Ribbens, 1991), alongside the fact that I have deconstructed this model of the subject in relation to interviewees, whilst retaining it to speak of us decision-making researchers!

In the same way that researchers set the terms for discussion in an interview, so public debate may already be framed in such a way – again by adults – that intervening within the terms of the debate is a compromise. A sense of perspective is needed to weigh up whether an idea is worth challenging, or whether granting it research attention bolsters its status. This can be thought of as a question about whether to try to make gains within the existing terms of the debate or to challenge those terms (Alldred, 1996; Kitzinger, 1987; Prince and Hartnett, 1993). The dilemma, again, concerns the risk of reification by critiques.

How specific to research with children are the dilemmas discussed here? It seems that the theoretical issues are not specific, but apply across the board in feminist and critical research. However, the precise meanings assigned to childhood in this culture make the detail of the dilemmas of research with children particular. Ideas about marginal groups may be structured similarly in relation to the presumed centre, but do not necessarily require the same responses. It is the specific forms of these dilemmas to which researchers must attend in relation to the participants' social group, and in relation to the precise moment and location of their research intervention. Thus, the possible losses and gains of employing the discourse of hearing voices must be considered in relation to children (as a rhetorical category), and perhaps in relation to particular children, and the discourse might then be drawn on with varying degrees of literality.

Whilst much feminist research is concerned with adequately recognizing difference, representing children within research is always characterized by Otherness across the construction of a defining adult–child difference. Unlike Women's Studies, Childhood Studies has not arisen from a politics of experience (Oakley, 1994) and is conducted by adults on those who are Other to them. Children do, of course, make political representations on their own behalf, as well as on behalf of others (Hoyles, 1989), but more often through direct action, rather than through re/presentational or symbolic politics. As adults representing children we can try to recognize the ways in which our researcher status may confound and exploit our adult status, and clarify whether we are representing children in the realist, photographic sense of portrayal, or using our political perspective to make judgements about the way they are represented as we engage in struggles about 'recognition' or meaning. Referring to 'children's perspectives', naming their particularity, even though inevitably drawing into play their Otherness and our cultural centrality, we may be able to make use of the benefits this can provide in claiming that people who are marginalized 'as children' ought to be heard. Researchers interviewing children need to consider how we hear children's voices, meaning not only the approaches we employ, but also how the representations we make of their voices will be heard in the public sphere. Children's voices need to be heard alongside critical attention to the way childhood is constructed. This should then inform a more preliminary question, which, as Alderson (1995) notes, is often bypassed: not how, but whether the research should be done, and, I would add, not just how, but whether each particular re/presentational act should be made.

References

Alanen, Leena (1990) 'Rethinking socialization, the family and childhood', in P.A. Adler, P. Adler, N. Mandell and S. Cahill (eds), *Sociological Studies of Child Development: A Research Manual*. Greenwich, CT: JAI Press.

Alcoff, Linda (1988) 'Cultural feminism versus post-structuralism: the identity crisis in feminist theory', *Signs*, 13 (3): 405–6.

Alderson, Priscilla (1995) *Listening to Children*. London: Barnados.

Alldred, Pam (1996) '"Fit to parent"? Developmental psychology and "non traditional families"', in E. Burman, P. Alldred, C. Bewley, B. Goldberg, C. Heenan, D. Marks, J. Marshall, K. Taylor, R. Ullah and S. Warner, *Challenging Women: Psychology's Exclusions, Feminist Possibilities*. Buckingham: Open University Press.

Barrett, Michèlle (1991) *The Politics of Truth: From Marx to Foucault*. Cambridge: Polity.

Brannen, Julia and O'Brien, Margaret (1996) 'Introduction', in J. Brannen and M. O'Brien (eds), *Children in Families: Research and Policy*. London: Falmer Press.

Bruner, Jerome S., Jolly, A. and Sylva, Kathy (1976) *Play: its Role in Development and Evolution*. Harmondsworth: Penguin Education.

Burman, Erica (1990) 'Differring with deconstruction: a feminist critique', in I. Parker and J. Shotter (eds), *Deconstructing Social Psychology*. London: Routledge.

Burman, Erica (1992) 'Feminism and discourse in developmental psychology: power, subjectivity and interpretation', *Feminism & Psychology*, 2 (1): 45–60.

Burman, Erica (1994) *Deconstructing Developmental Psychology*. London: Routledge.

Burman, Erica, Alldred, Pam, Bewley, Catherine, Goldberg, Brenda, Heenan, Colleen, Marks, Deborah, Marshall, Jane, Taylor, Karen, Ullah, Robina and Warner, Sam (1996) *Challenging Women: Psychology's Exclusions, Feminist Possibilities*. Buckingham: Open University Press.

Butler, Judith (1990) *Gender Trouble: Feminism and the Subversion of Identity*. London: Routledge.

Clough, Patricia Ticineto (1992) *The End(s) of Ethnography: From Realism to Social Criticism*. London: Sage.

Corsaro, William A. (1981) 'Entering the child's world – research strategies for field entry and data collection in a preschool setting', in J.L. Green and C. Wallat (eds), *Ethnography and Language in Education Settings*. Norwood, NJ: Ablex Publishing.

Corsaro, William, A. (1986) 'Discourse processes within peer culture: from a constructivist to an interpretive approach', in P.A. Adler and P. Adler (eds), *Sociological Studies of Child Development* (vol. 1). Greenwich, CT: JAI Press.

Diamond, Irene and Quinby, Lee (1988) *Feminism and Foucault: Reflections on Resistance*. Boston, MA: Northeastern University Press.

Edwards, Rosalind and Ribbens, Jane (1991) 'Meanderings around "strategy": a research note on strategic discourse in the lives of women', *Sociology*, 25 (3): 477–89.

Finch, Janet (1993) '"It's great to have someone to talk to": ethics and politics of interviewing women', in M. Hammersley (ed.), *Social Research: Philosophy, Politics and Practice*. London: Sage.

Foucault, Michel (1983) Preface, in G. Deleuze and F. Guattari, *Anti-Oedipus: Capitalism and Schizophrenia* (translated by R. Hurley, M. Seem, and H.R. Lane). Minneapolis, MN: University of Minnesota Press.

Fraser, Nancy (1995) 'From redistribution to recognition? Dilemmas of justice in a "post-socialist" age', *New Left Review*, 212 (July/August): 68–93.

Fraser, Nancy and Nicholson, Linda (1990) 'Social criticism without philosophy', in L. Nicholson (ed.), *Feminism/Postmodernism*. New York: Routledge.

Grossberg, Lawrence (1989) 'On the road with three ethnographers', *Journal of Communication Inquiry*, 13 (2): 23–6.

Hall, Stuart (1992) 'New ethnicities', in J. Donald and A. Rattansi (eds), *'Race', Culture and Difference*. London: Sage in association with the Open University.

Hammersley, Martyn and Atkinson, Paul (1995) *Ethnography: Principles in Practice* (2nd edition). London: Routledge.

Hoyles, Martin (1989) *The Politics of Childhood*. London: Journeyman Press.

James, Allison and Prout, Alan (1990) 'Re-presenting childhood: time and transition in the study of childhood', in A. James and A. Prout (eds) *Constructing and Reconstructing Childhood: Contemporary Issues in the Sociological Study of Childhood*. London: Falmer Press.

James, Allison and Prout, Alan (1996) 'Strategies and structures: towards a new perspective on children's experiences of family life', in J. Brannen and M. O'Brien (eds), *Children in Families: Research and Policy*. London: Falmer Press.

Kitzinger, Celia (1987) *The Social Construction of Lesbianism*. London: Sage.

Kitzinger, Jenny (1990) 'Who are you kidding? Children, power and the struggle against sexual abuse', in A. James and A. Prout (eds), *Constructing and Reconstructing Childhood: Contemporary Issues in the Sociological Study of Childhood*. London: Falmer Press.

Mandell, Nancy (1986) 'Peer interaction in day-care settings: implications for social cognition', in P.A. Adler and P. Adler (eds), *Sociological Studies of Child Development* (vol. 1). Greenwich, CT: JAI Press.

Mandell, Nancy (1991) 'The least-adult role in studying children', in F.C. Waksler (ed.), *Studying the Social Worlds of Children: Sociological Readings*. London: Falmer Press.

Marks, Deborah (1993) 'Case-conference analysis and action research', in E. Burman and I. Parker (eds), *Discourse Analytic Research: Repertoires and Readings of Texts in Action*. London: Routledge.

Marks, Deborah (1996) 'Constructing a narrative: moral discourse and young people's experience of exclusion', in E. Burman, G. Aitken, P. Alldred, R. Allwood, T. Billington, B. Goldberg, A.J. Gordo-Lopez, C. Heenan, D. Marks and S. Warner, *Psychology, Discourse, Practice: From Regulation to Resistance*. London: Taylor and Francis.

Mayall, Berry (ed.) (1994) *Children's Childhoods: Observed and Experienced*. London: Falmer Press.

Mayall, Berry (1996) *Children, Health and the Social Order*. Buckingham: Open University Press.

Mishler, Ernest G. (1986) *Research Interviewing: Context and Narrative*. Cambridge, MA: Harvard University Press.

Nencel, Lorraine and Pels, Peter (eds) (1991) *Constructing Knowledge, Authority and Critique in the Social Sciences*. London: Sage.

Oakley, Ann (1981) 'Interviewing women: a contradiction in terms?', in H. Roberts (ed.), *Doing Feminist Research*. London: Routledge and Kegan Paul.

Oakley, Ann (1994) 'Women and children first and last: parallels and differences between children's and women's studies', in B. Mayall (ed.), *Children's Childhoods: Observed and Experienced*. London: Falmer Press.

O'Brien, Margaret, Alldred, Pam and Jones, Deborah (1996) 'Children's constructions of family and kinship', in J. Brannen and M. O'Brien (eds), *Children in Families: Research and Policy*. London: Falmer Press.

Parker, Ian (1992) *Discourse Dynamics*. London: Routledge.

Parker, Ian and Burman, Erica (1993) 'Against discursive imperialism, empiricism and constructionism: thirty-two problems with discourse analysis', in E. Burman and I. Parker (eds), *Discourse Analytic Research: Repertoires and Readings of Texts in Action*. London: Routledge.

Patai, Daphne (1991) 'US academics and third world women: is ethical research possible?', in S. Berger Gluck and D. Patai (eds), *Women's Words: The Feminist Practice of Oral History*. London: Routledge.

Plummer, Ken (1995) *Telling Sexual Stories: Power, Change and Social Worlds*. London: Routledge.

Potter, Jonathan and Wetherell, Margaret (1987) *Discourse and Social Psychology*. London: Sage.

Prince, Jane and Hartnett, Oonagh (1993) 'From "psychology constructs the female" to "fe/males construct psychology"', *Feminism and Psychology*, 3 (2): 219–25.

Probyn, Elspeth (1993) *Sexing the Self: Gendered Positions in Cultural Studies*. London: Routledge.

Qvortrup, Jens (1987) 'Introduction: The sociology of childhood', *International Journal of Sociology*, 17 (3): 3–37.

Ribbens, Jane (1989) 'Interviewing: an "unnatural situation"?', *Women's Studies International Forum*, 12 (6): 579–92.

Roche, Jeremy (1996) 'The politics of children's rights', in J. Brannen and M. O'Brien (eds), *Children in Families: Research and Policy*. London: Falmer Press.

Rorty, Richard (1980) *Philosophy and the Mirror of Nature*. Oxford: Blackwell.

Rose, Nikolas (1985) *The Psychological Complex*. London: Routledge.

Scottish Law Commission (1992) *The Report on Family Law* (No 135). Edinburgh: HMSO.

Spender, Dale (1985) *Man Made Language*. London: Routledge.

Spivak, Gayatri Chakravorty (1988) *In Other Worlds: Essays in Cultural Politics*. London: Routledge.

Waksler, Frances Chaput (1986) 'Studying children: phenomenological insights', *Human Studies*, 9 (1): 71–82.

Waksler, Frances Chaput (ed.) (1991) *Studying the Social Worlds of Children: Sociological Readings*. London: Falmer Press.

Walkerdine, Valerie (1988) *The Mastery of Reason: Cognitive Development and the Production of Rationality*. London: Routledge.

Walkerdine, Valerie (1990) 'Some day my prince will come: young girls and the preparation for adolescent sexuality', in V. Walkerdine, *Schoolgirl Fictions*. London: Verso.

Weedon, Chris (1987) *Feminist Practice and Poststructuralist Theory*. Oxford: Basil Blackwell.

Woolgar, Steve and Ashmore, Malcolm (1988) 'The next step: an introduction to the reflexive project', in S. Woolgar (ed.), *Knowledge and Reflexivity: New Frontiers in the Sociology of Knowledge*. London: Sage.

10   Re/constructing Research Narratives

Self and Sociological Identity in Alternative Settings

Maxine Birch

In this chapter I discuss my experiences of research, registered for a PhD, as my journey of self-discovery in a sociological world. During this journey I experienced many dilemmas as I moved from a participant in the fieldwork research to the analysis and writing up of my research as a text (Birch, 1997). My perception of this journey derives from the way I have chosen to understand and interpret the data collected. When I started this journey I did not know that a mirror image would emerge between the substantive issue and the research process. I will briefly outline how I constructed the substantive issue before going on to consider how this was mirrored in the research process. I had chosen to explore the concept of self-discovery in alternative therapy groups. I had identified four such groups that promised to help participants know themselves. This knowing was enabled through a variety of techniques, which all depended upon a fundamental psychotherapeutic message. The message was to uncover, release and express emotions, and the result of this expression was perceived to be a deeper understanding of who you are. The achievement of this deeper understanding was argued to bring about positive changes to the individual through the presentation of healing and personal growth. Thus I defined the concept of self-discovery as the process each individual undertook in the groups in order to know her or himself.

During the stage of analysis I consolidated my way of interpreting and representing the data I had collected from three main sources. These were, first, my participation in the therapy groups, secondly, interviews with other participants of the groups, and, thirdly, interviews with the facilitators of these groups and other facilitators of comparable groups. Reading the transcribed interviews brought together my understanding of concepts such as narrative, auto/biography and stories that I had come across in the social sciences (Bruner, 1995; Corradi, 1991; Josselen and Lieblich, 1993; Nash, 1990; Plummer, 1995; Stanley, 1992). This way of reading the transcriptions represented a specific way of appreciating self-identity. This can be briefly summarized here by the term 'life stories', the telling about yourself, which involves the selection and organization of experiences to be recounted within a social setting. The social setting may frame this selection and organization in a particular way, as illustrated by the setting I had chosen with the alternative therapy groups. It is the telling of life stories that gives the individual a sense of who she or he is, a sense of self. I could use many terms here to illustrate the dynamic relationship between the constitution and construction of such telling about yourself, for example, it involves the relationship between the inner and the outer, the public and the personal, and the social and the psychological. The vital ingredient of this dynamic process is the reflexivity that informs a sense of self. Finally I arrived at the conclusion of a 'self in dialogue' (Burkitt, 1991; Wiley, 1995), to illustrate the interactions which construct life stories and inform a sense of self on many levels, within each individual and between individuals.

Having established the telling of stories and the construction of a sense of self-identity in the alternative therapy groups, I recognized that this was also applicable to the research process. I was selecting and organizing the sociological story that I told within a specific frame of PhD research. As I wrote my story of the research during the final stage of 'being here' I was constructing and informing my own sociological identity. So here I tell of my journey into this research process, from the theoretical exploration at the outset, *going there*, and the participation in the field, *being there*, to the final stages of analysis and writing up, *being here*. I argue that this final stage of 'being here' becomes a personal, private space even though I seek to create a more publicly acceptable story for my sociological audience. To me the dilemma of producing sociological knowledge from the stories of others remains both a personal and public dilemma. First, as it has taught me to select and assemble a representation that achieves a more prominent story, which covers the construction of the research process, and, secondly, this representation continues to support the main stream orthodoxy of what is considered to be acceptable knowledge.

The research journey

My journey in social research involved many different stages, which can be clearly identified in a web of relationships with myself at the centre. I am the research medium. I am the clear common denominator that has remained both constant and in flux as the many facets of my life criss-cross, each containing the possibility of understanding what I am doing in a different way.

Going there is the theoretical exploration before the field, that places the researcher in a particular position when entering, defining and gaining access into the field of inquiry. This stage involves the selection of how to understand, the researcher's way of knowing, and thus determines how the questions are asked. *Being there* in the field is the actual participation, involvement and relationships engaged and made. In the approach I used, these two stages have a distinct progression, from the theoretical preparation to the fieldwork, but the boundary between the two remains fluid as the researcher moves from the field research world to the academic research world. The moving between the two worlds of being a researcher in the field and then being a researcher in the academic world produces many contradictions and tensions. However, I suggest that in these two stages, in both worlds of academia and participation, I had a central pivot through my social interactions that occurred throughout both worlds. I was a participant in concrete social relationships in both areas. Yet the final stage of the research is predominantly located in an area that negates these social relationships.

Being here is the stage of me and my computer, the creation of a text; here the practical research world is distanced, and in many cases, like my own, any major involvement in the academic world is minimized, as time is taken to produce the final piece of work. Therefore the last processes of analysis and writing up become located primarily within my own private working space. The stories that I have gathered from others in the field now become my own.

Going there

Preparing my way

In my personal life I wanted to know more about myself, in order to seek satisfaction and happiness from my life. I had experienced many life changes, finally resulting in the breakdown of my marriage. Therefore I sought a counsellor. My access into this therapeutic world was an easy step for me as this type of support was familiar; I had friends involved both as recipients and as trained professionals. In entering this counselling relationship I became a part of a therapeutic culture reflected in contemporary social theories (Cohen and Taylor, 1992; Foucault, 1988; Gergen, 1991; Giddens, 1991). I belonged to this therapeutic culture in many ways, through my life opportunities and experiences, my education and my social networks. The counselling relationship taught me a different way of telling my 'life stories'. The psychotherapeutic emphasis upon myself as the creator of my experiences and on self-responsibility changed the stories I told about myself. My interpretations of my experiences were no longer just a result of circumstances but became my active creation of what I wanted. Continuing this exploration of myself, I started a course in Japanese massage, Shiatsu. Here my body became the main focus of understanding myself. I was taught an Eastern understanding of the body perceived as a field of energy. From this perspective I could understand my feelings in reference to a stream of energy that could become blocked and sluggish, or free and flowing. These two aspects of my social life, the new social networks I was involved in and the new knowledge I had learned, developed a certain awareness in beginning my research question.

My selection of the question

I had originally set a research question concerning the development of holistic health and general practitioners. This seemed in keeping with the field of inquiry and with the discipline of the sociology of health, where my post of teaching assistant was located and funded. My initial stage of searching the literature associated with holistic health was organized around the key words of complementary, alternative, health, medicine and therapy. During this search I came across research that showed how GPs in California had changed their orthodox medical practices for a holistic emphasis, where numerous complementary /alternative health services were provided alongside Western medicine. The GPs explained how this change towards holistic med- icine was not a response to consumer demand but took place because of their own personal experiences. Their way of understanding and seeing them- selves had been changed by life events that brought them to question certain values (Goldstein et al., 1987). This explanation of personal change comple- mented another central theme that underpinned many of the studies in this area: the understanding of 'the self' as a focal point for any personal change. I found definitions and explanations of 'the self' in approaches to comple- mentary medicine that are mainly physically orientated, as well as psychological and paranormal practices found in the area of alternative ther- apies (Fulder and Munroe, 1985; Gaier, 1991; West, 1992). The self appeared to be the shared concept in such a diverse area.

Continuing my literature search I noted the theoretical recognition of the psychological practices in this alternative health field, but found no empirical studies. I found the psychotherapeutic area was ignored in a recent report from the British Medical Association: their understanding of this area was divided into the physical recognition of diagnosis and treatment and the use of faith in 'miscellaneous systems of healing' (Saks, 1992: 225). This lack of attention to psychotherapeutic influences contradicted my own experiences as well as the theoretical proposition that the role of therapy is increasing in our contemporary life (Gergen, 1991; Giddens, 1991). It was because of my own personal experiences that I was aware of friends who attended self-discovery groups and of where to find information about such groups. It was these per- sonal relationships that provided me with a practical research area.

My involvement with how to research

Before entering the field, I wanted to understand how I could put social research into practice. Could I just go there and see what happened? The more I read concerning ethnography (Agar, 1980; Atkinson, 1990; Hammersley, 1992; Okely and Callaway, 1992), qualitative methodology (Hammersley, 1989; Silverman, 1985), feminist practice (Smith, 1989; Stanley, 1990; Stanley and Wise, 1983, 1993), and postmodern influences (Gifford and Marans, 1986; Lather, 1991), the more I became certain that I could be in the field in a way that acknowledged the research process and welcomed the subjectivity of the researcher. In particular I felt that the concept of autobi- ography (Okely and Callaway, 1992; Ribbens, 1993) and auto/biography (Stanley, 1992, 1993) provided me with a practical tool to bring the process of constructing research to the surface. The concept of autobiography as 'bring- ing yourself to language' (Benstock, 1988) reflected the ontological position of telling life stories about yourself and its relationship to developing a sense of self. The telling of life stories informs a sense of self-identity, where individuals negotiate at all times where they are and who they are (MacIntrye, 1985; Taylor, 1989). This understanding is reflected in Giddens' discussion of the 'reflexive project of the self' (1991: 244) and underpins the presentation and explanation of a social self (Burkitt 1991). The concept of auto/biography, developed in the work of Liz Stanley (1992, 1993) and the British Sociological Association Study Group in this area, offered me the possibility of using the hyphenated connection of auto/biography to distinguish the essential connection between the stories of others and the researcher's own story.

The recognition of my research story alongside others is a central addition to sociological understanding. Following this approach I hoped to use auto/biography not as a narcissistic exploration of myself but as a vital sociological tool necessary to understand the social within each individual and how social research is a social construction. It is through the individual's autobiography that her relationship to public or dominant discourses can be explored. How are knowledge structures retold in the individual's own life stories? It is through my autobiography of the research process that my relationship to sociological discourses can be explored in the construction of the research story that I tell. Hence my understanding of auto/biography gave me a methodology of how to record my experiences in the field, how to place my story of the research process alongside my observational story of the groups and the stories told to me by the facilitators and participants. However, I had set myself a complicated task that could sound all too simple in theory. The mirror image was beginning to emerge. Auto/biography became my way of exploring the construction of self-identity in the research groups and the start of informing my own sociological identity.

Being there

The research world

My fieldwork involved my participation in four alternative therapy groups. These four groups all shared the promise that emotional release – expression of the deepest feelings – can be uncovered to show an inner self. This inner self was described as containing a deeper recognition of the truth, the ability to experience yourself as more real in contrast to a feeling of superficiality experienced in the social world, and was said to provide a spiritual connection with life beyond the social milieu. The characteristics that define this experience of an inner self, realness, truth and spirituality, are said to give a deeper understanding of life and the potential for change at an individual and social level (Birch, 1996).

From an initial exploration of the approaches of the groups, I arrived at the concept of self-discovery to illustrate how this promise was realized in the groups. The approaches to discovering yourself in the groups varied, but exhibited a central core in the incorporation of Western psychology and Eastern beliefs. The psychotherapeutic work of Jung, Reich and Adler was combined with the Eastern beliefs of Buddhism, Chinese medical philosophy and Eastern body work such as yoga, to encourage an inner reflection and examination of yourself. The groups occurred over various times, from meeting one night a week for 12 weeks or meeting one weekend a month for a year, to a meeting called at seasonal festivals, usually every three months. Two groups had a mixed gender membership, approximately half women and half men, and one group was for women only. The fourth group, which I attended in order to compare the approach used, was a weekend workshop open to both men and women, but at this particular weekend only women attended. Members of the groups were middle-class as I defined it through access to higher education and professional jobs. However, many members could also be located within a lower income bracket because of unemployment and the choice to develop different lifestyles such as voluntary work and self-employment in this field of alternative health. Exceptions to this image of a middle-class membership were two working-class men who both had a background in the building trade, but who had worked and educated themselves in the area of psychotherapies for many years. This experiential aspect of learning was a major emphasis in the process of discovering yourself. It was your own inner feelings that were considered to be the most important part of this learning process.

Access

My access to the groups reflected the networking system of this alternative area. I was introduced to numerous sources of possible research material and was able to select the four groups that shared the promise of self-discovery. Negotiating access within these groups was especially facilitated by my use of the term auto/biography. In the beginning I used this term of auto/biography to describe my research aims, to acknowledge the subjective by being part of the research story, and also to provide a process where the members of the groups felt that they had some say in how the research was produced. This is where my first realization of difference between my two worlds arose. In my speech 'autobiography' remained one word: I did not display the hyphenated distinction between my story and the stories of others. Even if I had, at this stage it would not have made any difference, as I did not understand the full implications of the final stage that I discuss later on in this chapter. The facilitators and members of the groups interpreted 'autobiography' to mean my own story of self-discovery in the groups; in other words I would be my own research subject. This reveals the mismatch between the everyday understanding of 'autobiography', where I am the research subject telling my own story, and auto/biography in the sociological world, that places the emphasis upon the stories of others as research subjects with myself as the researcher. This particular dilemma illustrates the way that academic language becomes removed from its everyday use (an issue discussed further in the chapter by Kay Standing in this volume).

Moving between the two worlds of academic life and the research groups permitted me to use the mismatch between autobiography and auto/biography to my advantage. Academically, 'auto/biography' gave me the theoretical support that I needed, the perception of intellectualism. In the field, 'autobiography' gave me the ability to stress the importance of feelings and emotions, my personal involvement. My research field notes questioned this research role. 'Where is my research role'? 'Are the relationships I am developing with the other group members friendships'? 'Do they really know what I am doing'? These questions expressed my feeling of being a fraud. It was hard to use my membership of these groups, which encouraged intimacy and trust, as research data. Nevertheless, the reflexivity highlighted in my field notes did not hinder my actual participation in the social relationships I had made in either the therapy groups or at the university. It was through concrete interaction in social relationships that I was able to return to be 'myself', either as just another member of the group or the postgraduate student. I was able to resort to just 'being there' in either space because I was relating to others. This was my first hint of the difference I would find in the final stage: the difference between my feelings of being involved, and then retrospectively and reflexively forming some textual representation of this involvement. My initial concern of being an over-involved researcher was alleviated by the theoretical development I had made in the stage of 'going there'. Texts on qualitative research that emphasized the values of reflexivity and the awareness of the research as a social construction gave me permission to try and be myself (Douglas, 1985; Holstein and Gubrium, 1995; Lather, 1991; Stanley and Wise, 1993). In the movement between my academic world and my fieldwork, I could be myself and return to my everyday understanding because values and feelings had been placed on the research agenda. I did not need such words as 'professional stranger' (Agar, 1980), 'subjects', 'collaborators' or 'informants' (Okely and Callaway, 1992) to describe a research relationship, but I was able to refer to friends and group members of which I was one. The term I adopted to satisfy the demands of both being in the research world and present in the academic setting is 'participant'. With this term I am also included; we are all participants. However, it was only in the later stage of 'being here' that I realized we are all not participants of the same world, at the same time.

Being here

Creating a different world

I am now able to look at these different stages of the research process in relation to my interpretation of the data. As previously mentioned, I have been drawn towards an explanation and understanding of narratives and stories. Philosophical, psychological and sociological theories and research have developed a clear connection with the telling of life stories or narrative and understanding social life (Josselen and Lieblich, 1993; MacIntrye, 1985;

Plummer, 1995; Ricoeur, 1992; Somers, 1994). The central link made in this area is how the telling of such stories informs and constitutes a sense of self-identity, as illustrated by the attention towards autobiography and auto/biography (Bruner, 1995; Griffiths, 1995; Stanley, 1992). Whichever term is used (stories, narratives, autobiographies) the same end result is perceived: the telling about yourself and your experiences is the assembly of life episodes that the researcher can use to show how individuals see themselves and place their understanding of social life. This understanding is easily recognized from the interactionist and feminist tradition that has prioritized listening to people's accounts and has attempted to present any interpretation as closely as possible to the original meaning. In current social theories this focus upon stories and narrative assembly adds the dimension of listening to the way, the style and nature of the whole set of social relations engaged with such telling and listening (Josselen and Lieblich, 1993; Plummer, 1995; Somers, 1994).

I have drawn on these academic theories to explore the alternative therapy groups I participated in during my research. My analysis of these groups argues that self-identity stories are reconstructed in these groups (Birch, 1997). Past, present and anticipated future experiences are placed in the context of the groups, which provide different relationships and reference points by which to organize the experiences told. Therefore the self-identity stories of the participants change through the learning experiences in the groups. As I stated earlier, I did not know that a mirror image would emerge in this research project. As I have progressed and learned more sociological knowledge, and my social relations within the sociological setting have become more established, the stories I tell continue to inform myself about my sociological identity. Just as the systematic reflexivity used in the alternative therapy groups encouraged the reinterpretion and retelling of experiences, so has my journey into this research given me a systematic reflection of where I want to locate my sociological understanding.

'Being here' describes the stage where the analysis and writing of the thesis transforms the research data. In the first part of the research, my physical movement from the academic world to the research world and back again permitted me to be in social relationships that I argued should not be ignored by the research process. In the final stage, these social relationships are interpreted as data. It is the stage of analysis that makes a break in these social relationships. I suggest that it is here that the sociologist has to return to herself. The selection and editing of what is told, how it is told and what is left out enters her own inner dialogue to form what is said, being here now. To understand this further I will now briefly describe the analytical stages I undertook.

Analysis as the first step in creating a textual world

From the recorded interviews, I transcribed each word on the tapes. This textual representation was the first transformation that left out many aspects of what had happened: how the interview felt, the unspoken meanings shared through gesture, the relationship that had developed between myself and the interviewee. I was left with a text. While I was transcribing I was often transported back to the setting in which the interview occurred. I remembered simple images, from sitting in my kitchen having a cup of coffee, to more complex feelings such as empathy and a sense of closeness. Through the act of transcribing I had relived the telling. The final transcribed text offered a different sort of reading, more distanced as if the words had been told by anyone. Changing the interview into a textual representation created the jump I needed to enter the world of analysis, which presented me with the greatest challenge that any of the research stages had encompassed until then.

In preparation for this stage I had attended a course on qualitative analysis, and had selected 'how to do it' texts that gave me more insight into what exactly is supposed to happen (Dey, 1993; Fielding and Fielding, 1992). I had inquired into computer analysis (Fielding and Lee, 1991), and succeeded in getting the department to order a copy of 'NUDIST' (Non-numerical Unstructured Data Indexing Searching and Theorising) to analyse my data. At the end of all this information, I was stuck; all I could do was read and recognize the recurring themes that appeared. From the transcriptions I found I was reading a definite whole, but if I started cutting and splicing, linking and indexing, I felt that the nature of the story and the social setting disappeared. Therefore I started a thematic analysis from the facilitators' interviews where I identified the key theme of self-discovery as a journey with a path to follow. From the recognition of a self-discovery journey I was able to identify and place the transcripts and what happened in the groups into an analysis of stories as put forward in Ken Plummer's invitation to a sociology of stories (1995).

Once the nature of the story had been interpreted, it felt easier to separate sections as the whole remained present. Therefore, from the whole I continued to explore themes, knowledge influences, social influences and narrative structure in great depth. I developed several analytical strategies and concepts to illustrate differences and similarities in the content and structure of each story. For example, I used the descriptive terms of major and minor keys, taken from their musical meaning, to illustrate a different quality in hearing the private intimate details of life events and a more public presentation of self-discovery. This public presentation involved the definition of an inner self. The detailed investigation of the narrative structure of defining this inner self in each story revealed a distinct pattern of telling about an inner experience, placing this in a frame of reference, and coming to a conclusion about what this revealed to yourself. However, the minute details of this structure were not central in the understanding of the process of story telling engaged in within the groups. It was the structure of the whole story that kept the person telling the story and kept the social setting in focus.

This analysis fitted with the data in an ideal way. What had happened in the groups was analysed by the strategies of story telling identified by Plummer (1995). I was able to bring my field notes into the analysis and explore the central role of the 'confessional' in transforming a personal emotional episode into a shared group story. I found I was constructing a meeting place, between the theoretical way of knowing social life, life stories and self-identity, and the experiences of the alternative therapy groups. It is this construction of a 'fit' that became a personal, private decision of interpretation. It provided me with the academic credibility but also felt right. I felt that this focus on story telling echoed my own experiences in the field on a personal intuitive level.

My experiences in the stage of analysis echo many of the issues raised in Dorothy Smith's discussion of how feminism has enabled 'being there', but it still has not provided us with a way of producing a different form of sociological knowledge when interpreting data:

> . . . we have developed methods of working with women that are fully consultative and open, (yet) a moment comes after the talk has been inscribed as texts and become data when it must be worked up as sociology. (Smith 1989: 35)

It is this 'working up' of data into disciplinary knowledge that changes the data from the original. As a process, this transformation inevitably leaves some things out and places a greater emphasis upon a different way of knowing about social life. Often the issues that are neglected, such as subjectivity and the research process, become a small part of the end product that seeks to be a sociological representation. The open responsive stance available in the fieldwork becomes a private act of selecting and organizing the research story. This is where the act of writing up enabled by the analysis begins to reconstruct the original narratives heard in the field. This is described by Dorothy Smith as the textual forms of discourse that change the location of the original experience.

> A central problem for a feminist sociology is the continual and powerful translation back of our beginnings in women's experience, whether our own or others, into the textual forms of the discourse placing the reading and the writing subject outside the experience from which she starts. (Smith 1989: 35)

By exploring in detail my experience of this stage of analysis, I hope to show how this central problem, which I extend from Dorothy Smith's definition of feminist sociology, is the creation of a textual world. Sociology has a distinct textual world in the representation of ethnography (Atkinson, 1990, 1992), which creates a systematic, analytical understanding of how others construct their own understanding. In this way textual explanations constructed in the academic setting are contrasted with those shown in journalistic explanations or dramaturgical scripts of social life. This raises the question of how the social researcher tells about others in a way that seeks a social science explanation in contrast to a description or portrayal of social life that any good journalist or playwright could produce. For many in this academic setting, explanations of social life demand a judgement of seriousness and reliability founded upon the understanding of objectivity. Dorothy Smith (1989) describes how this understanding of objectivity in the social science world pervades all understanding and judgements of what makes good research, valid research, reliable research. Thus it is precisely because the understanding of 'autobiography' has become removed from its everyday understanding to become a sociological concept of auto/biography that it has come to be accepted as a serious sociological way of providing explanations of social life. Not only has such a presentation of auto/biography been removed from an everyday understanding, but it can now only be portrayed in text; the solidus does not exist in speech. It is because story telling has received the credibility of analysis that empirical explanations of life stories can be made. The telling of stories is not just regarded as a social event but is analysed with strategies of story telling, and as the consumption and production of stories. In this way the telling of stories becomes sociologically acceptable. I suggest that it is these strategies of analysis upon which the whole notion of sociological understanding depends; they are at the heart of the sociological text. Without such analytical devices our text could and would resemble many others.

Intellectual concepts

I am now going to introduce two concepts I developed and used to embed the analysis of the transcribed interviews and observation of the groups into a sociological understanding: *framing* and *social practice*. These concepts provided a simple way of describing the different (albeit connected) influences in an individual's life that are knowledge and the practice of this understanding in a social setting. By looking at what is learned and how this learning is placed in concrete social relationships I could illustrate the ways that the individual understands. It was with some regret that I found myself developing my own sociological jargon, but it is a strategy that I also engaged in willingly as it gave me the means to construct my sociological way of knowing.

Framing   During my thematic analysis of the self-discovery story I was able to identify what body of knowledge had influenced the development of a particular theme. For example, I was able to recognize the theme of connection from Buddhist philosophy, and to explore how this had been incorporated into the psychotherapeutic message of discovering yourself.

Social practice   By looking at the social practice of story telling, I was also able to explore another way of understanding the telling of the self-discovery story. The social practice of the alternative therapy groups showed the importance of relationships within the group, and explored the importance of belonging to a group. In this way my distinction between framing and social practice enabled me to present the untold parts of the story telling, the concrete physical relationships of being a member of the group.

Yet this recognition of the social practice of telling stories still becomes a textual construction. I return to my suggestion that the stage of 'being here' remains void of such tangible social relationships, and that my analytical concepts of framing and social practice are an artificial device imposed on the data to seek sociological credence. 'Working up', as identified by Smith

(1989), is the analysis of data; that is the retelling of the research story in a new frame and social practice. Stories, narratives, accounts, do not remain unchanged, but are edited, rewritten and interpreted away from the social relationships in which they occurred. Within this process of 'working up' data into a sociological research account, the interpretation depends more and more on my own inner dialogue, on finding my own way of telling my story of others. It is the recognition that my analytical stages applied to the data could also be applied to my production of the research story that finally formed a mirror image for me.

The mirror image

I was able to begin to write about the stories told to me because I was telling my story of their stories. As my analysis developed, and my story of the research participants became established, I found I was disappearing from the text, despite my original auto/biographical emphasis. In order to place myself back into the story, I had to recognize that the analytical stage of story telling looks at how stories are produced and consumed. This recognition enabled me to look at my own production and consumption of my sociological story, the research process. The analysis of telling stories enabled me to bring my construction of the research world into text, to build a bridge between the fieldwork and my representation. The analytical concepts of framing and social practice could be applied in the same way to the research story I was producing. As I have discussed earlier in the chapter, my stage of 'going there' was vital in developing a distinct approach, to produce a way of knowing that I wanted to develop. Therefore, on one level of analysis, I could look at how the self-discovery stories were framed, and on another, show how my own sociological knowledge was framed by the selection and assimilation of sociological theory into the research story told. I could also recognize the social practice of postgraduate research in the academic setting. Hence my concepts of framing and social practice applied to the data could also be applied to the research process. Because I was trying to present a serious explanation to a sociological audience it was important that the analysis I constructed met some sort of shared understanding of objectivity. I had been able to distance myself, to develop an intellectual, systematic way of dealing with the data. I was able to take the words of others and place them into my own interpretation. This was the mirror image, and the recognition that I was also producing a story eased my conscience of transforming the data away from its original setting. I was able to say, yes, this is my story of others, and this is how my story of those others is produced.

From this I question what had happened to my original hopes and ideals of creating a research environment where my story would be told alongside the stories of others? These ideals did not disappear. In an effort to meet this ideal I did send back my initial stages of analysis to many of the facilitators for their comments. However, to continue this sort of participation throughout the analysis became too difficult with the constraints of time and finance. Nevertheless, I also suggest that the production of my own story was a question of authorial authority. The more I progressed into the analysis and the writing up, and so into my own personal, private space, the more I became aware of the emergence of my own sociological identity. I was the author who was choosing to make certain arguments and explanations. Hence it is the recognition of the mirror image that was my own inner journey of self-discovery. The more I told my sociological story the more my sense of self as a sociologist was discovered. This does not negate the existence of another story that could be told about my participation in the self-discovery groups, which have taught me a great deal about other aspects of myself. However, this story is for another time and another audience. In the research story the identification of how my sociological identity is formed is important as it reveals how I constructed the research. My sociological identity is therefore my awareness of the research process, which has been the most difficult but valuable area that I have experienced. The final stage of 'being here' has taken a great deal of inner dialogue, self-examination, and self-reflection to enable me to feel comfortable, confident and content with what I am doing, why I am doing it and how I am doing it. These are important issues for me to address as I continue in my sociological career and negotiate where I want to belong and be accepted in the sociological world.

At the end, though, my dilemma remains, as to whether the focus upon story telling as part of the presentation of an acceptable sociological identity has removed me from my original aims of doing research in a different way. I agree with Dorothy Smith (1989) that the textual form has indeed placed the reading and writing subject outside the experience from which she starts. However, the recognition that this also places me outside the experience from which I started can only be a positive addition to the presentation of research texts, as shown in the final production of my text, told as my story of the substantive area and how this story was formed. My key resolution to the dilemma of textual representation has been to keep myself in the text as much as possible. I have also tried to keep myself clearly visible in this present text, but even here there are limitations to what I have told. In this chapter I had hoped to give a much clearer presentation of the inner dialogue that made me question what, why and how I wrote my thesis, but in the end this aim was overruled by my need to make myself clear. Again, within myself I have reached a comfortable compromise, where I attempt to show 'myself', or, as Jane Ribbens discusses in her chapter, 'hear my own voice', but I still place this 'me' into an acceptable academic text for this audience. Moreover, I have learnt a great deal from such acceptable texts. I would not have developed this discussion if I had not.

References

Agar, Michael (1980) *The Professional Stranger: An Informal Introduction to Ethnography*. London, Academic Press.

Atkinson, P. (1990) *The Ethnographic Imagination: Textual Construction of Reality*. London: Routledge.

Atkinson, P. (1992) *Understanding Ethnographic Texts*. Newbury Park, CA: Sage.

Benstock, S. (1988) *The Private Self: Theory and Practice of Women's Autobiographical Writings*. London: Routledge.

Birch, Maxine (1996) 'The Goddess/God within: the construction of self-identity through alternative health practices', in Kieran Flanagan and Peter Jupp (eds), *Postmodernity, Sociology and Religion*. Basingstoke: Macmillan.

Birch, Maxine (1997) 'The quest for self-discovery: the reconstruction of self-identity stories in alternative therapy groups'. Unpublished PhD dissertation, Oxford Brookes University, Oxford.

Bruner, Jerome (1995) 'The autobiographical process', *Current Sociology*, 43 (2/3): 161–77. (Special issue: Biographical Research.)

Burkitt, Ian (1991) *Social Selves: Theories of the Social Formation of Personality*. London: Sage.

Cohen, S. and Taylor, L. (1992) *Escape Attempts: The Theory and Practice of Resistance to Everyday Life*. London: Routledge.

Corradi, Consuelo (1991) 'Text, context and individual meaning: rethinking life stories in a hermeneutic framework', *Discourse and Society*, 2 (1): 105–18.

Dey, Ian (1993) *Qualitative Data Analysis*. London: Routledge.

Douglas, J. (1985) *Creative Interviewing*. Beverley Hills, CA: Sage.

Fielding, N.G. and Fielding J.I. (1992) *Linking Data*. London: Sage.

Fielding, N.G. and Lee, R.M. (eds) (1991) *Using Computers in Qualitative Research*. London: Sage.

Foucault, M. (1988) 'Technologies of the self', in L.H. Martin, H. Gutman and P.H. Hutton (eds), *Technologies of the Self*. London: Tavistock.

Fulder, S. and Munro, R. (1985) 'Complementary medicine in the UK: patients, practitioners and consultations', *Lancet*, 7 September: 542–5.

Gaier, G. (1991) 'Complementary medicine and the European Community', in G. Lewith and D. Aldridge (eds), *Complementary Medicine*. Saffron Walden: C.W. Daniel.

Gergen, Kenneth J. (1991) *The Saturated Self: Dilemmas of Identity in Contemporary Life*. New York: Basic Books.

Giddens, A. (1991) *Modernity and Self-Identity: Self and Society in Late Modern Age*. Cambridge: Polity Press.

Gifford, J. and Marans, G.E. (eds) (1986) *Writing Culture: The Poetics and Politics of Ethnography*. Berkeley, CA: University of California Press.

Goldstein, M., Jaffe, D., Sutherland, C. and Wilson, J. (1987) 'Holistic physicians: implications for the study of the medical profession', *Journal of Health and Social Behaviour*, 28 (2): 103–19.

Griffiths, Morwenna (1995) *Feminisms and the Self: The Web of Identity*. London: Routledge.

Hammersley, M. (1989) *The Dilemma of Qualitative Methodology*. London: Routledge.

Hammersley, M. (1992) *What's Wrong with Ethnography?* London: Routledge.

Holstein, J.A. and Gubrium, J.F. (1995) *The Active Interview*. Thousand Oaks, CA: Sage.

Josselen, R. and Lieblich, A. (eds) (1993) *The Narrative Study of Lives* (vol. 1). Newbury Park, CA: Sage.

Lather, Patti. (1991) *Getting Smart: Feminist Research and Pedagogy with/in the Postmodern*. New York: Routledge.

MacIntrye, A. (1985) *After Virtue*. London: Duckworth.

Nash, C. (ed.) (1990) *Narrative in Culture: The Uses of Storytelling in the Sciences, Philosophy and Literature*. London: Routledge.

Okely, J. and Callaway, H. (eds) (1992) *Anthropology and Autobiography*. London: Routledge.

Plummer, Ken (1995) *Telling Sexual Stories: Power, Change and Social Worlds*. London: Routledge.

Ribbens, J. (1993) 'Fact or fictions? Aspects of the use of autobiographical writing in undergraduate sociology', *Sociology*, 27 (1): 81–92.

Ricoeur, Paul. (1992) *Oneself as Another*. Chicago: University of Chicago Press.

Saks, M. (ed.) (1992) *Alternative Medicine in Britain*. Oxford: Clarendon Paperbacks.

Silverman, D. (1985) *Qualitative Methodology and Sociology*. Aldershot: Gower.

Smith, D. (1989) 'Sociological theory: methods of writing patriarchy', in Ruth Wallace (ed.), *Feminism and Sociological Theory*. London: Sage.

Somers, Margaret. (1994) 'The narrative constitution of identity: a relational and network approach', *Theory and Society*, 23 (5): 605–50.

Stanley, Liz (ed.) (1990) *Feminist Praxis. Research, Theory and Epistemology in Feminist Sociology*. London: Routledge.

Stanley, Liz (1992) *The Auto/biographical I: The Theory and Practice of Feminist Auto/biography*. Manchester: Manchester University Press.

Stanley, L. (1993) 'On autobiographies in sociology', *Sociology*, 27 (1): 41–52.

Stanley, L. and Wise, S. (1983) *Breaking Out: Feminist Consciousness and Feminist Research*. London: Routledge and Kegan Paul.

Stanley, L. and Wise, S. (1993) *Breaking Out Again: Feminist Ontology and Epistemology*. London: Routledge and Kegan Paul.

Taylor, Charles (1989) *Sources of the Self: The Making of Modern Identity*. Cambridge, MA: Harvard University Press.

West, Ruth (1992) 'Alternative medicine: prospects and speculations', in Mike Saks (ed.), *Alternative Medicine in Britain*. Oxford: Clarendon Paperbacks.

Wiley, Robert (1995) *The Semiotic Self*. Chicago: University of Chicago Press.

11 Writing the Voices of the Less Powerful

Research on Lone Mothers

Kay Standing

In this chapter I discuss one of the final stages of the research process over which we, as researchers, have power and control – the process of writing up. In particular I consider the language we use when we write, and how this may play a role in sustaining hierarchies of knowledge. I do this by looking at my research on low income lone mothers in the inner city, and my own experiences as a white working-class woman re-entering the academic world. I explore the differences and power relations between academic writing, including much feminist work, and working-class women's everyday language. The dilemma I want to address in this chapter is of how we write our research in a language which is acceptable to the academic community but does not alienate the people who took part in our research. This issue is central for feminist research which claims to be 'on, by and *for*' women.[1] It is a particular dilemma for feminist researchers researching groups of less powerful people – that by the ways in which we write, and represent their words to an academic audience, we may in fact reinforce and contribute to inequalities of power.

I have tried to write this chapter in a way which is understandable to most people, not just those of us from academic backgrounds, or taking part in feminist research. It does contain some complex language, the 'technical terminology' of sociology, that illustrates that it is not always possible to write about complex issues in everyday language – often the language does not exist outside the discipline – but I have tried to write as simply as possible in order to make this chapter accessible. The dilemma in this of course is that this very chapter may not be taken seriously, it may be seen as simple, untheoretical, not sufficiently academic. So be it. Part of the reason for this chapter is to challenge those assumptions, to make you, the reader, stop and think about how you write up your own research, about who you are writing for, and what the purpose behind the research is.

However, I have a confession to make about my own use of language. I do not always write in this way. I have written other articles in quite different, more 'academic' language. My PhD is written in quite dense, often complex, theoretical language – it is concerned with the discursive construction of lone motherhood and lone mothers' subjectivities – how lone mothers are seen in society (or specifically, in the education system) and how they see themselves.

It was through writing the thesis that dilemmas discussed in this chapter arose. I am instrumental in my use of language. We need to recognize that research does not take place in isolation – it is always for someone or some purpose – it always has a chosen audience and cannot be separated from this. The audience we choose to address all too often affects our language and accessibility. I want to challenge that this should be so. If a piece of writing or research is not accessible, because of the language it is written in, to those who take part in the research, what is its purpose? Who is the research for?

This chapter then is more of a 'raising issues' chapter than a 'how to do it' textbook. Its purpose is to challenge and contest, to make you, the reader, think and question some of the taken-for-granted assumptions about the language of feminist research, and the purpose of the research.

Background: language in the field

This chapter is based on the dilemmas that face me as I write up my research for a doctoral thesis. My research is on lone mothers' involvement in their children's schooling. I am interested in exploring their understandings of their lone motherhood, and how these understandings may differ from those of, and affect their relationships with, their children's school. The research is based on interviews with 28 lone mothers, all on low incomes (all claiming income support, housing benefit, and/or family credit). The women are of various ages (from 20 to 48), of differing ethnic backgrounds, have children of different ages and live in differing household situations (some with their parents, some with live-in partners, all with their children). All of the women live, or work, on a large North London council estate.

I began the research in the summer of 1993, in the midst of the demonization of lone-mother families in Britain in government rhetoric, policies and the popular media. A moral panic over lone motherhood arose, with lone mothers portrayed as a 'social threat' or a 'social problem'. Newspaper headlines screamed, 'Wedded to Welfare – Do They Want to Marry a Man or the State?'; 'Once Illegitimacy Was Punished – Now It Is Rewarded' (*Sunday Times*, 11 July 1993). A BBC television *Panorama* documentary, *Babies on Benefit* (BBC1, 20 September 1993) portrayed lone mothers as irresponsible, young, single, never-married women, having babies in order to obtain social security (welfare) benefits and council housing. The language used in these debates was inflammatory and derogatory, as Michelle, a white working-class mother with one daughter and one son commented:

> . . . we had all this thing about single parents were like the root of all evil you know. It just got ridiculous. I mean all the pressures we was getting like the government saying we're doing this, that and the other you know, and people believe it.

When I began the research, dilemmas of difference were at the forefront – I was not a lone mother (I was not, at the time, even a mother). I had never lived in a lone-mother family – the attacks on lone mothers seemed to have little relevance to my life. Yet the social construction of appropriate mother-hood, and control of women's sexuality through a dominant discourse of normative mothering (in a heterosexual, married relationship – a white middle-class model of the nuclear family) are issues that concerned me as a feminist. All women are defined in relationship to motherhood (either posi-tively or negatively) (Gordon, 1990). This construction of all women as potential mothers (and some women as potential 'bad' mothers) is one which impacts on women's lives and identities in various ways, organizing them in particular relationships with institutions, such as schools.[2]

The women were contacted through snowballing methods, starting with my own social network on the estate. During the course of the fieldwork I became pregnant and gave birth to my daughter – the newly acquired identity of 'mother' opened up contacts with many women (through baby clinics, toddler groups and the like).

I had initially intended to use more 'sociologically acceptable' methods of contacting women by sending out letters through the local primary schools: I had sent out 30 letters in one school and received no replies at all. Again the use of language is important here; other researchers (for example Glucksmann, 1994) have found that working-class women often do not respond to requests for interviews in written form, especially on 'official' sta-tionery. The reasons for this are complex, partly due to a mistrust of authority, but also partly due to the style and language that letters may be written in.

Unlike Tina Miller (this volume) I had little difficulty in gaining access by using snowballing methods. It was slow and time-consuming, with each net-work running out after about five women, but it allowed me access to women who may not have responded to more 'conventional' methods. Snowballing also gave me access to women whom I would not have contacted otherwise, because they did not fit my definition of a lone mother (for example, if they had a partner). It allowed the women to define their own situation and iden-tity as lone mothers.

Snowballing also helped to break down some of the power relations between myself as the 'researcher' and the women as the 'researched'. It allowed for a relationship of trust to be established because the women were always approached by someone they knew – at first, myself, but as the snow-balling progressed, the women who I had interviewed asked their friends and neighbours to take part. In this way, each new 'interviewee' had some idea of what the interview would be like. In this way, snowballing is a useful method for contacting groups of women, such as low income lone mothers, who are vulnerable and stigmatized in everyday life (Lee, 1993). Because I had begun my research in the midst of the British Conservative Party and popular media demonization of lone-mother families, many of the women were initially sus-picious of my agenda and the ends the research would be used for. Lone mothers' lives are constantly under supervision, from school, health, welfare and benefit agencies, and many of the women were simply tired of having to explain their lives again. Jane, a white working-class lone mother with one daughter summed up the feelings of many lone mothers:

> I think lone mothers are tired of having to defend ourselves. It's, 'Oh no, why pick on us again?' especially after Peter Lilley [the secretary of State for Social Security who launched a particularly vicious attack on low income, inner city lone mothers in 1993] when everything can be turned against us.

Snowball techniques meant that my sample was not representative of lone mothers nationally, but they allowed me to 'sample explicitly with reference to the social structure' (Coleman, cited in Lee, 1993: 66) of the locality. My sample, although small, is diverse and reflects the varied age, class, ethnicity and family status of lone mothers in the area.

The interviews were in-depth and tape recorded, lasting between one and four hours, depending on the amount of time the women were able to spare in their busy timetables of childcare, housework and paid work. Occasionally, if we ran out of time, an interview would continue the following day or week. Most of the interviews took place in the women's own home, but some also took place in my home. As other researchers have noted (Ribbens, 1989), the interview situation, especially in-depth interviews, gives the interviewee some power to control the interview – the power over what to tell, and the power to decide what to talk about. For me, the interviews seemed to be both like, and unlike, conversations. Often they involved a dialogue between us, and often the women would ask me questions, especially about my family and relationships. Sometimes I felt that our roles were reversed, and I was the one being interviewed. However, at the end of the day, I held the research agenda; it was my questions that led the way the interview went.

In the interview situation, especially when we are women interviewing women about family and household issues, the language that we use, and the issues we discuss are private and shared (see Finch, 1984; Oakley, 1981; Ribbens, 1994). It is when we take the interview tapes and the women's words away for analysis and writing that the dilemmas, for me, begin to appear. However equal the methods of access and interviewing, we, as researchers, still hold the real power when we take the women's private words into the public world of academia. It is in producing the written text, the thesis, research report, journal article, book, that we have the most power (see Pam Alldred, this volume). Researchers hold the power of which data, which parts of the interviews, to use, how to interpret the women's words, what to use the research for, and how to represent the women's voices – what language to use to write. It is, as Maxine Birch argues (this volume), the dilemma of moving from the research world to the sociological world – of moving from being a participant in the research relationship to being in a position of power to translate and interpret.

Dilemmas of speaking and writing

As I began writing up my thesis I became increasingly aware of the differences and contradictions between how I speak, and how I write. Listening to th tapes of the interviews as I transcribed them, I was aware that there was very little difference between the spoken language of myself and the women I interviewed. We had different regional and ethnic accents and dialects, and the interviews were full of laughter, slang, pauses, idioms and ungrammatical speech that were impossible to reproduce on the written page. I transcribed the tapes as I heard them, as a constant monologue or dialogue, with pauses, hesitations, both of us speaking at once, but with no formal sentence structure, commas, colons and full stops. We do not speak in grammatically correct sentences. We speak in a flowing, haphazard way. But to put the women's voices in the written text in this way looked 'wrong'. It jarred against the complex sentence structure of my academic writing. The language in which the women, and I myself, spoke (and indeed in which most of us, you the reader included, speak) is very different to the language of academic writing. To put the two side by side seemed to reinforce the unequal power relations between me, the researcher, and the women, the researched. Moreover, as Beverley Skeggs points out, it made their words look '. . . authentic and simple' (Skeggs, 1994a). The issue is not just one of the gaps between the written and the spoken word, but between the spoken word and the academic presentation of the spoken word. It is the ways in which we represent and interpret the women's voices which reinforces hierarchies of knowledge and power.

I had made a conscious decision to 'tidy up' the transcribed words of both the women and myself, for example to edit out some of the 'ums, ahs, errs, you knows', the swearing, and my own constant 'yeahs', and make 'gonna' and 'innit' into 'going to' and 'isn't it'. The before and after example below from Maria, a white working-class lone mother with three daughters, illustrates the dilemmas I faced in transcribing the taped interviews as I heard them, and then translating them into a form more suitable and acceptable for an academic piece of research. Maria's style of speech is distinctive. She speaks quickly and passionately, at '90 miles an hour', barely pausing for breath (and certainly with no respect for grammatical conventions!). During the course of the interview she became upset and emotional, angry and heated. In the passage below she talks of her anger at her ex-husband not paying Child Support:[3]

> I got that letter and I think . . . it just don't . . . oh I was fuming this morning you know how if one person had just said one thing to me I'd've jumped down their throats you know but that's it . . . I think oh sod the lot of them you know I mean they've done no investigation at all I told 'em when they phoned me it's a lie he's living with someone I even spoke to me mother-in-law, I said why is he telling me this 'oh well erm she's not working' and I said 'so fucking what?' that's not my problem and what is the big deal [shouted] 'cos he's expected to pay something for his kids [yeah] it's pathetic you know [yeah], so erm, I can't say to the kids 'oh this is what you're gonna get [oh no] it's an insult it's like oh yeah this is what you're worth, you ain't even worth a pound each to him you know [yeah] yeah yeah, and it's hurtful you know . . .

The lack of punctuation marks makes the passage difficult to read, and sits uneasily in conventionally written text. Yet at the same time, unedited, it captures Maria's style of speech, it captures her passion and anger, the emotions which became lost in the tidied up, neutralized, 'safe' version of the same passage. The words remain the same, but much of the meaning is lost:

> I got that letter and I think . . . It just don't . . . Oh I was fuming this morning. You know how if one person had just said one thing to me, I'd've jumped down their throats. But that's it. I think, oh sod the lot of them you know. I mean they've done no investigation at all. I told them when they phoned me, it's a lie, he's living with someone. I even spoke to my mother-in-law. I said, 'Why is he telling me this?' She said] 'Oh well, erm, she's not working.' And I said, 'So fucking what?' That's not my problem, and what is the big deal 'cos he's expected to pay something for his kids? It's pathetic you know. So, I can't say to the kids, 'Oh this is what you're going to get.' It' s an insult. It's like, oh yeah, this is what you're worth, you're not even worth a pound each to him. And it's hurtful you know.

The editing out of many of my interventions, the 'yeahs', also negates the experience of the interview, when often both of us would be talking at once, and has implications for where we place ourselves in the research text.

By tidying up the transcripts in this way, I homogenized the women's voices, making them all sound (or read) the same. I took away their own (and my own) distinctive way of speaking, which reflects their background and culture, and made standard English the 'normal' means of communication. This raises a further dilemma: by doing this, am I further negating the worthiness of the women's language, and indeed of my own? Am I just playing into the hands of the 'establishment' by saying black and white working-class women's ways of speaking are wrong, are inadequate, are not as valid as the academic discourse? However, the women themselves often did not feel that their words were valid as academic discourse, and wanted to tidy up their speech to sound 'more English'. This compromises the character of both their speech and the data and has implications for the production and validation of knowledges.

I tidied up the women's language partly in response to feedback from some of the women after giving them their interview transcripts to read. Initially I asked everyone who took part in the interviews whether they wanted copies of the transcripts. About half of the women did, with others asking for copies of articles or papers written as a result of the research because 'I'd like to see what other single mothers are saying' (Sian, white, one son). Although most did not read them (nor did those who asked for copies of articles or papers I had written), mainly through lack of time,[4] the comments I did get were not on the contents of the interviews, but on the style and language used – such as, 'Do I really say "you know" all the time?', 'Don't I um and err a lot?' This in itself has important repercussions for the meaning of the interviews. Statements such as, 'You know', and bodily gestures may point to implicit shared understandings between research participants.[5] Although none of the women actually asked me to alter their style of speech, there was an implicit feeling that it was not good enough for the public world. As Marlene Packwood argues:

> . . . [working class-women] at times experience the English language as alien, full of subtleties and nuances which are available to the middle classes. Certain words are

totally out of our area of experience [. . .] It is another aspect of the middle-class lifestyles which reiterate the different world we were bought up in [. . .] Lack of confidence with language mirrors our nervousness inside [. . .] Sometimes the words come out coarse, harsh, clumsily expressing what we need to say. The basic need, language itself, almost as basic as breathing, is still not ours for the asking. (Packwood, 1983: 12)

Many of the women wanted to challenge, and speak (or write) about, the representations of lone mothers, but did not know how to. Maria again:

Maria: I hear and read all this crap about single mothers and I want to go on telly, or write an article and tell them what it's really like, how hard it is . . .
Kay: Why don't you?
Maria: Who'd listen to me? I mean I could talk for hours about my woes, but what difference would it make, they wouldn't take me seriously now would they? Come on, a working-class cockney like me – yeah, they're really gonna have me on Newsnight or something [. . .] I don't know how you're supposed to write things for papers and that [. . .] Maybe they'll listen to you.

The women not only did not have access to the resources to get their voices heard, but they also did not know the correct conventions in which to speak and write. In this way, language acts as a barrier, a way to reinforce inequalities of gender, class and race – the denial of access to the 'correct way' to speak creates hierarchies of knowledge. This again raises issues for us as feminist researchers of what the expectations for the research are.

Often I felt that the women expressed ideas and concepts in plain language much more effectively (and powerfully) than complex theoretical explanations would have done. Yet the process of producing an academic piece of work demanded that I took the women's words and theorized from them, juxtaposing their language with that of the academy. In this way, the women's knowledge becomes invalidated – their ways of saying things and expressing ideas are judged to be not as valid as those of the 'experts', the researchers in the academy. As Maxine Birch (this volume) found, to be reflexive over the use of language, to try to represent the women's words in their own voices brought the dilemma of '. . . not being sociological, but just being descriptive'. In this way, language becomes one of the ways in which hierarchies of knowledge are reproduced.

The dilemma, however, of the difference between the spoken and the written word is a more general one, and one which goes beyond the difference between the spoken and written word *per se*. Very few of us write in the way that we speak, yet, when we, as academics, write articles and research reports using empirical research, we *do* transcribe our participants' words as they were spoken – their spoken language enters the text to make our work 'authentic' and real – *our* spoken language does not. As researchers we too feel discomfort at the disjunction between our spoken voices and written words. However, as researchers, our voices are hidden behind the academic conventions, contrasting the words of the interviewed with the technical and often abstract language of the social sciences. We need to ask, what does this do to the women (and men) we research? The worlds we investigate are often those of the less powerful, for feminists, often those of women. What representation, what image of these women are we constructing? We claim we are being 'true' to our respondents by recording their voices accurately, but if their words and language are different from the other written text – the analysis – does this make them seem less valid? For black and white working-class women we need to consider the implications of our use of language – does using their words as they are next to academic language simply reinforce stereotypes of strong and angry women fighting against the system, or of depressed and downtrodden mothers? As feminist researchers one of our roles is to translate between the private world of women and the public world of academia, politics and policy. The dilemma remains of how we do this without reinforcing the stereotypes and cultural constructions we are challenging.

For me, in researching lone mothers the issue of language was crucial. My research practice was (is) informed by feminist theory and an interest in poststructuralism. Above all, I tried to follow Kum-Kum Bhavnani's definition of a feminist project, that

> . . . any study whose main agent is a woman/women and which claims a feminist framework should not reproduce the researched in ways in which they are represented within dominant society – that is, the analysis cannot be complicit with dominant representations which reinscribe inequality. (Bhavnani, 1994: 29)

In this context the use of language and the ways in which I represented lone mothers through the use of their own words was important in challenging the ways in which lone mothers are represented.

It was important to me that I did not use language in a way that would reflect, or reinforce, the negative stereotypes of lone mothers. However, my very use of the term 'lone mother' is in itself an academic construct[6] – it is a use of language that I, as an academic, have imposed on the women's understandings. All of the women in my research referred to themselves as 'single parents' – regardless of their previous marital status (whether they were divorced, separated, never-married, or had new partners). They rejected the term 'lone' because of the connotations of 'being alone', as Jackie, a white working-class mother with one son stated: 'I'm not on my own am I? I have a family, we are a family.'

Most of the women also used the ungendered term single *parent*, rather than single mother, perhaps as a way of distancing themselves from the negative discourses which focus on single mothers. Here I faced a dilemma with my own use of language: do I use the preferred term of the women I interviewed – single parent – and stay true to their language, or do I use my preferred term – lone mother – a term seldom used outside of academic writings? I decided to sacrifice staying true to the women's words for two instrumental reasons. Firstly, the term lone *mother* emphasizes that it is overwhelmingly *mothers*, women, who are single (lone) parents; to refer to ungendered parents prioritizes fathers and makes invisible the gendered dimensions of lone motherhood. Secondly, the term *lone* mother, is inclusive –

it includes all mothers who define themselves as single (or lone, or self-supporting, or solo or autonomous, all terms used in academic writings), it includes women who are divorced, separated, widowed as well as those conventionally called single – never-married mothers. This example illustrates one of the dilemmas of language – that in gaining a wider definition (or academic credibility) you must often lose part of the 'authentic' voices of the women in research.

The issue of language then is especially important for feminist researchers trying to do research 'on and for' marginalized and less powerful groups of women, such as lone mothers (see also Pam Alldred, this volume). In the next section I want to explore how the mystification of academic language serves to alienate and disempower these groups of women.

How academic discourse negates everyday language

The language conventions of academic discourse (the language used in academic books and articles, in spoken discussion by some members of the academic world) is different from, and more complex than, the everyday private language of most people. There is no reason why academic language should be different – it is just a convention (Madoc-Jones and Coates, 1996), but it is a convention that excludes others from taking part in academic discourse. It is also a convention that serves a particular purpose – to uphold notions of knowledge as abstract, rational and detached from women's everyday lives (see Smith, 1988, 1989). Language is not simply a means of communication. It is also an expression of shared understandings and assumptions, and as such it transmits certain (hidden and implicit) values to those who use it. Language is '. . . at once the expression of culture and part of it' (Mills, 1989: xi). In the academic world, the language used often expresses values and understandings held by white, male, 'scientific' culture. It seems to me that, as bell hooks argues, one of the many uses of academic language is to reproduce an intellectual, white, male, middle-class hierarchy where the only work seen to be theoretical is work that is '. . . highly abstract, difficult to read, and containing obscure references' (hooks, 1994). This ensures that certain knowledges are heard, while others are obscured and hidden. These knowledges may be different from, and in opposition to, those of our own as feminist researchers, and the differing knowledges of the women we interview. This is a point that I will return to later, but first I want to explore some of the implications of the use of this abstract language for feminist research.

Feminist research is concerned with challenging dominant assumptions and representations. I assume if you are reading this book you have some interest in, or familiarity with, feminist research. You may have read the main texts, entered the theoretical debates. You may be engaged in political action inside or outside the academy. If, like me, you came to your research believing you could challenge and contest taken-for-granted assumptions and question dominant knowledges by using feminist research, you may have been surprised by the ways in which different feminisms seem to reproduce and create hierarchies of knowledge through using complicated 'male-stream' academic language. My experiences of feminist research are mixed. I left academia after completing my MA in women's studies because, much as I loved the subject and found the theory stimulating, I could not relate it to what I was doing, socially, economically and politically, outside the university setting. I felt I had two lives – my academic one, and my personal one where my friends, social network and family were not academic. The feminisms I was learning seemed to be from the standpoints of white middle-class women. They were experiences different from my own, as a white working-class woman. Dorothy Smith (1988, 1989) writes of how, as feminist academics and women, we operate in two worlds – our everyday life, and the sociological world in texts, whose conventions are embedded in the relations of ruling (. . . 'that internally co-ordinated complex of administrative, managerial, professional and discursive organisation that regulates, organizes, governs and otherwise controls our societies', Smith, 1989: 38). The texts that we write – '. . . the moment after talk has been inscribed as texts and become data when it must be worked up as sociology' (Smith, 1989: 35) – are written in a style and language that conform to sociological discourse – removed from the realities of women's everyday lives.

I returned to academic life seven years later to begin a PhD. I believed feminist theories had 'moved on', begun to deal with differences, and not just the acknowledgement of difference, but the unequal power relations in differences between women (Olson and Shopes, 1991). Yet many of the dilemmas remain unresolved, not least the question of how we write, how we use the words of women who are different from us in a way that represents the realities of their lives, and does not serve to marginalize and oppress further.

Despite the growth of 'difference' feminism, discussions of difference and diversity downplay or ignore questions of language (hooks, 1994). The feminist demands for the primacy of diverse voices that are often silenced, marginalized and/or censored all too often do not question the language used in these demands. Diverse participation does not necessarily mean diverse language. As the audience for feminist writing and speaking grows, and becomes increasingly diverse, it is still assumed that 'standard English' will be the main way of communicating feminist thought.

For feminist researchers in higher education a further dilemma arises – not only must the research be written up in 'standard English', but, with the growth of an academic theoretical 'meta-language', also written in a style that is acceptable to male-stream academia, even if the style and language is inaccessible to the people who take part in research. Despite the increasing number of feminist journals and publications, the growth of women's studies as a discipline, and increasing numbers of black and white working-class women entering social science disciplines, the language of feminism grows increasingly complex and convoluted. This concern is not new – socialist feminists in the 1970s took issue with the complex language of Marxism

(Segal, 1987) – but it seems to have escalated as feminism becomes increasingly interested in debates around postmodernism and post-structuralism.

Feminist theory has recently embraced post-structuralism, or '. . . turned to culture', (Barrett and Phillips, 1992; Nicholson, 1990), a move from a concern with 'things' to a concern with 'words' (Barrett, 1992). As a materialist feminist I was initially hostile to the concepts of post-structuralism. It seemed to form a vacuous theory, with no grounding in the material realities of everyday life. Power seemed to come from everywhere and nowhere. The emphasis on deconstruction seemed to me to alienate theory from practice, to individualize and leave me, as a feminist, with nothing to organize around politically. Postmodernism seemed to represent '. . . the politics of privilege' (Skeggs, 1994a). Its basis in language meant you needed to understand the language in order to participate. However, as I read more, I found some post-structural feminism (for example, Weedon, 1987) useful in providing a way to deal with competing and often contradictory accounts of life in my data, of theorizing the women's (and my own) constantly changing identities and accounts of reality. Post-structuralism seemed to present a change from portraying women as 'passive victims' of oppression to a recognition of the '. . . possibility of resistance, struggle and active defiance' (Maynard, 1994: 274). A recognition of the diffuse nature of power is useful, as long as we remember that not all power relations are equally balanced; some of us are more oppressed than oppressors, and vice versa.

It is interesting then that the language of difference, post-structuralism, that offers the most possibility for change and difference, is written in the most inaccessible, exclusionary and complex language (hooks, 1991). It speaks to a very specialized audience, namely those who share the knowledge of the language in which it is based.

This presents a dilemma for feminist researchers, who, like myself, believe post-structuralism offers possibilities for challenging and contesting dominant ideas and the way less powerful groups are represented. This dilemma is perhaps best illustrated by the example of a well-known feminist methodology text, *Breaking Out* (1983), by Liz Stanley and Sue Wise. The first edition was written in simple, easy to understand language. However, the second edition, *Breaking Out Again* (1993) used the complex academic language. Defending their rewrite of *Breaking Out* in the 'specialist language' of postmodern and post-structural social science, Stanley and Wise write that as academic feminism has become professionalized, that is, accepted by malestream sociology '. . . it has become necessary to participate in its languagegames in order to be taken seriously as a member of its epistemic community' (Stanley and Wise, 1993: 231).

They themselves acknowledge that this approach will alienate many readers from their ideas because of the complex and mystificatory way in which the book is written. This again raises the crucial issue of who feminist research is for, especially if, as Stanley and Wise acknowledge, one of the aims of feminist research is to challenge male-stream academic conventions:

. . . feminist praxis should be the goal – as enhanced political engagement, rather than a preoccupation with textuality and intertextuality for its own sake. We also need to keep in mind that a part (but not the whole) of such a praxis is a feminist political engagement within academic life itself; we are here to change it. (Stanley and Wise, 1993: 231)

If part of our role as feminist academics is to challenge academic conventions which exclude and marginalize less powerful groups, how can we hope to do this if we continue to 'play by the rules'? This is a dilemma for feminist researchers questioning and challenging dominant representations of less powerful women's lives if part of the aim of the research is to use knowledge in a way that challenges oppressions and inequalities. These are the dilemmas which Rosalind Edwards and Jane Ribbens discuss in Chapter 1 of this volume, of how the researcher is inevitably placed in the position of 'translator', and the difficulty/impossibility of escaping the dominant discourses.

The dilemmas of class and differing knowledges

The dilemma of language is particularly acute for feminist researchers who, like myself, are from working-class backgrounds. In order to succeed in higher education, working-class students have to surrender part of their working-class identity (hooks, 1994; Lynch and O'Neill, 1994). Working-class knowledge, language and culture do not 'fit' into traditional academic conventions. For people moving outside poor working-class backgrounds, language is important. To fit into the mainstream, working-class and black students have to adopt, in public, a different style of speaking and writing to their private voice at home and in the community. In this way, language becomes a 'source of estrangement' from your background, culture and ways of knowing (Childers and hooks, 1990; hooks, 1989). Although I identify myself as being from a working-class background, through education I am no longer 'working-class'; my ways of knowing are different from those of my neighbours and the women I interviewed.

For black and white working-class women, lone mothers and others, their ways of knowing are different from, and do not translate easily into, conventional academic forms. For black and white working women, knowledge is based in the family, community and 'common sense' (Luttrell, 1992), not in academia and 'rational science'. For the lone mothers in my study, knowledge of the schools, educational system and welfare agencies was gained through people they knew and trusted, family, friends and neighbours whose common sense came from experience, and the sharing of common problems, not from 'professional experts'. Their knowledge was partly acquired through their individual, personal and private experiences of mothering, but again this knowledge was shared with other mothers in the form of practical or emotional help.

Knowledge is differentiated by race and ethnicity, as well as by class. Black women have to negotiate racism in their everyday lives, and their knowledge can be seen as part of a collective identity as black women, learnt through l relations and everyday interaction with a white racist society (Collins, 1990).

For lone mothers, their knowledges are localized knowledges shared by mothers, rather than part of the academic or professional 'scientific' discourse. Because women's knowledge is seen to come from their mothering and domestic responsibilities, it is seen to be private and individual, and therefore it becomes structurally excluded from academic thought (Luttrell, 1992; Smith, 1988). Through using a language which is different from that used by working-class women to describe their experiences and knowledge, and often inaccessible to them, a hierarchy of knowledge is set up. The researcher is seen to have more knowledge, to be able to interpret the words and worlds of the women in a way that, by its complexity and difficulty, implies that the researcher has greater, or better, knowledge, better understandings, than the women who form the research.

Women's use of language, both written (letters, diaries) and oral (gossip, chat) are private forms, confined to the space of the home, family and community. In the public world, especially in the cultural domain (the ways in which society represents itself through institutions, rituals and 'official' knowledge), women's language forms have '. . . little or no currency, let alone value' (Cameron, 1990: 4). In society's most important and prestigious spoken traditions – religion, ceremonial, political rhetoric, legal discourse – women's voices are silenced, both by social taboos and restrictions and by custom and practice (see, for example, the historical exclusion of women from public debates and the ongoing debate over women priests).

Writing is also something that women are seen to do in private, in the domestic setting within the structural and emotional constraints of women's family and domestic roles. For women living on a low income, the sheer day-to-day effect of living in poverty leaves little time or energy for anything else (Lynch and O'Neill, 1994; Smith and Noble, 1995), and writing becomes the preserve of the more powerful. For less powerful groups of women, access to academic work is then restricted both by lack of time and the inaccessibility of the language in which it is written – differences that much feminist research has failed to address.

In conclusion: different audiences, different languages?

As this book has shown, the research process does not end with the field work, but power relations continue into our analysis and writing. This chapter has begun to raise some of the ways in which how we write, and the language we use, may contribute to these power relations, and exclude less powerful groups. It has questioned if it is enough simply to state our own personal position and social location, where we, as researchers, are 'coming from', and to use this to explain any limitations of our speech and writing. This is what working-class and black women, and other less powerful groups outside academia, have always had to do. We need rather to challenge and ntest the use of academic language, to forge new ways of writing and new methodologies that do not exclude and alienate. (Quite how we do this in the current academic climate of individualism, competition and the educational marketplace I am not sure.)

Research, however, does not take place in isolation. The use of language and the issues of power involved are situated within specific cultural, historical and ideological circumstances which influence our writing and use of language. As Beverley Skeggs states:

> . . . all writing occurs within particular histories and within an academic mode of production. This presupposes that we are writing for a particular audience. (Skeggs, 1994a: 85)

As a doctoral student, I write in a particular style, for a particular audience, and for a specific end product. The doctoral style of writing in particular is not accountable to those outside the academic establishment, especially those who have taken part in the research. This raises a dilemma for feminists – for whom is the research carried out? We need to be honest when doing research about the outcomes of that research. The writing of a doctoral thesis will gain for me a PhD. It will not alter the material realities of the lives of the women I interviewed. It will not provide adequate housing, childcare, employment. Anne Opie (1992) argues that we empower the 'socially marginalized' in our research by taking their experiences of marginality and making it central. We also need to make it public, and accessible. One of my concerns in doing my research is to give space and validity to working-class lone mothers whose voices are not heard elsewhere. In order to do this, and to write a thesis that will be seen as an acceptable piece of academic work, I have tried to use some of 'the master's tools' of language for my own purposes. However, in other situations I may write, and speak, quite differently, in a style and manner closer to my everyday language. This decision is again instrumental. We need to 'translate' ideas to different audiences, to formulate different styles of writing and presentation for different settings and make connections between academia and the everyday world. As bell hooks argues below, the separation of the public world of higher education from the private, everyday lives of mothers, through the use of exclusionary language, is one of our own making:

> . . . the use of a language and style of presentation that alienates most folks who are not also academically trained reinforces the notion that the academic world is separate from real life, the everyday world where we constantly adjust our language and behavior to meet diverse needs. The academic setting is separate only when we work to make it so. It is a false dichotomy which suggests that academics and/or intellectuals can only speak to one another, that we cannot hope to speak with the masses. What is true is that we make choices, that we choose our audiences, that we choose voices to hear and voices to silence. (hooks, 1989: 78)

In everyday life we write and speak in different styles; our use of language is not fixed, but varies according to our audience. We write for an audience, academic or otherwise, using different styles with different groups. By the very use of language we can serve to reinforce inequalities of knowledge, by presenting our findings in our academic voice, in the specialized language of sociological discourse, positioning this next to the women's words in a way that makes them look 'authentic and simple'. By doing this, we reinforce divisions and hierarchies of knowledge across the lines of gender, class and race (see also Pam Alldred, this volume).

There are, however, other ways in which we can use language, to challenge and contest these divisions and hierarchies, to reshape the dominant language as a site of resistance. Language is powerful (see, for example, the historical and cultural exclusion of the less powerful, women, the working classes, black people from literacy). As many black writers have observed, the language to describe oppression has, until very recently, been in the hands of the oppressors, but this language can be reshaped and used to challenge the oppressors. bell hooks writes how black people under slavery took standard English and transformed it into their own language, which was both subversive and threatening to white authority:[7]

> By transforming the oppressor's language, making a culture of resistance, black people created an intimate speech that could say far more than was permissible within the boundaries of standard English. The power of this speech is not simply that it enables resistance to white supremacy, but that it also forges a space for alternative cultural production and alternative epistemologies – different ways of thinking and knowing that were crucial to creating a counter-hegemonic worldview. (hooks, 1994: 171)

It is not language itself, but access to knowledge of that language, that is exclusionary. It is not simply an issue of differing knowledges, but how those differing knowledges are translated into the research. We need a language that incorporates black and working-class women's idioms of speech, but does not subsume them.

I hope this chapter has made you think about your use of language when you write up your research and the implications of it for the production of knowledge.

As I said at the beginning, I do not have any answers; the one that I use, writing differently for different audiences, is in itself a compromise. There are no easy answers. I do not believe that we can, or should, research only those who are like us (see also Edwards, 1996) – that would result in the silencing of the voices of many less powerful groups who do not have access to the academic world and the publishing opportunities it brings. It would mean the knowledge that we promote is that of the privileged. Our choice is how we use the privileges that access to academic knowledge brings us, whether we use it mainly to further our own careers, and to reaffirm hierarchies of knowledge, or whether, through thinking about how we write, how we represent the voices of those who are less powerful, we challenge and contest the dominant knowledges – including the growth of an academic 'meta-language', and write in ways that are accessible to those outside the university setting.

The dilemmas we face as feminists writing the voices of the less powerful are those of translation and compromise. How much of the women's voices and experiences do we lose by translating them into more academic language? Yet, if we do not translate, mediate and alter their words, how do we stop reproducing dominant cultural constructions of poor and working-class women (see also Armstead, 1995)? It is the dilemma of trying to challenge, not reproduce, hierarchies of power and knowledge; the dilemma of not losing the 'authenticity', emotion and vibrancy of women's voices, whilst not positioning them as 'Other', and distancing ourselves from the political challenge of feminist research in the so-called 'objective' language of academia.

Notes

1 Not all feminist research claims this.

2 Dorothy Smith (1989) argues this relationship is a negative, deficit one.

3 The Child Support Act was introduced in Britain in 1993 to enforce maintenance payments from absent fathers.

4 This raises a further dilemma for feminist researchers: how far do we go in the spirit of 'reflexivity'? When does empowering the women who take part in research by letting them have a say in the data analysis and writing process become exploitation, taking advantage of women's (limited) time and energy by getting them to do our work for us?

5 Thanks to Jane Ribbens for this point.

6 Thanks to Rosalind Edwards for this point.

7 A contemporary example of this resistance is Beverley Skeggs' (1994b) work on black female rappers.

References

Armstead, Cathleen (1995) 'Writing contradiction: feminist research and feminist writing', *Women's Studies International Forum*, 18 (5/6): 627–36.

Barrett, Michelle (1992) 'Words and things', in Michelle Barrett and Anne Phillips (eds), *Destabilising Theory*. London: Polity Press.

Barrett, Michelle and Phillips, Anne (eds) (1992) *Destabilising Theory*. London: Polity Press.

Bhavnani, Kum-Kum (1994) 'Tracing the contours: feminist research and feminist objectivity', in Haleh Afshar and Mary Maynard (eds), *The Dynamics of 'Race' and Gender: some Feminist Interventions*. London: Taylor and Francis.

Cameron, Deborah (ed.) (1990) *The Feminist Critique of Language: A Reader*. London: Routledge.

Childers, Mary and hooks, bell (1990) 'A conversation about race and class', in M. Hirsch and L. Fox Keller (eds), *Conflicts in Feminism*. London: Routledge.

Collins, Patricia H. (1990) *Black Feminist Thought: Knowledge, Consciousness and the Politics of Empowerment*. Boston and London: Unwin Hyman.

Edwards, Rosalind (1996) 'White woman researcher – Black women subjects', *Feminism and Psychology*, 6 (2): 169–175.

Finch, Janet (1984) '"It's great to have someone to talk to": the ethics and politics of interviewing women', in C. Bell and H. Roberts (eds), *Social Researching: Politics, Problems, Practice*. London: Routledge and Kegan Paul.

Glucksmann, Miriam (1994) 'The work of knowledge and the knowledge of women's work', in Mary Maynard and June Purvis (eds), *Researching Women's Lives from a Feminist Perspective*. London, Taylor and Francis.

Gordon, Tuula (1990) *Feminist Mothers*. London: Macmillan.

hooks, bell (1989) *Talking Back: Thinking Feminist, Thinking Black*. Boston: South End Press.

hooks, bell (1991) *Yearning: Race, Gender, and Cultural Politics*. London: Turnaround.

hooks, bell (1994) *Teaching to Transgress: Education as the Practice of Freedom*. London: Routledge.

Lee, Raymond (1993) *Researching Sensitive Issues*. London: Sage.

Luttrell, Wendy (1992) 'Working-class women's ways of knowing: effects of gender, race and class', in J. Wrigley (ed.), *Education and Gender Equality*. London: Falmer.

Lynch, Kathleen and O'Neill, Cathleen (1994) 'The colonisation of social class in education', *British Journal of Sociology of Education*, 19 (3): 307–24.

Madoc-Jones, Beryl and Coates, Jennifer (1996) *An Introduction to Women's Studies*. London: Blackwell.

Maynard, Mary (1994) '"Race", gender and the concept of "difference" in feminist thought', in Haleh Afshar and Mary Maynard (eds), *The Dynamics of 'Race' and Gender: Some Feminist Interventions*. London: Taylor and Francis.

Mills, Jane (1989) *Woman Words*. London: Virago.

Nicholson, Linda (ed.) (1990) *Feminism/Postmodernism*. London: Routledge.

Oakley, Ann (1981) 'Interviewing women: a contradiction in terms?', in Helen Roberts (ed.), *Doing Feminist Research*. London: Routledge and Kegan Paul.

Olson, Karen and Shopes, Linda (1991) 'Crossing boundaries, building bridges: doing oral history among working class women and men', in Sherna Berger Gluck and Daphne Patai (eds), *Women's Words: The Feminist Practice of Oral History*. London: Routledge.

Opie, Anne (1992) 'Qualitative research, appropriation of the "other; and empowerment"', *Feminist Review*, 40: 52–69.

Packwood, Marlene (1983) 'The Colonel's lady and Judy O'Grady – sisters under the skin?', *Trouble and Strife*, 1: 7–12.

Ribbens, Jane (1989) 'Interviewing – an "unnatural situation"?', *Women's Studies International Forum*, 12 (6): 579–92.

Ribbens, Jane (1994) *Mothers and Their Children: A Feminist Sociology of Childrearing*. London: Sage.

Segal, Lynne (1987) *Is the Future Female? Troubled Thoughts on Contemporary Feminism*. London: Virago.

Skeggs, Beverley (1994a) 'Situating the production of feminist ethnography', in Mary Maynard and June Purvis (eds), *Researching Women's Lives from a Feminist Perspective*. London: Taylor and Francis.

Skeggs, Beverley (1994b) 'Refusing to be civilised: "race", sexuality and power', in Haleh Afshar and Mary Maynard (eds), *The Dynamics of 'Race' and Gender: Some Feminist Interventions*. London: Taylor and Francis.

Smith, Dorothy E. (1988) *The Everyday World as Problematic: Towards a Feminist Sociology*. Milton Keynes: Open University Press.

Smith, Dorothy E. (1989) 'Sociological theory: methods of writing patriarchy', in Ruth A. Wallace (ed.), *Feminism and Sociological Theory*. London: Sage.

Smith, T. and Noble, M. (1995) *Education Divides: Poverty and Schooling in the 1990s*. London: Child Poverty Action Group.

Stanley, Liz and Wise, Sue (1983) *Breaking Out: Feminist Consciousness and Feminist Research*. London: Routledge and Kegan Paul.

Stanley, Liz and Wise, Sue (1993) *Breaking Out Again: Feminist Epistemology and Ontology*. London: Routledge.

Weedon, Chris (1987) *Feminist Practice and Poststructuralist Theory*. Oxford: Blackwell.

Epilogue

Jane Ribbens and Rosalind Edwards

At one Workshop meeting, the women researchers whose work we were going to discuss, and several others, were unable to attend as a result of a strike on the London underground system.[1] So those of us who were there began talking about the concerns of this book, about our feelings about being involved in academic life, and about the dilemmas that always remain.

As we talked, we realized how much we shared a feeling of marginality to academic worlds, and a doubt about whether or not we want to 'be here' (in Maxine Birch's terms, this volume). We expressed a shared sentiment that the Workshop itself is situated on the edges of academic life, a part of it and yet trying also to offer something else (as we discussed in Chapter 1). We felt that we are constantly compromising, between what seems to be required of us as academics, and what we want to express as women with a certain view of the social world. There is a continual balancing, and weighing up, of the gains and losses entailed by our academic participation.

We have argued in this book that exploring domestic and intimate private and personal lives and relationships in particular reveals a range of dilemmas that we face as social researchers, in a context where such explorations are marginalized within mainstream disciplinary knowledge. The chapters collected together in this edited book have revealed the details and nuances of these dilemmas in practice.

One central dilemma has been how we show that our work has relevance to theoretical, conceptual and formal 'public' traditions and conventions of knowledge, and present our work in an acceptable fashion within the public domain, while remaining faithful to our research participants' 'private' experiences and accounts. Can and how do we, from a position constituted within dominant discourses (as disciplinary researchers in the public academic sphere), reconstitute and represent privately based knowledges and personal understandings, without reproducing the dominance of those public disciplinary knowledges and colluding in their intrusive 'colonization' and blocking of alternative ways of knowing and being?

Another, related, dilemma has concerned how we shift across the edges of our own personal lived experiences, our research explorations of others' private lives, and our transformation of these into the format of public knowledge. We may often find that the boundaries between our personal lives and our academic concerns become very loose and permeable (which we may or may not find valuable), and yet we also have to remain aware of the different worlds we are moving between. For many of us within the Workshop, the presence of children in our lives has significantly affected the ways in which we think about the position of women in our academic work. Even if we are central participants in the privately based social worlds we study (as mothers, sisters, wives or partners, and so on), or our topic has formed part of our biographical history (for example, as children or mature women students), or we have strong privately based social contacts among those we study (such as alternative therapy groups, or lone mothers), the very act of researching these social worlds places us in a different position and can remove us to the edges of that private and personal world, positioning us on the edge of another, public, world.

Moreover, on the one hand, if we reflexively make ourselves visible within our research as embodying and constituting those edges, we may risk muting the voices of our research participants. Yet, on the other hand, if we do not do this, we perpetuate the illusion that we are not actively present in the data collection, analysis and writing up of our research. But where do we set the limits to self-revelation? Many of us in the Workshop have made decisions at times about what to put in, and what to leave out, in terms of self-revelation. Does this mean we are looking for an openness from our research participants that we are not prepared to show about ourselves? Or are we really in a different position since we are the embodiment of the edges between public and private worlds, and there is no-one else to give us the protection of anonymity that we offer our research participants within the public knowledge forum? Yet it is precisely these established ways of producing public knowledge that we are questioning and rethinking.

These dilemmas raise the further issue of who our research is 'for'? Is it for our research participants, so that collective alternative public representations of their private lives and personal understandings are available and sustainable (which brings us back to the risk of making them also more vulnerable to colonization or appropriation)? Or is our research for ourselves, as we pursue topics to which we have a personal attachment or seek to gain a PhD and/or academic credibility? Or, linked to these points, is our research for academic and public audiences, either as part of a desire to make privately based interventions into public representations and theorizing, or for their recognition and approval of our academic competence? Most often, the answer to who our research is 'for' is a combination of all the foregoing, with the dilemma being where the balance lies. Certainly, many of us have found PhD research to be personally empowering, enabling us to find a greater sense of our own voice and our own authority. And while we may seek to de-construct 'expert' knowledge, we may also at times want to assert our authority and 'expertise', perhaps making strategic use of such contradictions in different contexts. Indeed, there is also the likelihood that such dilemmas and contradictions may themselves be a source of insight and creativity.

The dilemma of where the balance lies brings us to the final dilemma, underlying the choices we make in our contingent 'solutions' to the knotty theoretical, epistemological and methodological issues that confront us: how do we know when we have 'sold out'? It is a dilemma with which Patricia Hill Collins confronts herself and her students, balancing the aim of intervening in dominant understandings and representations of black women's lives in public and private spheres, with the desire for academic qualifications and credibility (as discussed after her plenary paper presentation, 1997).[2] Perhaps, if we do 'sell out', we will no longer care that we have done so, and this will be the surest sign that we have indeed 'bought in'. So maybe our discomfort and feeling of living on the edges is something to be valued in itself, as reassurance that we retain our critical perspective. If we start to feel too comfortable, it may be too late.

There are no easy resolutions to the dilemmas we have outlined here. As feminists working within the 'reflexive turn' of social research, the only suggestion we can offer is that we need to recognize ambiguity, to be open about the dilemmas we face and the choices we make, and to think through the implications of these choices for the knowledge we produce. Our aim, in this edited collection, has been to demonstrate how we have sought to do this in practice, within an area of research which sharply highlights these intermingled public and private issues. At the end of this day, we seem to be still 'here', still living with and debating the contradictions and dilemmas and hopefully turning them to good advantage.

Notes

1 The Workshop refers to the Women's Workshop on Qualitative Family/Household Research, which we describe in Chapter 1.

2 See reference in Chapter 1.

Index

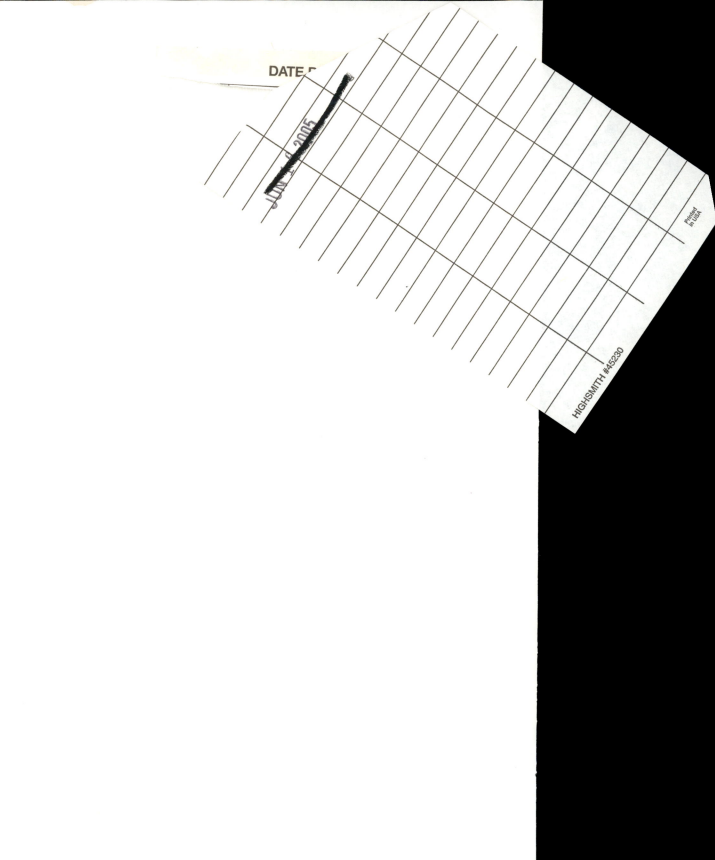

DATE

JUN 2005

HIGHSMITH #45230

Printed In USA